FROM NAZARETH TO THE CITY OF ANGELS
THE STORY OF A FOREIGN STUDENT

GHASSAN S. BISHARAT

From Nazareth to the City of Angels

Copyright © 2024 by Ghassan S. Bisharat

All rights reserved.

Published by Red Penguin Books

Bellerose Village, New York

Library of Congress Control Number: 2024923052

ISBN

Print 978-1-63777-655-1 | 978-1-63777-656-8

Digital 978-1-63777-654-4

No part of this book may be reproduced in any form or by any electronic or mechanical means, including information storage and retrieval systems, without written permission from the author, except for the use of brief quotations in a book review.

The main cover pictures beginning with top left- Ma'Alool's remaining Catholic Church, Nazareth panorama, Mary's well, and the watts Towers. Thus, From Nazareth to the City of Angeles.

Contents

Prologue and Dedication	1
Introduction	7
PART I The Nazareth Years	15
PART II The Gas Station Years	149
PART III The Transition Years	201
PART IV The Trial Years	225
PART V A Life Well-Spent	275
Conclusion	400
Appendix	421
Acknowledgments	429
About the Author	431

Prologue and Dedication

When I began writing my daily memoirs at age eighteen in the city of Nazareth, Palestine/Israel (aka: "The Holy Land" but in my opinion, "The Tragic Land"), I did not imagine that I would revisit them at age seventy-two. Now, here I am, living in the city of Sierra Madre, California, almost 7,700 miles from the city of Nazareth. My daily habit of writing my thoughts and impressions began after my oldest brother, Nabil, opened a checking account for me with $80.00 in it on January 13, 1968. This took place at Bank Al-Omal (in Arabic), also known as Bank Hapoalim (in Hebrew), and "Workers Bank" (in English). It was in downtown Nazareth, and he opened that account for me as payment for my brewing Arabic coffee and tea for his laborers, among other boring stuff, at his construction company in downtown Nazareth. As a promotion for opening this new account, the bank manager gave me a free, 3" x 5" blue-colored, 1968 calendar. This was the first time that I had ever received something for free as part of a promotion and I was so excited that, before going to bed, I wrote in it all the events that took place that day.

2 From Nazareth to the City of Angels

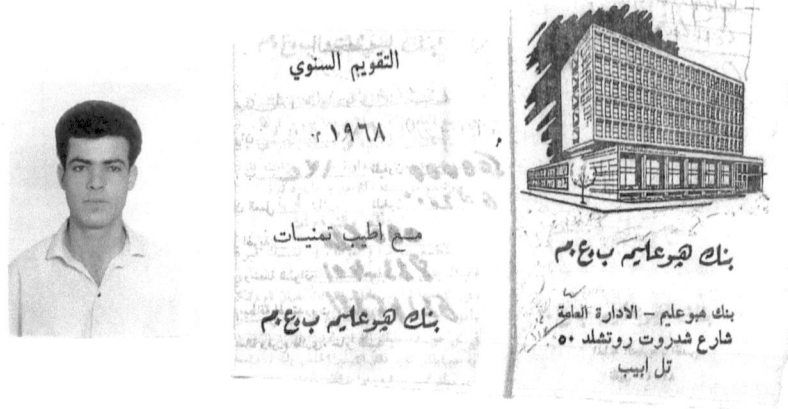

LEFT: Undated photo of the author's older brother, Nabil. RIGHT: Copy of the front cover of the author's calendar (dated 1968).

That event spurred my interest in continuously writing and recording my impressions and has continued to this very day with the "bug" of writing still blazing. At age 72, I have accumulated 54 years of daily, handwritten journals in calendars of all sizes and shapes, written in many different colors of ball-point pens. And that original calendar remains with me today in mint condition as it is very precious to me.

Upon my retirement, in April 2010, from my teaching career in the Greater Los Angeles Basin, I began straightening up my library's books, including those many calendars. It was then that I realized what a treasure I had before me. I immediately began reading each one, which turned out to be a timely but worthwhile endeavor as it recorded my life-long story of long-forgotten happy and sad memories, back home as well as here in the United States. I have woven my stories around my parents, family, friends, education, work, teachers, students, religious Fathers, workers, and merchants. Most significantly, my stories tell of my life, the Palestinian Nakba [1] (see Appendix) and The Israeli/Palestinian People's Tragic Kismet (TIPPTK), all of which have played significant roles in shaping my values and making me the person who I am today.

Thus, I began seriously thinking of how I could utilize my journal entries to write my own memoir, which began long before entering the United States on a Foreign Student Visa on March 21, 1971. As a Palestinian Foreign Student with an Israeli Citizenship [2], I wanted so badly to complete my studies as I was propelled by my love of education and the promise I made to my parents. That promise was that if they agreed to let me fly forth from their family's nest that I would sacrifice as much as was needed to get a Doctorate Degree in their honor. Leaving my parents was a heartbreaking experience that I still feel to this day; I have always felt guilty about leaving them. However, my love for education was tied to the love I had for my parents. Without the first, there could be no second and without the second, there could be no first. This is how entrenched those two pillars of my life were, then and now.

Those two twin pillars also stood on a solid foundation cemented by all the people who I came to know as I was growing up in the city of Nazareth. Without them, those twin pillars could have collapsed and with them, my values, as well. That solid foundation was in the making long before I was born. I just inherited it from all the indigenous people who lived in Palestine for at least four thousand years before my birth.

This educational journey tested all the values that were inculcated in me. By holding onto my values, I was able to successfully overcome many difficult challenges that I encountered, including the heavy price that came with leaving Palestine, achieving my educational goals and later, in building my own family.

It was, then, no surprise to me when during the early 1980s, I became a high school, college, and university teacher in the Greater Los Angeles Basin. I anchored my teaching philosophy by invoking my love of education and sharing my family values with my students. What motivated me as I continued this journey was my desire to share my heart-filled stories of love, pain, and struggle with my inner-city students who I had the privilege and honor of teaching.

For starters, I wanted to encourage my students to take the time to record their thoughts and feelings in a journal as I have done. It is never too late to begin this process and, as I have found, this exercise will dramatically change their lives. For in the years to come, when they look back on these journals, they will become a valued treasure. While this treasure might not contain gold and diamonds, it will hold something even more precious: it will be filled with the memories of all the people who they have loved and those who helped shape them into being who they have become today. I believe that the people who they write about will be very similar to those people who helped shape my life.

The process of reading my journal entries has brought to life many good and bad memories as I re-read my stories about life's ups and downs, twists and turns and its ugly and joyful moments of pain and suffering that I witnessed. In some ways, it has taken its toll on me, but it has also brought me a great many gifts. It has led me to question my conscience and my reason for recording my thoughts, which remains at the very heart of this process. If there was no person or cause to dedicate these memories to, it would have deprived me of this lifelong journey. So, I believe that one must have something to live for—a personal reason that drives this process forward. Otherwise, why would I want to revisit and re-read years of calendar entries that are often painful? That very question kept me awake many nights until I realized that the answer was easier than I had previously thought.

I realized that with writing my memoir, I could accomplish some very important goals that I still have, starting with honoring all the people who loved me and cared for me back home in the city of Nazareth, Palestine, before I came to live in the U.S. at nearly 21-years of age. Those people taught me the Palestinian values of love of education and family. With those values always in my mind and heart, I was able to endure times when I struggled with hard work, pride, and sometimes, a lack of hope. With these twin pillars guiding me, I was able to maintain my dignity, integrity, and love for others as it was a part of my DNA and made me who I am today.

My memoir is also dedicated to the American people who I have met throughout my life, starting with those who granted me my Foreign Student Visa, which gave me the vital opportunity to live in the United States and become a humble and thankful citizen as I excelled in my education, to all my teachers and professors, and all those people who I have worked and intermingled with. Despite the U.S.'s shameful policy toward the unjust and painful trauma that befell the Palestinian people and became known as their "Nakba," I shall always respect and appreciate this opportunity. To date, I have never been aware of any negative or racist behavior projected toward me for being of Palestinian or Arab descent.

As important as my education has been to me, so has the opportunity I have had in my role as a teacher for over 30 years at the high school, college, and university levels in Greater Los Angeles. Specifically, my teaching journey with my South Central and East Los Angeles inner-city high school students have mirrored my own life experiences of growing up in the city of Nazareth. It was there that I came face-to-face with the wounds of poverty, racism, discrimination, neglect, bigotry, and my own people's painful Nakba. In my memoir, I will share how my teaching of inner-city students helped me to heal some of my oldest wounds as I also helped these young people heal their own. As such, my memoir is my way of letting them know that I loved them and was honored to be in their company.

By watching my students' struggles to overcome the many challenges placed in their environment daily—in the process of just walking to school or riding the bus—I saw their tremendous endurance. That very condition created a tremendous resonance for me of the Nakba's long-lasting trauma on myself, my family, and the Palestinian people. Our struggle was not so different from that of the indigenous American Indians, African American and Hispanic children who I taught. We all shared a struggle to overcome life's difficulties in our survival against occupation, discrimination, and racism. By teaching these young adults, I grew to appreciate and respect them despite the utter failure of our national policies in addressing the miserable, socio-economic conditions of our inner-city schools.

Most importantly, I learned that poverty, racism, violence, discrimination, and lack of equality does not preclude their ability to be generous, loving and caring to each other. They never intentionally hurt me or messed with my teaching materials, including dangerous machine shop equipment and tools. Nor did they hamper or attempt to open my desk drawers or my briefcase. Instead, they protected me with their own lives. Despite the many injuries and surgeries that I sustained teaching them, my happy teaching memories outweigh the pain I endured as it strengthened my respect for my students' instinct and resiliency in navigating their harsh socio/economic environment so reminiscent of my own. Thus, I have dedicated the last intimate and emotional chapter of my memories to those very cherished memories.

Finally, this memoir is dedicated to my children and grandchildren in the hopes that, one day, they will read it and appreciate my heritage, my teaching experiences, and the long-running history of foreign occupation that has left behind the scars of pain and suffering for so many people, including the Palestinians, Arabs, Muslims, Christians, and Jews and all their descendants.

My story is very similar to the stories of hundreds of thousands of foreign students who have struggled to achieve their goals in the hopes that their children and grandchildren would not have to go through the same hardships and struggles that they have endured.

Ghassan S. Bisharat, September 2023

Introduction

So, what do those early years of writing journal entries in Nazareth say about what my life was like before I left for the U.S. on March 21st, 1971?

Undated photon of the Nazareth skyline.

Typically, I recorded the time I woke up, went to school and came home, the homework I did, the subjects I loved and hated, the grades I got, the meals I ate, any jokes I heard, and the soccer games I listened to on the radio. I also described things that happened at work, the main political events that were shaping the landscape of the Middle East, especially The Israeli/Palestinian People's Tragic Kismet (TIPPTK) activities in which I was involved, the frequent visits to my nearby family and neighborhood homes, friends I saw, movies I watched, extra books I read, and other items that I now find boring.

When I wrote about the meals I ate, it usually included the typical breakfast before school: a boiled egg, a glass of milk, and green and black cured olives with hot, flat Arabic bread topped with labneh and zaatar. *Labneh* is a creamy paste very similar to cream cheese while zaatar is crushed, dried thyme mixed with roasted sesame seeds. Both are very tasty!

My meals were almost identical since my mother was physically unable to cook two different meals for nine people every day, and financially, it would have been a burden. Thus, whatever I ate for lunch, I also ate for dinner without any complaint.

My favorite meals consisted of freshly cooked vegetables, soups, and steamed rice, in addition to raw fruit, nuts, and vegetables. Cucumbers and tomatoes were my favorites. These were consumed more frequently because they were less expensive than meat, which I did not especially like due to the fat in it. But by far, tabbouleh [3] was and continues to be my favorite dish of all time.

In honor of the author's love of tabbouleh, his cousin, Sou'ad (left) and aunt, Blanche (right) feed him tabbouleh in an undated photo taken circa 1973 or 1974.

On a few occasions, I helped my parents entertain family and friends. And while I rarely mentioned any intimate time spent with my brothers and sisters, when it came to my parents, I always talked about how I loved to tease them, especially my mother who I drove crazy. I will always remember my mother as my angel, and my father as my hero.

When it came to academics, I was a good student and rarely missed a day of classes, regardless of the weather conditions or illnesses. I frequently mentioned different events that took place on the campuses, especially listening to my teachers, arguing with classmates, and playing soccer in my notes.

Interestingly, I failed to record some important events that I still remember, such as the titles of my short stories that I sent to the British Broadcasting Corporation; why I was unable to convince my principal at Don Bosco High School to publish a school newspaper; and the content and title of the speech I delivered to the 10th graders during their graduation ceremony at Don Bosco when I was visiting my family in 1978.

While my love of education and family was repeatedly mentioned and elaborated upon in my memories, I also spoke about my values. I repeatedly emphasized my respect for my fellow human beings, gratitude to those who loved and cared for me, loyalty to those who trusted me, and the constant friendly greetings I shared with and received from those who I knew. I also spoke about the constant helping hands that were always present for those in need and the uttering of tender words that always included "please" and "thank you."

Many of my entries described my stand against racism, bullying and arrogance. I questioned two-faced friends and relatives and refused to accept many of my family's long-cherished and outdated inherited customs and beliefs. Later in life, I would question the expression "truth to power" when confronted with unfair principles and department chairs' evaluations, arrogant supervisors and corporate executives.

I took a firm stand against the United States of America's unfair and unjust policies toward TIPPTK in my journal entries. I saw the U.S. repeatedly taking Israel's side while ignoring the legitimate and moral side of the Palestinian people's struggle for justice and peace. This saddened me and I began questioning the basic moral and just values that my country—the USA—stood for.

Finally, there were many entries in which I emphasized my continued defense and support for all legitimate freedom-seeking people in their struggle against racism, inequality, and bigotry. These included the struggles against brutal dictators in the Arab world, Latin America, Africa, Europe, and elsewhere. I was focused on the continued struggle for civil rights for all people long before I became an inner-city schoolteacher. This strong belief that I held was a factor in my teaching as I reminded my students of the roles played by

Martin Luther King and the Mexican farm leader Cesar Chavez and many others.

However, on many occasions, I paid a heavy and painful price for speaking out. The way I saw it, I was morally and ethically obligated to stand up for what is just and fair, a value I first expressed at the age of four when I first stood up to my teacher. This stand has grown within me as my life has been strengthened by the foundation of those twin pillars that always guide me and make me a better human being.

But those same values and beliefs also tested me, to a great extent, in my resilience to survive and thrive throughout my difficult journey as a foreign student in the United States of America. I had left behind a safe, caring, and loving family environment for an uncertain, scary, and unknown foreign living environment. This kept me in a state of constant fear of financial insecurity with the potential failure of my educational mission and the fear of failing as a teacher, husband, father, and grandfather looming just ahead. It also created additional difficulty for me in finding a job that could pay for my tuition and my family's needs.

Timeline of Events

Most of the events that I mention in my memoir took place before I began writing them down at the age of eighteen. But these were events that I still vividly remember and were chiseled in my mind, never to be forgotten.

The first early imprint began for me at the age of four. One day, at that tender age, I asked my kindergarten teacher if I could go to the bathroom. She said, "No." At the same time, her nephew, who was my classmate, also asked for permission to use the bathroom. This time, she said, "Yes."

Even as a kindergarten student, I felt that I was being treated differently and my response was to cry and throw the wooden blocks that I was playing with at her. She immediately punished me by telling me to stand facing the wall of the classroom. She then sent a student to inform the principal, Mother Superior, of my behavior.

I remember Mother Superior: she was a tall, French nun with blue eyes and extremely white skin. When she entered the room, she asked the teacher why she was asked to visit her classroom. My teacher told her that I was throwing wooden blocks at her and because of that, she had demanded that I stand facing the wall as punishment.

Mother Superior asked me why I had thrown those blocks at my teacher. I told her that she would not let me go to the bathroom, yet she allowed her nephew to do so. I admitted that I threw the blocks at her and told her that I was sad and angry as I felt that she had been unfair to me. I then began crying as all kids do at that tender age.

Mother Superior then told me to go to the bathroom and to take my time, that she would wait for me to come back. When I returned to my classroom, she took my hand and stopped all the classroom activities as she told the students that "Ghassan did the right thing by being courageous in expressing his feelings regarding his teacher's decision, which was unfair. Take this as a lesson to all of you: stand firm, be courageous, and demand fairness when you are right."

Since that time, Mother Superior's comments have stayed with me to this day.

While I could not have understood the meaning of justice, fairness, discrimination, or integrity at the age of four, I deeply felt at that moment in that classroom, the universal feeling that every child feels when they realize they cannot have or do what another child can.

Now, at the age of 72, I held my head between my palms and began thinking very deeply about the roots of that stand. Where did it come from? Was it from the values my parents raised me with or the DNA imprint of my descendants, who for thousands of years have lived in occupied Palestine? Was it something I learned from the stories I was told by my loved ones as they described our collective *Nakba* with anguished and painful looks that penetrated the core of my bones, heart, and conscience? I strongly think it was all the above and much more.

To find the factors that contributed to my taking a stand at such an early age, I need to go back to the twin pillars upon which my values were built. The whirlpool of confused feelings and thoughts in my heart and mind takes me back to my early childhood memories of Nazareth and that is where I shall begin.

However, I must confess at the outset that there are many instances where I will elaborate more on certain historical events than others in the hopes that those elaborations will enhance the context in which they have shaped my overall life story.

Part One
The Nazareth Years
1950-1971

16 From Nazareth to the City of Angels

Clockwise from the top: the author's parents on their wedding day (1942); the author's mother in an undated photo; the home in which the author grew up in Nazareth (1970); the author's father in an undated photo; the author at age 18 (center).

Chapter 1
In the beginning...

I was born on June 23, 1950, to Palestinian parents. My father's name was Suleiman Ess'aid Bisharat. My mother's name was Miriam Awad Bisharat. They were cousins and after they married, they lived in a one-bedroom apartment in a place called "Deir Blanche," located at the heart of the city of Nazareth. Deir, in Arabic, is used to describe the place where priests and nuns lived and worked while "Blanch" is a French word that means "white."

The Deir Blanch campus in Nazareth was a self-contained, enclosed community made of many separate buildings resembling present-day apartment complexes. This complex included its own schools, hospitals, places to rent, and places to worship and was run by a French Catholic Mission.

At the time of my birth, I had two older brothers, Nabil and Emil, and two older sisters, Hana and Hiam. As I was told, the seven of us lived in a one-bedroom apartment with a communal kitchen and a bathroom.

In Arabic, Nazareth is called "Al Nasirah," meaning "the one who grants victory" or "the victorious one." A few years ago, an Israeli anthropologist at Tel Aviv University discovered the remains of the upper jawbone of one of my ancestors. This person was a homo sapien who lived approximately 190,000-170,000 years ago. This fossil was embedded in the sediment of an archaeological site known as the "Misliya Cave," approximately seven miles south of the present-day city of Haifa. It was ten miles from my family's destroyed village of Ma'Alool and twenty-five miles from where I was born in the city of Nazareth. Back then, there were no Arabs, Palestinians, Jews, Israelis, Christians, Muslims, Holy Land, Ma'Alool, Haifa or Nazareth; that all came thousands of years later [4].

Therefore, one must assume that the past and present indigenous inhabitants of this geographical space, which for the last 4,000 years was and is called Palestine, are the direct descendants of those people (excluding those who recently immigrated to Palestine). These original inhabitants settled here long before the other foreign occupiers, including: the Egyptians, Romans, Greeks, Jews, Persians, Arabs, Ottomans, British, and very recently, the Israeli/Zionist occupiers.

We do not have any DNA traces of those far away people. The best recorded written history that we have goes back approximately 10,000 years ago. So, there is a certain probability that the present inhabitants of this geographical space have a mixed DNA of all the people who settled or occupied it.

Then and now, Nazareth was influenced by the many religious missions, established a long time ago, during the tragic history of its foreign occupiers. The most well-known religious missions came from Britain, Italy, France, Russia, Greece, Armenia, and Germany. The missions owned and occupied a lot of land in Palestine, especially in Nazareth, Jerusalem, and other religious places along the shores of the Mediterranean Sea.

Each mission, of course, wanted to have a footprint in Palestine. In fact, the name "The Holy Land" was invented by them as a way of legitimizing their narratives of occupying Palestine in defense of this invented Bible. None of the above missions ever asked the opinions of the indigenous Palestinian people's acceptance of their missions or the occupation of their lands. The fact that the history of Palestine and its indigenous people goes back thousands of years before the Bible was invented meant nothing to all of those missions. This same Biblical narrative was exploited by the present occupiers to legitimize a Biblical claim to the land of Palestine.

The Expulsion

After the invention and the creation of the State of Israel in 1948, Nazareth's population suddenly increased due to the flood of refugees from nearby villages and towns that were destroyed by the newly created State of Israel's army. Israel's creation was completely dependent upon the assistance and support of the mighty British Empire that occupied Palestine after World War I in pursuit of its imperial self interest in the Middle East.

The creation of the State of Israel directly resulted in the Palestinian Nakba as almost 800,000 Palestinians were forcefully evicted from their villages, towns and cities to become refugees in the surrounding Arab countries. Out of almost 900 villages, a total of 400-500 were destroyed; some, being blown away by dynamite while their residents were asleep. To hide their crimes, many overseas supporters of Israel contributed resources to plant trees among and between the destroyed villages, which served also as a future cover.

Only about 130,000 Palestinians remained in Palestine by the end of 1948. My parents were among this group who fell directly under the new Israeli/Zionist State's occupation, which made them a third-class, if not a fifth-class citizen, to this day.

Most, if not all the properties owned by those missions, were strategically located with excellent views of downtown Nazareth. With its growing population and Israel's policies of forced confiscation of almost 50% of Nazareth's original land, it was apparent that the mission's real estate was urgently needed for any further real estate expansion of the growing population.

My parents, like many other Palestinian families, were driven out of their destroyed village of Ma'Alool, a Cananite name that meant a large entrance door which replaced the old Roman name of Ahalol. Ma'Alool's location was roughly ten miles west of the city of Nazareth, and again, barely ten miles from the ancient Misliya Cave where my ancient relatives once lived. My parents managed to rent a one-bedroom apartment in Deir Blanche where I was delivered by a midwife on June 23, 1950.

My Parents

My father was a cobbler. He rented a shop in downtown Nazareth where he repaired old shoes and made new ones. My mother, like many women of her generation, took care of the family's needs, including raising myself and my other four siblings.

Author's family. L-R: author's father, sister Hanna, mother, brother Nabil, brother Emil, sister Hiam, the author (nine months old). Photo taken March 18, 1951.

My parents' education was limited due to lack of public education policies during the Ottoman Empire and that of the British mandate of Palestine following World War I. I was told that neither of my parents attended any formal public education beyond the third grade. Yet, in my humble opinion, the way they raised and loved us deserves a post Ph.D. diploma and a Nobel Prize. (I strongly believe that the Nobel Prize committee must include "Parenting" as part of its Nobel Prize considerations as it outweighs all others.)

I do not remember much about my life in Deir Blanch. I heard many stories about the priests who managed this complex as being racist, arrogant, and mean-spirited. For example, my mother and my aunt told me the following story:

Undated photo likely taken during the 1980s. L-R: author's aunt Wardeh, aunt Hana, who was responsible for pushing the priest out of the author's home, author's mother.

When I was one year old, my mother and Aunt Hana were in the middle of giving me a hot bath in a large bowl during a cold winter night when, suddenly, a priest pushed open the door without asking anyone's permission. Demanding that the rent be paid, he left the door wide open regardless of the cold wind that rushed in. My mother shielded me to protect me while my aunt pleaded with the priest to leave immediately. When he refused to do so, she pushed him out the door and closed it on him as he cursed and insulted them.

This incident caused them to protect me even more. In fact, they would tease me by saying that they should not have done so because it made me too stubborn when it came to standing firm and defending one's Al Haq or "justice." I have always replied that that incident made me a good-looking man and a hater of organized religions.

When I was four years old, my family moved to a two-bedroom home which sat on a half-acre of land and had a kitchen and an outside bathroom. My father had borrowed some of the money to buy the land and build our house there. The land was located at the far fringes of Nazareth in a place called "Hay Al-Ke-room," meaning "the neighborhood of orchards." However, there were no orchards; this area was full of rocks, dirt roads, and wild animals. I still have friends and family members who say, "Abu Nabil moved to where the coyotes lived."

The word for father in the traditional Palestinian saying is "Abu." Because my father's eldest son was named Nabil, he was the father of Nabil, meaning Abu Nabil. To keep my father's memories as Abu Nabil alive, I have also called my first male child Nabil, thus, I am also Abu Nabil or Abu Nabil, Junior.

I have memories at that age of walking a half mile, each way, to school with other students escorted by a mother or two. My kindergarten school was run by French nuns and was part of a huge complex called Don Bosco Catholic Foundation that included churches, schools, and farmland.

Until I left Nazareth, and with it, Palestine, I lived for 21 years as an Arab/ Palestinian/ Israeli citizen with my singular identity as a "Palestinian" erased from all my formal documentation. The Israeli/ Zionist strategic government's domestic and foreign racial policies were, then as it is now, based on erasing the word "Palestine" from all forms of its state communications and documentation. At the heart of this strategy is the illusion that, by eliminating the word "Palestine" and its history, the Israeli/Zionist project could be portrayed as the settling of the Jewish people in an empty land that had been promised by God through his prophet, Abraham, 2,000 or more years ago.

Chapter 2
Nazareth's Topography

When flying over on Aladdin's Carpet, Nazareth's typography looks like an elongated canoe. The two elevated sides of the canoe contain the city's residential neighborhoods, which are dissected by Nazareth's main boulevard where all the downhill roads of the two neighborhoods meet. The boulevard runs the length of the canoe where it meets at its two, east and west sides with additional boulevards that connect it to the rest of the country.

Undated photo of the Church of the Annunciation.

In the center of Nazareth stands the Church of the Annunciation, built on top of a cave where we were told Jesus' mother had lived and an angel was sent by God to tell her that she would be pregnant with a future king. This church is the largest church in the Middle East. It is one of the numerous churches that dot Palestine and are affiliated with various Eastern and Western Christian missions.

What the angel failed to disclose to Mary was that her future son would become a rebellious, justice-seeking, charismatic leader called "Jesus of Nazareth," (who I count as my cousin). I do not know at what age Jesus became a rebellious person, but assuming that he was my cousin, I would speculate with a fair amount of certainty that he became so at the age of four. Why not?

Jesus' destiny was to fight the Romans and free Palestine, while mine was to teach inner-city students in a far-away country. His destiny brought him death and fame while mine was marked by injuries and painful surgeries with no one to blame.

Undated photo of Mary's Well.

Not far from that historic church stood Mary's Well where the inhabitants of that time got their drinking water and gathered to gossip. I did the same, years later, with many of my school friends.

Nazareth is also the home of the many mosques that serve its majority Muslim population. There is also one Jewish synagogue that I know of, located in Nazareth, adjacent to my kindergarten school.

Chapter 3
Grades 1-3

Episcopate Catholic Church of Nazareth / Kanisat Al-Masih/ Christ's Church

At the age of five, I began first grade at Kanisat Al-Masih "Christ's Church" school (aka: KALM), which was in the heart of old Nazareth's bustling Bazaar. The school and the church followed the Melkite Roman Catholic traditions. The Melkites split from the Greek Orthodox Church in 1724 A.D. and are one of five other Middle Eastern rites that follow their own Catholic traditions and liturgy while accepting the Pope as their spiritual leader, like the rest of the Roman Catholic Church.

LEFT: *Undated photo of Kanisat Al-Masih "Christ's Church" school (aka: KALM), situated in the heart of Nazareth's old bazaar.* RIGHT: *Undated photo of Nazareth's bazaar.*

I still can hear my mother's voice ringing in my ear saying, "Do not make comments and sing while the priest is reciting rhythmic Eastern verses from the Bible at your Kanisat Al-Masih Church."

I did not like the priest at KALM who served as the principal and ran the show. During Sunday's masses, which I hated to attend, I would sing Palestinian folklore songs and the songs of the famous Egyptian singer Oum-Kalthoum while the priest and the parishioners were reciting traditional Eastern church rhythms. Of course, the priest could hear my voice but was unable to pinpoint where it was coming from as I was sitting or standing among the rest of my fellow students. I can still picture the look of annoyance on his face when I did this.

Adjacent to KALM was a synagogue where Jesus' so-called "Silent Years" of preaching took place. At that time, Jesus' messages were controversial to the ears of, mainly, Palestinians farmers who lived in Palestine among many other fragmented tribes, including the Jewish tribe. Through it all, Jesus endured many angry rebuttals and responses from the crowd. He was on his guard all the time fearing that the Roman soldiers, who were the occupiers at that time, might arrest him for preaching that his father's heavenly powers were more powerful than those of Caesar's.

Undated photo of the interior of Nazareth's only synagogue.

He also preached that the population needed justice, liberty, and equality rather than Caesar's brutal occupation of the land and its inhabitants. His teaching at the time laid the foundation of a recent Palestinian as well as Latin American movement called "The Theology of Liberation." This theory invoked the teaching of Jesus and used his personal charisma as a way of gathering his believers to overthrow their un-elected dictators.

Jesus' preaching took place mainly in the northern part of Palestine, popularly known in Arabic as "Al - Jaleel" or Galilee in English. The farmers there were the first to become his followers. Like all charismatic movements, it could not evolve without having followers who believe in their leader's charismatic appeals. Without those Palestinians or Galileans who believed in Jesus of Nazareth's charisma, Christianity could never have been born.

Kanisat Al- Masih had a single, enclosed playground of almost 80 x 80 square feet that was paved with solid cement and had no grass.

You had to be very careful not to fall or you would get hurt–but to a first grader, this warning was never taken seriously.

The church stood on the southern side of the yard, the synagogue to its west, there was a tall wall to its north side, and to its east stood two floors. The first floor contained bathrooms while the second housed three separate classrooms.

The school was at least three miles from my home, which was located at the highest edge of that canoe. It was all downhill from my house, so it was much easier to walk to school in the morning than to return home after a long day of studying.

My mother made me lunch every day so that I could avoid having to walk home during the lunch break. It was too exhausting for a young boy to walk that distance – especially the uphill part, although I did it almost every day. Walking that six miles kept me slim, athletic, and fit to play soccer and it provided other health benefits, as well. Complaining got me nowhere as there were no cars to pick me up or drop me off. I had two legs, which I called "number eleven" (spider legs) and that was my basic transportation.

On my way to and from school, I was always greeting passersby, a habit I still practice to this day. I also paid attention to the beauty of Nazareth's natural environment, comparing the local Palestinian architecture with that of the surrounding massive European churches and their living dwellings.

This long walk, to and from school, increased my stamina and determination to excel in my education. It opened my eyes to the value of education and the price that I had to pay to receive it. This made my parents very happy and proud of me for not only getting excellent grades but for my endurance of these conditions without complaint.

Memories of My Dad

As time passed, I began stopping by my father's shoe shop, which was located a few yards away from my school. I would wait for him to close his shop so I could accompany him with his grocery shopping. Shopping for groceries then became another life lesson that is still with me today. My father showed me how to pick the freshest produce by feel and smell and how to bag them in a way that they did not damage the more tender produce. The top items in the bag were always either tomatoes or grapes with the larger, firmer produce on the bottom.

 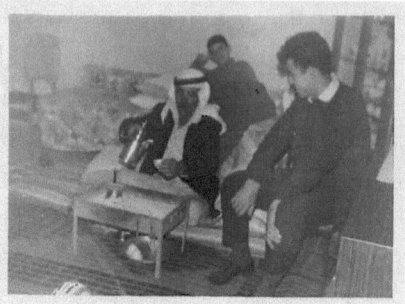

LEFT: *Author's father gardening (1968)*. RIGHT: *Photo from 1968 of the author's father serving coffee over a portable fire* (kanoon) *with the author's brothers, William (background) and Nabil (foreground), inside the author's home. The* kanoon *was the family's main source of heat during the winter.*

As my father felt sorry for me having to carry heavy groceries all that distance home, he would occasionally hire a taxi. This required waiting at the taxi station for other people who would split the cost of our ride as he was unable to pay for a private ride. On rare occasions, when it rained or was extremely hot, he would pay the full price for our taxi. While I knew money was very tight, I saw how happy it made him to do that for me.

Along the way, he would tease me by asking how I was doing at school. He also shared stories with me about his life experiences. I really loved those taxi rides home with my father enjoying that strong father-son connection. This experience taught me about the difficulties and sacrifices that a father must endure to raise his family. Seeing him struggling to keep his family's dignity and pride intact increased my respect and love for him. I knew that, one day, I would be a father, as well, and must honor my family's dignity and pride and keep my family united.

My biggest surprise, regarding my father, came about when I first ran to his shop to proudly show him my excellent grades, hoping that he might give me a few cents as a reward. Instead, he quickly glanced at my report card and said, "This is what I expect from you. You do your work and I do mine." Suffice to say, there was no reward.

On many occasions, he would respond to my educational accomplishments by reminding me to fill up the chicken's water container when I got home. He was more concerned about the wellbeing of the chickens than in inflating his son's ego. Still, I recall a few rare occasions where he gave me twenty-five cents, which was enough for a pack of gum and a few candies.

My dad's stories about his days as a resistance fighter against the British occupation of Palestine opened my eyes to the Palestinian tragedy that resulted in the destruction of his village of Ma'Alool, among hundreds of others. The years 1936 – 1939 were especially significant in my dad's life as a young man. Those heroic years saw an eruption of support by the Palestinian people to stand firm against Britain's brutal occupation of Palestine. For almost four years, the people stopped working and went on strike. This resulted in one of the longest work strikes in history. The way the British managed to quell it was by using severe punishment, assassination, hanging and jailing most of the strike leaders (and they call themselves a civilized people).

Hearing these stories at such a young age, I could not fully comprehend why stronger nations became so cruel in their treatment of the people who they occupied. Regardless, I was very proud of my father's identity as a Palestinian-Arab armed with the spirit to resist and struggle against oppression, while at the same time, being kind to others. After all, Jesus was a distant Palestinian cousin of ours.

My father's pride in his identity and heritage extended to his love of reading the great Arab epic "Taghribat Bani Hilal" [5], also known as Siret Bani Hilal or Al- Sirah al-Hilaliyah.

I remember, very well, seeing many men and women gathering at my parents' house where they would sit separately in our two bedrooms. I can still hear their cries and vocal support for or against the main, two rivals battling each other for supremacy in their defense and attacking each other's armies.

My father used to read the tale loudly and then recite the poetry with his nightingale voice that evoked the heroic and suffering tale of the Banu Hilal. He was so evocative that men and women would begin to cry and chant their heroes' names. This strange encounter repeated itself at least once every three to four months until my mother could no longer bear the responsibility of hosting these gatherings, which drew many people from our neighborhood and the surrounding villages. Soon, this in-house tradition spread to other neighbors' homes where my father would be invited to perform his readings.

His voice is still ringing in my ears as I try to recall the way he sang those sad and evocative poems. Like father, like son: years later, when I would place my own newborn children in my lap while feeding them their milk from their bottles, I would sing to them what I could remember of these poems. Suddenly and from nowhere, I start crying and sometimes weeping while looking straight into their eyes and they look into mine wondering what they are thinking about? This habit continued with all my children and grandchildren until they began eating solid food and the bottle of milk no more.

The other characteristic appeal about my father that surprised me came about when I was helping him in his shop during my Spring and Summer school breaks. I would assist elderly women by carrying their grocery bags as they passed by his shop on their way to the bus station. These were Jewish, Christian, or Muslim women. Especially on the Sabbath (Saturdays), many Jewish shoppers who lived in their newly-built Jewish community of "Nasserite Elite" or "Upper Nazareth" on Nazareth's northern and eastern sides, would come down to shop at Nazareth's Bazaar. This modern city was built on expropriated land from Nazareth and other adjacent Arab municipalities in 1957. This was part of a government campaign to Judaize the Galilee and maintain a strong military presence over Nazareth under the cover of accommodating the increasing immigration of Jews to Israel.

To encourage Jews, who were reluctant to immigrate to Palestine, the government launched a massive brainwashing campaign with the promise of giving the stolen land to them free of charge. These enticed thousands of immigrants to settle in Nasserite Elite. Why not? The government did not pay for it in the first place; it stole it like the rest of Palestine by the barrel of the gun. The indigenous Palestinian population had no one to appeal to for justice, like the situation today, almost eighty years later.

I used to be bothered by my father's request to carry the shoppers' groceries and I would say, "I can understand helping an elderly Palestinian woman but a Jewish one?" Then, I would add, "Remember Ma'Alool? This woman's army destroyed your village."

His answer was always, "Helping the elderly is in our blood regardless of the tragedy that befell us. She probably has her own story to tell, who knows? She might have been brainwashed to immigrate to Israel to begin with. No one knows what she is feeling about what the Israeli Army did in her name."

And so, I would carry these elderly shoppers' bags as instructed. Once on the bus, this woman would open the window and say in Hebrew, "Ta-da-ra bah," meaning "thank you." As I looked into her eyes, I realized that they reminded me of my grandmother's face. (More than half of Israel's population migrated from many parts of the Arab world, thus the similarities.)

Honestly, I felt a deep sense of fulfillment when I helped these women. When leaving the bus station, I used to walk with a swagger, twisting my body to the left and then to the right, for I was happy and content that I did something nice for someone. My father's tender, beating heart taught me to be kind to people everywhere and give the ones who you do not know the benefit of the doubt.

Looking back, it's clear that my father was less concerned with my grades and more concerned with my behavior. He always chose his heart rather than his mind in his relations with others. His kindness, humor, and generosity were his trademarks, which I tried to carry on when I came to the United States and began teaching in the greater Los Angeles Basin.

Class Economics

When I was growing up in Palestine, our financial situation was not the best. Like most of Nazareth's families, we were a semi-middle-class family, closer to the poor class than the middle one. Luxury food items, such as meat, fish, cheese, and canned food, especially tuna, were saved for special occasions. Poultry, fruits, and vegetables were more in our everyday diet as they were more affordable.

One day, my father purchased a can of tuna and told my mother to open it up. He made his favorite alcoholic drink, which we call *Arak*, and heated up Arabic bread. When the tuna was ready, my father sat on the floor and placed all the food items on an elevated wooden table as he prepared to eat. My brothers and sisters and I watched him, wishing that my father would share his tuna with us.

Realizing what was going on, he immediately took all the food items off the table and threw them away. My mother and the rest of us were astonished. After throwing them outside, he came back in and began cursing about his financial situation saying, "Either we all eat tuna together or none will. I just cannot look at your faces desiring that tuna and eat it in front of you without being able to purchase more for all of us to eat." He then told my mother to bring what she had already cooked for us, which was a vegetable soup with rice and garbanzo beans.

That soup was the best meal that I had ever eaten in my life, and to this day, I have always shared any food that I have with my family, students, and friends, if they have desired it. Like my father, I cannot eat food in front of others who desire it without the need to share it – and this came from my father's example with that can of tuna, so many years ago. I cry when I think about it as I felt sorry for my father who was unable to enjoy a good meal after a long and hard workday. My love for this man is chiseled in my bones forever.

That incident also enabled me to understand the evils of poverty when I began teaching in South Central Los Angeles. I never ate in front of my students, I always dressed modestly, and never turned away any requests for financial help when my students needed me to purchase food items, learning materials, or to pay for their transportation.

My Mother's Love

Photo from 1968 with the author's brother, Emil, seated next to their mother while she prepares vegetables for a meal. Moments like these were her favorite.

My father was not alone in shaping my values at that time: my mother's impact was just as strong as his. Her love manifested itself in so many ways as she always put her needs second to ours. She kept the house very clean and welcoming and always prepared warm meals for us to eat every day. I still remember the mountain of clothes lying there waiting for her to wash with her bare hands, which made me feel sorry for her. We did not own a clothes washer or a dishwasher at that time as we could not afford it. I recall that she would complain of severe, lower back pain and her fingers and palms became very wrinkled. She would always invoke that God's and the

Virgin Mary's mercy and love be bestowed on all of us; she prayed to the Virgin Mary every night before going to sleep.

A photo taken circa 1944 of the author's parents along with his sister Hanna and brother Nabil.

At that time, women throughout the Middle East lacked equality with men. Women's liberation and equality with men was just not a part of my mother's life. Even today, women still lack full equality with men all over the world. And I always felt so bad for all those silent women doing everything it took to keep their families well fed, loved and intact.

My father was part of the generation that did not help women with house chores. On many occasions, he behaved harshly toward my mother but he never physically or mentally abused her. He would always say something funny to ease the pain of his behavior. Sometimes, he would even make hummus and *shish kebab* with his own hands, which surprised my mother. My father was good at what he loved to cook. Rarely, did he say he was sorry. That would reduce his manly stature and it was something that I always hated. But then, manhood was what men held onto at the time, regardless of how soft they were.

Physically, my mother was slim and had black hair and brown eyes. When you stared into them, you could see love emanating from them like sparkling stars. I would stare into her eyes and feel a deep calmness and a sense of belonging. Even now, at the age of 72, it is too hard to describe those looks without crying. Her kisses and hugs made me feel protected and secure. I used to leave home on my way to school feeling happy and at peace knowing that my mother would be there when I returned home.

My mother was content with our overall financial situation. She always purchased what was needed rather than what she or we wanted. Her frugal management of whatever my father was able to provide made us feel that we always had what we needed. During holidays, especially Christmas and Easter, I loved walking with her to the Bazaar to shop for a new shirt, pants, and a pair of socks. The new shoes, however, were my father's responsibility. After all, he was the shoemaker par excellence.

On our way to the Bazaar, she would meet many women from her old village, Ma-Alool, and they would greet each other with warm words and hugging. Their conversations always referred to the good times living in Ma'Alool and their family's situations. I used to beg my mother to stop talking because I was in a hurry to shop with her, keeping in mind my new clothes.

With the limited income she had, my mother would spend a lot of time trying to bargain for the best deals. This habit taught me the power of being nice when bargaining with others as well as being content with whatever means I had. It also taught me to be careful with how I spent my money, focusing on what I needed rather than what I wanted.

Our daily exchange in the morning would start with me greeting my mother with "Sabah Al-Khair Yama" (Good Morning, mother), to which she would respond, "Yess-Aid- Hatha-Al Sabah Yama," which means, "Happy this morning shall be for you, son."

Wow. This morning becomes mine and hers at the same time and it will bring me as much happiness as it will bring to her. (*Yama* is also used as a term of endearment as though calling the child, "Darling".) And off I would go to school, happy and content. Above all, she made me realize the heavy and extraordinary job that women, and especially mothers, contribute silently to the betterment of humanity without the need for macho vengeance. The tenderness that all females are born with is a most powerful gift that we men must appreciate. It reduces life's stresses and the urge for male violence.

My memories of Easter differ from those of Christmas. A month or so before the start of Easter, the cookie season begins. The smell emanating from the neighborhoods of both the Muslim quarter and that of the Christian one was full of the sweet smell of cookies. I remember very vividly how my aunts used to gather at my house to complete making Easter cookies, a process that would repeat at each of my aunt's homes as they took turns making the cookies.

I am not talking about a small batch: I'm talking about three to four hundred of them for each family. These cookies were filled with a special mix made mainly of ground dates, to which was added a heavenly spice mix that only skilled women were able to perfect. This mix was rolled into about a third of an inch diameter and then inserted into a flat piece of dough made of flour or semolina, similar to rolling a cigarette. The cookies averaged 3-4 inches in circumference with a diameter of about one half of an inch. The final product looked like a bracelet, and after baking in the oven (I still remember the smell!), they would harden and turn brown and white in color. I used to place three to four of them around my hand as if they were bracelets and eat them one at a time.

To complete our cookies, my mother and sisters used to prepare all the needed ingredients the night before. My aunts would arrive in the morning to help my mother complete the process. Her main job was to cook and serve her guests while they were making the cookies, while singing, gossiping, laughing at a dirty joke, and complaining about the bad behavior of their husbands and kids.

My aunt Zahra was the only sister among her seven brothers, and she holds a special place in my memory. In addition to her cookie-making expertise, she would also watch us little ones try and stop us from sneaking in and stealing that heavenly date filling. You were in deep trouble if she caught you doing so, and I was scared of her catching me. My aunt Zahra never got married and instead chose to take care of her mother and to enjoy the company of her brothers, including my father. In addition of witnessing the passing of her parents, she also witnessed the passing of six of her seven brothers. We all feared her but respected and loved her. She always prepared something for me when visiting her, either a coffee or a cookie (of course).

In addition to my aunt Zahra were my aunts Eessa, Jeries, Joseph, Khaleel ,Farah and my sisters. On the second day of cookie-making, they would meet at another aunt's house and repeat the same process all over again. One common theme that they all followed was to make a special cookie for the youngest in the family. The cookie was always almost half the size of the regular ones decorated with special symbols for the littles one. Love was at the center of it all. No one dared to eat it, as it was for the youngest of them all. In my case, it went always to my youngest brother, William.

I miss this cookie tradition a lot and think of it when Easter arrives... all have passed on now, but I still live with their memories.

It Takes a Village

I strongly believe that it takes a village to raise a child. This was my belief long before Hillary Clinton began using it as a slogan for her election campaign. Most of the men and women in my family and in my neighborhood knew who I was, and when I misbehaved outside the house, they used to reprimand me as if I was their own child. Most parents did not make a big deal out of it as the neighborhood parents were your parents, as well. This meant love, companionship, and strict discipline—no one called the police.

Those three years at KALM shaped many of my early values as well as my outlook on life. I began questioning God's presence, priests' rigidity, and the many divisions among God's three religions, who all were fighting each other in his name. At that age, I did not understand what the main differences were among these three religions that surrounded me. Yet, it was very easy for me to realize that all of them shared the belief of one God and that each occupied Palestine in his name. Furthermore, the name of God was used to extend their brutal power and use it as an excuse for their crimes against the occupied people.

During those years, I also learned how to navigate the complex relationship between students and teachers as I knew I had to live with my teachers' strict disciplinary policies while also being able to appreciate their kindness. Not only did they teach us how to read and write, but they taught us a love of country, parents, family, and friends. In return, they demanded we listen to their instructions, attend school daily, attend mass on Sundays, and study hard. Not following those requests meant that we would be completing our homework at school rather than in the comfort of our own homes. It also meant our parents would be told about any major infractions.

I hated the last as it always resulted in further disciplinary punishment by my parents. Our parents trusted our teachers, and as such, they took the place of our parents during the school day, so I had to listen to them.

My first encounter with a teacher was with a strict but fair teacher known as Mr. Khouri. To keep us warm during winter months, as our building had no central A/C or heating systems, he would light a pile of wood in a large steel bowl. At the beginning of our math class, he would give us division and multiplication problems which were to be placed, when completed, on top of his desk adjacent to the fire pit. To stay warm, you needed to be first in line when he was correcting the papers so you could be closest to that fire pit.

Well, I had my math problems solved as fast as I could to ensure that I would be nearest to the warmth generated by that fire pit. The issue was that I did not always make time to ensure the accuracy of my answers. Other students may have been better at math, but they took too long to solve the problems. Thus, they were further away from the fire. I figured out that making a mistake and being warm was much better than being cold and correct. I always felt that I could always catch up later when the summer heat arrived.

Photo of the author's favorite teacher from grammar school, Mr. Khouri, dated circa 1970.

I tended to be much better in my other subjects of reading, writing, history, and reciting poetry, but overall, my grades averaged between a B and B+, even with my less than stellar grades in math.

Mr. Khoury had other ways to keep us in line during our "physical training session." Once out on the playground, he would divide the class in two halves. One half stood against the northern wall of the yard while the other stood to its southern side. We were 30 to 40 students, as I recall. He would walk toward the synagogue's western wall and with a pencil hidden in his left palm, he would write a number on the wall between one and 50. He would then ask each of us to figure out the number he had written by asking the first student standing in line on the north side, followed by the first student standing in line on the south side, alternating back and forth until a student shouted out the correct hidden number.

Depending on which side that student stood on, those standing on the losing side would have to carry the winning team's students on their backs, one time around the yard. So, 20 or so losing students would be carrying 20 or so winning students, who would be laughing as they got their free ride. Meanwhile, those carrying the load on their backs would be trying their best to breathe and get this done as fast as possible.

I loved this game! I always prayed that the student standing on the opposite side facing me was not too tall or heavy. But just in case, to avoid that outcome, I used to switch my place in line with the student standing next to me without being observed by my teacher. When such an illegal plan failed, I always paid the price by not being allowed to partake in the fun or by being assigned to pick up trash. Mr. Khoury did not accept any excuses and he showed no mercy. If you broke the rules, you paid the price.

One day, Mr. Khoury performed the exact same exercise, yet this time, when he held the pencil under his palm, I saw that his right hand went up and down. Then he moved his hand a bit to the left and again, his right hand went up and down. I immediately figured out that the number was 11 -- and so it was! Number 11 in Arabic is identical to that in English. After all, English numbers derived from the Arabic numbers, which we still use today.

As a result of my observation, my team won, and we rode on the backs of the other students around the yard. It was a great feeling, thanks to my powerful eyesight and my power of observation when his hands moved up and down.

After that success, Number 11 became my favorite number. When my kids were born and started their soccer practices, I always asked their coach to put Number 11 on their jerseys, and now, I do this for my grandchildren. To this day, when I select lottery numbers or play roulette at the casino, I always select Number 11, even though that number has never shown up, so far.

Unfortunately, when I moved up to the third grade, Mr. Khoury's year came to an end and a teacher named Mrs. Rose became my nightmare. She was short and wore heavy makeup and she was *mean*. She used to punish me for the kinds of silly things that a 7-year-old would do, such as: chewing gum, throwing pieces of paper at other students, making funny noises, talking in class, giggling and so on. And her punishments were always severe: standing to face the wall, not being allowed to participate in playground activities, extra homework, picking up trash, or worse, informing my parents. The few days that I behaved well by her standards, I was allowed to play soccer with the rest of the students.

Mrs. Rose used to knit while observing us playing. She would place her big purse, that contained cotton fabrics, on top of a table that we carried out from the classroom. We also had to carry out her favorite chair so that she could sit and knit. Her purse covered her face, which was a blessing for us troublemakers. For me, it created the perfect opportunity to release some of my frustration against her repeated punishments.

While playing soccer, I would purposely aim the ball directly at her purse and kick it, hoping to hit her purse and in turn, her face. I figured that if I missed, I could always run after the ball, apologize, and claim that it was just an errant kick. But when on a few occasions the ball hit the purse and then her face, she would get very angry and stop all the fun. Her face would turn stern, and she would launch an FBI-like investigation to find out who did it.

Somehow, she always failed to pinpoint me as the kicker. This amused my classmates, who looked forward to my next attempt, so no one turned me in. Why spoil the fun? I was always loyal to them, as well, and never snitched on anyone.

Despite my bad experiences with Mrs. Rose, I enjoyed singing in her class. One song was dedicated to her ego, while the second was for our school and education. The first goes like this:

Sit Rose Ya Eyoony. (Mrs. Rose you are my eyes, or inside my eyes.)
Khasrek khasr al-laymooneh. (Your abdomen looks like a beautiful lemon tree.)
La-ma betfuti ala' al saff- zay al Aum Alhanooneh. (When you enter the classroom, you look like a tender mother.)

The second song is much longer and more enduring. It is a song full of love of school, education, and our parents. (I wish that all students around the world could learn it and its meaning.) It goes like this:

> *Madrasti Ma ahlaha.* (My school is so beautiful.)
> *Calbi Mo walla'a fi hawaha.* (My heart is full of her love.)
> *Tool omri ma bansaha.* (For the rest of my life, I will not forget it.)
> *Baffeeq al subeh bakeer* (I get up early in the morning)
> *Kabel ma ya-tiru al asafeer.* (before the birds fly away.)
> *Bakul lel mama Sabah al-khair.* (I say good morning to my mom.)
> *Walil baba ya Nour El Ain* (and to my father: you are the light of my eyes.)
> *Radu Alayah then etnen.* (They both answer me together:)
> *Sabah al khair Sabah al noor.* (Good and bright blessed morning.)

And so, when the media and our leaders began associating madrasah (Arabic for school) as a places where terrorists learn how to terrorize and kill, I wish they would remember that, overwhelmingly, a madrasah can also be a place where teachers teach peace and love in addition to providing a great education. My madrasah was a warm place where education took place, friendships were built, and excellent values were born, cherished, and strengthened.

Because of its great meaning to me, I sang the *al madrasah* song to my children and to my grandchildren. Why do I still remember both these songs and not the others I learned? I really do not know.

After almost 30 years, I met Mrs. Rose at my sister's house during one of my visits to see my family. I confessed to her that I was the one who kicked the soccer ball at her purse. She told me that she always had a hunch that it was me. We laughed and she gave me a big hug and told me how proud she was that I had completed my Ph.D. but then insisted on harshly twisting one of my ears as a payback. This ear-twisting was one of many punishments she used to discipline troublemakers like me.

Before the start of classes, all students were directed to stand in line in three columns that indicated grades one, two and three. We were all asked to pull our handkerchiefs out of our pockets and place them on the back of our palms exposing our fingernails. This was how the teachers of each grade inspected the cleanliness of our fingernails, as well as our handkerchiefs. If what they saw was not to their satisfaction, they would hit us with the edge of a ruler, inflicting severe pain, so that we would not forget our hygiene the next day. To this day, I make sure that I always carry a handkerchief in all of my pants' pockets.

Another lesson I learned was how to handle bullies. Bullying by cowardly classmates required different survival strategies than those I used with nice or kind classmates. I quickly learned how to defend myself, protect my friends, and stand firm when I was bullied. I tried to be honest and loyal to those classmates who were kind to me and meant no harm.

No one was more of a bullying student than "Hani," who, like me, was a good soccer player. Hani was unable to use his bullying techniques inside the classroom but he made up for it outside and especially when playing soccer. Hani lived very close to our school's building so he felt he was more at home than others who lived farther away.

Since neither one of us could afford a soccer ball, we relied on "Mounir," a student who came from a wealthier family, to buy a new soccer ball. Since Mounir lacked a strong personality, Hani was able to use his ball whenever he pleased, and more so than me. With this privilege, the first thing Hani did was try to prevent me from playing soccer. He would choose different classmates for the soccer teams, excluding me. It was painful and hurtful to me, but I swallowed my pride and abided by Hani's decision.

But when Mounir let me be the one in charge of the ball, I would pay Hani back by doing the same thing to him. The main difference between Hani and me was that when Mounir put him in charge, I swallowed my pride. But when I was in charge, Hani showed no such decorum. He would threaten Mounir and intimidate him after school. As Hani's house was close to school, he knew many hiding places from which he could ambush Mounir. I used to tell Mounir that he should stand tall and do as he pleased, and I made sure to always let him know that I would have his back regardless of whether he put me in charge of his soccer ball or not.

Chapter 4
Middle School: Grades 4-8

When third grade came to an end, I began attending the fourth grade at a Roman Catholic High School called St. Joseph. It was also known by two more popular names: Al-Madrasah Al-Eklerikiyah (school of the Eklerikiyah) and Madrasat Al-Mutran (the Bishop's school). The second name was the more popular reference, but then take your pick.

Madrasat Al-Mutran (MAM) served only male Muslims and Christian students who mostly lived in Nazareth and the surrounding cities, towns, and villages. Students there were a mixture of diverse socioeconomic backgrounds.

The Israeli/Zionist racist policies at that time, as it is today, discouraged Israeli students from registering at any Palestinian schools to prevent assimilation with the Palestinian population, who were viewed as enemies of the State of Israel and inferior to them. We were not the "chosen people" like they were, and thus, we were treated as second class, if not fifth class citizens. How could you mix God's chosen people and the most intelligent people on earth with those lesser people who were occupied, forgotten, and neglected by this same invented God.

This policy worked both ways: it also prevented me from making any Jewish friends my age. They lived in a privileged world while I lived in my occupied world. All my life, I have wondered how I would have behaved if I had lived in a Jewish neighborhood. How about inviting Jewish friends to my house and vice-versa? At this time of my life, I did not understand the racist supra-nationalist ideology of Israel's Zionist agenda against the Palestinian indigenous population.

Not having the opportunity to assimilate meant there was also no understanding or appreciation of one another's religion, culture, history, habits, and norms. What a waste. Nothing good or positive comes out of racism.

At the time of MAM's opening in 1956, it was under the leadership of Bishop George Hakim or Al-Mutran Hakim. (In Arabic, bishop translates to "Muttran," while "Hakim" means "the wise one" or "medical doctor.") The bishop's reputation and influence were widespread among the Palestinian communities; you did not want to mess with him.

At MAM, the main administrative powers were in the hands of its Principal Father or "Abuna" in Arabic, by the name Kerrillos Habib ("the loving Kerrillos" or "K" for short and I do not mean "K" as in Kissinger). I remember Principal Abuna-K as being tall and overweight with a black and white beard, walking quickly as if he was in a hurry all the time. He was a very mean disciplinarian, and while his name "Habib" meant "the lovely one," he was not lovely at all.

The so-called "Lovely K" had another abuna assisting him named Father Abuna Ghazal (Ghazal in Arabic is the name given to the majestic animal, the deer. The word "Ghazal" was, then as it is now, popularly used by poets to compare the Ghazal's beautiful eyes to those of a beautiful woman's eyes. Poets also associated the beauty of the deer's eyes and its slender body as having a romantic night with a woman with the same bodily beauty of that of the deer's.)

Father Abuna Ghazal was a heavy cigarette smoker and wine drinker. He was short and skinny and had a very short fuse, coughed a lot and rumors had it that he used to molest students. I can still hear his loud and abusive voice directed at us little ones.

Lastly, the teachers, most of whom were local Palestinians, formed the other group of disciplinarians.

Then there was a pecking order based on your age. Twelfth grade students received better treatment from the administrative personnel than the rest of the students, followed by the eleventh graders, and so on. As I was at the lower end of the above scale, I was often cursed, bullied, and pushed around. If it was not for my older relatives, who were attending the same school, and for running too fast and hiding in very hard to find places including trash canisters, I could have gotten myself in more trouble.

I only managed to attend MAM until the eighth grade. By then, I became a confused and disillusioned student who wanted to just get the hell out of MAM. There were good, bad and ugly reasons that influenced my negative attitudes (in reference to one of my favorite movies: *The Good, The Bad, and The Ugly*).

The Good

To start with, MAM was located at the top of Nazareth's canoe-shaped topography, which was almost the opposite of KALM's location. It was also nearly two miles from my home. That meant no more walking three miles, one way, downhill as I did at KALM. MAM was built at the far northwest rim of that canoe-shape so it meant that if I walked fast enough, I could eat a hot, homemade lunch and still make it back in the nick of time before afternoon classes began avoiding further punishment by those priests. As I recall, the lunch break was one and a half hours long.

So, I made sure that I woke up early enough to have plenty of time to have fun with the neighborhood kids on my way to school. We did many funny, stupid, and innocent things as we passed between and among family and friends' homes. We encountered many women who were drinking their morning coffee on their balconies as a way of socializing after their husbands had left for work.

Undated photos of the author's neighborhood in Nazareth.

Undated photo of the author's uncle, Radwan.

Neighborhood women would drink coffee as a way of maintaining their strong bond with other women to gossip, complain about their husbands and kids, tell funny and nasty jokes, discuss what they wanted to shop for or cook, and other boring family issues. Once they had their fill, they would go back into their homes and do whatever they had to do until the next morning's coffee break. The smell of coffee would fill the air as they encouraged us to walk faster and get to school on time. They would also remind us to behave and to get excellent grades—or else.

One of those homes we passed was that of my Uncle Radwan and his wife, whose name I have forgotten. She used to tell me all the time to stop by her garden on my way to school and pick her fresh produce, especially tomatoes and cucumbers. (I cannot remember a day that passed without eating both vegetables.) I would do this while preventing the others from picking my uncle and aunt's produce so her husband would not get mad at me.

A few yards away from her house stood a large, old house where

Dar-Al-Hawwary's family lived. Their son Nimer ("Tiger" in English) was inflicted with a mental disability. Most of the time he roamed the streets singing and dancing his 'unique' dance. He was at least 25 years old. As a kid, I did not understand why he behaved this way. The people called him Maj-noon, meaning "idiot" or "without brains." His family was poor, so they did not have access to medical or psychological help for him.

I remember very well that I used to force him to dance and sing for us as we laughed at him. To this day, I feel terribly ashamed of what I did to Nimer. Yet, his memory is imprinted in my mind, and it makes me extremely upset when I hear our political leaders advocating cutting funds and programs designed for the treatment of mental illness, homelessness, or basic research to cure them. Among the many songs that Nimer used to sing, I still remember one and only one. It goes like this:

Akhdar Ya kern Al Bamiyeh: (The okra stem is green.)
Josy etjawaz alaieh: (My husband married another woman behind my back.)
Wa ana sabeieh wa kamleh: (While I am still young and physically attractive.)

Why did Nimer mention okra, a husband and betrayal? I do not know.

While he sang, he used to lift his right leg up and down, then lift his left leg up and down. He repeated the above song many times over until we had our fill. (Wow, I was eight years old then. Who knew that at age 50, I would be teaching physically-challenged students at Narbonne High School in Los Angeles?

After such fun, we passed through a small forest before arriving at school. This forest was called Hursh Schneller or Schneller's Forest. It hid a huge hospital that was built, as I was told then, by the Germans as a military garrison for a show of force and further intimidation of Nazareth residents.

As kids, entering the forest meant all fun stopped and instead fear set in. We would run as fast as we could to reach its edge and enter an open field that was not far from the school's campus, that was planted with tobacco plants. We feared roaming dogs or other animals, as then, most dogs were not kept at home. They were wild and ate whatever they could find around the neighborhood so they could be very dangerous, hungry, and vicious.

On our way back, after passing through this ugly forest, we would chase each other, sing, dance, laugh, throw pebbles at each other, cuss and run. But the most disgusting habit I recall, for us boys, was when we would take our male organ out and try to pee as we walked or ran. The winner was the one who left behind the longest trail that was clearly shown on top of the dirt covering the road. Most of the time, I won. Wow, what a victory!

It was during those years at MAM that my father's work in downtown Nazareth ended abruptly. He began looking for a job and found one as a watchman on the (scary) hospital's afternoon shift. His courage and horse-riding skills were what the hospital administrators were looking for, thus, he was hired immediately. His horse-riding skills dated back to his outdoor activities during the Palestinian political and military struggle, both against the British. These horse-riding skills were also used to impress my mother while he was engaged to her. He used to ride his horse during the night, passing through very dangerous, uninhabited areas to show her his love. The problem was that he would arrive too late so no one would open the door, except her father, who would inform him that "Miriam went to bed a long time ago."

To tease him, my mother used to say, "If you really wanted to see me, you should have purchased a faster horse, unless you were not that good of a horse rider."

My father would answer her by saying, "You went to bed too early rather than waiting for the horse rider," and then we would all laugh.

Chapter 4 53

Undated photo of the author's parents sharing a romantic moment (and coffee) over the kanoon.

When word spread that my father had become the watchman, we rejoiced because the hospital's huge garden was full of fruit, ready for us to pick up or steal. Now that my father was the guard, we felt that even if he caught us, the punishment would not be that severe. And so, my older cousins, brothers, and their friends, all of whom attended the same school, cut a hole in the fences surrounding the garden and began stealing fruit while we, the little ones, acted as watch guards.

Undated photo of the author's father displaying his rifle skills.

Unfortunately, this made it harder on my poor father, who began complaining to my mother that he was unable to catch the thieves. I heard him often saying that "God would need to protect them, once I caught them and let my dog Max go after them."

Max was my father's assistant watchman. My father used to tie his hand to Max's neck while taking a nap. Once Max began barking and trying to run, he would pull my father's hand, which caused my father to wake up, grab his rifle, and follow Max. Most of the time, Max was only barking at other dogs or coyotes.

Soon, my father figured out that most of the stealing was taking place after four o'clock in the afternoon when students were dismissed from school. So, he began hiding in a place that was hard to see while he waited. As my older cousins and brothers began entering the garden through the hole that they had cut, my father caught them with their hands in the cookie jar. He became very angry and gave everyone an ultimatum: either stop stealing the fruit or he would report this to their parents, the principal, and the head of the hospital.

And so without much option we gave up the few peaches and oranges we were stealing rather than face the severe punishment of parents and priests. All of us promised my father that we would never steal again and that was that.

Another fun event I recall was sharing snacks that our mothers had given us with other students. I hated sweets so I always traded them for fruit and nuts, especially almond and pine seeds that the other students brought with them. When my mother gave me money to buy a snack at school, my favorite was Raha, a 2" x 2" dried Guowei fruit, which I would place between two unsweetened flat cookies, similar to marshmallows between two cookies.

For lunch, I began visiting the homes of my Muslim friends who lived nearby the school. The repeated lunch invitations were overwhelming. I realized, very quickly, that there is no difference between a Palestinian of Muslims descent and that of a Christian background in terms of national identity, customs, and norms. I learned that we all shared a strong connection to our Arab and Palestinian heritage. On many occasions, I would inform my mother, before leaving for school, that I would eat my lunch at Al-Shahbari's Muslim house, which saved me having to walk two miles to my house.

My mother also repeatedly encouraged my Muslim friends to come eat lunch with me and if they refused her invitation, she would forbid me from eating at their houses anymore. And so it went. Eating together further strengthened our bonds, protecting one another from bullies and scary priests.

In my case, this exchange of brotherhood between a Palestinian Muslim and Christian began a long time ago when my father began having a close relationship with Muslim Bedouins, having visited their villages and towns. I remember his friends visiting our home and eating with us on many occasions. They loved us a lot and shared many of their customs, habits, and pictures of their families.

Undated photos of the author's father with his Palestinian Bedouin Muslim friend, who were all living in the Negev Desert at that time.

I heard many stories from my family regarding the unity of the Palestinian Muslims and Christians that came from each living side-by-side in my parents' village of Ma'Alool. They shared all the Palestinian traditions and norms, equally, and without prejudice. I still remember my father and his brothers gathering at our house, then giving their holiday wishes to our Muslim neighbors' and vice-versa.

Knowing so many students from different parts of Palestine made me feel that I belonged to a much larger community, united by similar history, language, and customs. I got to know students whose parents were refugees, like mine. We began sharing the names of those places, especially the names of the destroyed villages and towns. Additionally, I learned a lot from the older students about the history of the creation of the State of Israel and how it led to the Palestinian Nakba, especially the saga of the Palestinian refugees living in miserable conditions all over the Middle East and the world.

The Bad

There were many bad things also about those years. My school's curriculum was much harder than it had previously been and included subjects that I was not ready for, especially beginning Algebra and Religious Studies. Learning other languages, such as Hebrew, French, and English in addition to Arabic, confused my little brain and my grades began to plummet. I do not remember when the above subjects were introduced, but what I am sure of is that my grades in those subjects were not very good.

The classes that I excelled in were History, Beginning Physics, Poetry, and Sports. The excellent grades I received in these subjects saved my overall grade, which averaged at a "C," but not much better. Despite my hard work and repeated attempts to improve my grades, there were always other students who did much better than I. Realizing this, I became less and less enthusiastic about keeping up with the competition and the pressure of studying.

The author's final eighth grade report card for the 1964-65 school year.

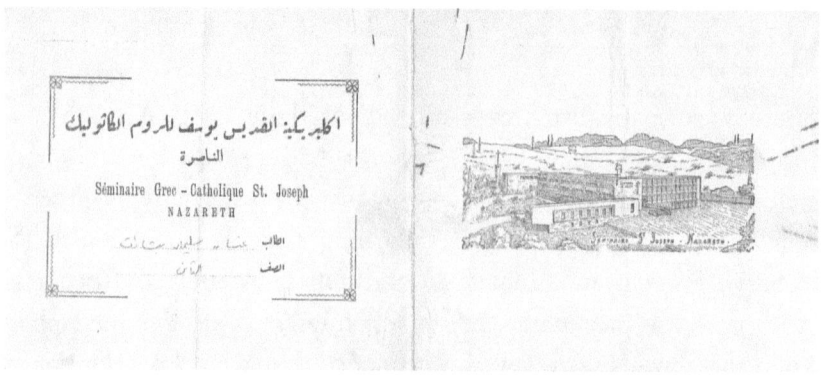

Our grades were given out twice a year: before Christmas break and at the end of the year. Teachers would submit our grades and ranks to the principal. The principal was Abuna or Father K, and he would enter the class with our grade reports and call our names, beginning with the highest-ranking students and ending with the lowest. There were no secrets at all.

I used to hide my face and wait for my name to be called. Of course, I waited for a long time. My name was always called among the last ten students. My grade report shows that my grades were poor in the four languages that I was studying (Arabic, Hebrew, English and French), as well as religion. But I excelled in history, as well as geography and physics. This added more humiliation and bitterness to how I already felt; I hated this school's tradition.

During this time, my love for soccer decreased, as well. The soccer field was too large, full of dirt, and held scattered small rocks that made falling very painful and bloody. I also had to play against much larger kids. I had been good as a forward player but always being harshly tackled by bigger and meaner defenders caused my goal scoring to decrease. Playing soccer also made me too tired to study. Therefore, I decided to drop soccer all together and pick it up later.

Most teachers were kissing up to "K" and behaving worse toward us than even he did. If you were late by one minute because of bathroom congestion or you did not stand straight in a perfect line, you were disciplined. You were also punished if you missed Sunday mass, made a slight joke, spoke while in line, or did some other meaningless action, as a few points would be shaved from your grades.

We, students, did not openly discuss the occupation of Palestine for fear of retaliation by the Department of Education for deviating from its curriculum. The subject matter that we were taught ignored the price that all Palestinians had paid for the creation of the State of Israel. Class discussions were limited to subject matter only. Any new ideas or explanations by students that differed from that of their teachers were not accepted and, in fact, were ridiculed. My rebellious voice was silenced all the time and eventually, I lost interest in voicing it anymore. Those teachers and so-called priests damaged my freedom of expression and I hated that.

The Ugly

I attribute "the ugly" to the repeated punishments by the two priests, especially Abuna K. I hated going to the mandatory Sunday mass. Father K used to take attendance just before the mass started. On the following Monday, he would enter the classroom and remove those students who had been absent. I think I was removed from my class more than any other student.

The punishment was to kneel against a wall for at least twenty minutes during lunch break, which prevented me from walking home and having my lunch. Father Ghazal or "G," raised the punishment bar even higher. He used to ask me to go and pick up small pebbles and bring them to him. Then, he used to lay them down and demand that I kneel on them. My pain was so severe that blood popped out of my knees very frequently.

I kept all the above to myself by making excuses to explain my injuries to my parents. Most of my friends and family members at school urged me to attend mass more frequently, which I did, but not all the time. At my young age, I reasoned that what I was hearing from those priests at Sunday mass about how much Jesus of Nazareth suffered for our sins, contradicted the way they were treating me. If I did not sin, then why were they treating me as a sinner? In my mind they were the sinners, but then, where was Jesus to save me and punish them?

When I asked my parents to explain this to me, their answer to such a confusing question was, "You have to have faith and believe in the messages given during the mass." But how could I have faith in the messages when the messengers were so cruel?

The ugliest incident which changed me forever was when my father received a letter from Father K informing him that I would be expelled from school unless my father fully paid the late tuition. My father became very angry and took me with him to Father K's office. He then closed the office door behind him and told Father K that his son would attend this school whether he liked it or not and that the backbone of this school was and is the Bisharat family. He reminded Father K of the many students from my family who attended the school and told him that he was paying for my two other brothers here as well as his two daughters at a Catholic school. And for those reasons he was unable to pay for all of them at the same time.

Flouting his arrogance, Father K continued his threatening to expel me. Suddenly, my father took his Palestinian Hattah (a head cover) and shirt off, and placed them both on his desk saying, "This is what I have: Take the shirt off my back and sell them and use the proceeds as a down payment for my son's tuition. My son will continue his education. If you keep refusing, I promise to bak-tulak."

Bak-tulak has two meanings: to physically kill and the threat of punishment that is yet to come. This word is widely used by parents to scare their children for behaving badly. Other adults used it to threaten us kids, but we rarely got punished. Fear of the punishment was enough to make us obey (just as we use the words "I will kill you" as a threat).

Father K took my father's threat very seriously. I had never seen my father so serious and angry. Father K immediately relented and told my father, "When you have the money, you can pay the tuition in installments."

At this point, my father gathered his clothes and we both left Father K's office. (This was the first time I saw my father without a shirt on and I did not know that he had so much black chest hair.)

This incident changed me for life. Seeing my father being humiliated and willing to threaten the priest to keep me in school made me very proud of him. Although, I must say, my father never hurt anyone. He showed his unconditional love for me and he believed in my educational abilities. I swore then, to myself, that I would complete the highest educational degree on earth for my parents, no matter what the price.

When my mother heard the story of what had taken place, she sat me down and gently told me, "I know that you are not happy at this school. Yet, God has given you hands made of gold. You could do anything with those hands. Why not go and attend a vocational school where your cousin Salim teaches?"

I told her that I would think about it but said I would not attend the ninth grade at my hated school.

She then told me something that I will never forget as it is chiseled in our Palestinian conscience and it goes like this:

"If the parents are happy with what their children are doing, and those children listen to their parents' advice, those children will always be successful in their lives."

We call this in our tradition *"Ridah Al-Wali-Dane."* Ridah carries two meanings at the same time: On one hand, it means that your parents are happy with what you are doing by listening to their advice. It is also a blessing from God. Al-Wali-Dane simply means "the parents: father and mother."

She then took my hands and placed them between hers and told me, with a few tears rolling down her beautiful face, to make up my mind as soon as possible. What could I do? Coming at the heels of what my father had done, my heart raced, and I felt so guilty for not wanting to go to school. I immediately told her, "Okay, I will attend that vocational school."

This parental advice was the key to my survival in the United States.

Chapter 5
Summer Break–Games We Played

During my five years at MAM, I and the other neighborhood's students patiently waited for summer break to play and have fun without teachers, priests, or Sunday masses. One of our favorite games was Hide and Seek or "Al-ghomedah" in Arabic.

We played this game at the only open field in our neighborhood. It was covered with rocks of all sizes, weeds, and wild green plants, most of which had sharp needles that poked you and left you with scars and pain.

Before starting the game, we would randomly choose someone to begin counting while the rest of us all sprang to hide before his count ended and he began seeking us out.

As kids do, we didn't pay attention to whether the grass was wet, dry, poking your skin, or hiding sharp rocks. One time, when the seeker was Boutros or "Peter," he stood on my hand while gazing out at the field to look for the kids who were hiding. I did not move, despite the pain it caused, as I didn't want him to find me. When dinner time arrived, you would hear all the mothers calling for us to get home fast or miss our dinner, and boy, we ran faster than rabbits with our clothes full of green stains and needles.

Flying kites was another popular summer break activity. I, along with the other kids, built my own kite. I used three identical 15" x 25" flat, wood pieces that are attached to each other with a nail hammered in the center of the three. Then I would fold them like a star with six points and place them on a flat sheet of paper and glue the end of this paper to the strings that I used to form the outside shape of this star-like kite.

We flew them when the wind was strong enough to lift them up. But when the wind was not strong enough, we still tried to fly them: One person would hold the kite and lift it up, while the other would hold the string's handle and run as fast as possible hoping to generate enough momentum to lift and keep the kite up. Most of the time, it was to no avail. We just wasted our energy for nothing.

Later in life, I began building kites for my children and now, for my grandchildren. Manhattan Beach, California, was our favorite place to fly kites and I am proud to say that the kites I built have always been the ones that flew the highest. People always ask me how I manage to build such fine kites, and I am happy to share my technique in detail so others can enjoy them.

In addition to building kites, we built scooters and small, wooden cars using used ball bearings as wheels after collecting them at the auto repair shops in downtown Nazareth. We raced those scooters downhill and then carried them back up again.

We also invented our own Israeli money from newspapers. We cut varying size pieces and assigned them different money values. We would then use this money to buy items at our friends' stand. They would pretend to sell us all sorts of items like sugar, coffee, beans, salt, peppers, and nuts, all made from a variety of small rocks and dirt found around the neighborhood.

We also played with tops, marbles, and poker cards. When friends would win my marbles and tops in the morning, I would win them back plus get theirs, playing poker in the afternoon. Now and then, I was good at poker despite losing more than winning. (Recent research shows that playing poker delays dementia and keeps seniors' minds young and alert, so, do you blame me?)

Another game we loved to play was Army. We would pretend to have two armies on horseback. The horse was a long, round stick of wood that you placed between your legs and pretended to ride or walk. For swords, we usually used items made of wood or hard rubber. Our shields were items we stole from our mom's kitchen, such as thin cooking pans, trash can covers or a frying pan.

I was always the General In Charge. My friends, who were the soldiers, would obey my orders and salute me. I vividly remember an incident where a passing soldier saluted me while I was peeing—after all, I was his commander. To this day, I still laugh with those same friends when I go back to see my family and friends in Nazareth.

Hunting birds was something else we boys liked to do. We would chase birds hoping that we could hit some of them with well-rounded marbles or small rocks flung from our slingshots. When we were able to hit and kill a bird, after a long and exhausting chase far away from our homes, we would clean off the feathers, remove the inner body parts, built a fire, and barbecue it for a meal. This exhaustive exercise tired us out and was not worth it. Yet, the chase experience and the togetherness of our little group of friends was what made it worthwhile. That barbecued bird meat was the best that I have ever eaten. It is by far much better than all the hamburger meals that I have eaten. The experience was not only worthwhile but outstanding.

Since we were too young to purchase cigarettes, we would model our fathers' smoking by making look-alike cigarettes out of dry pine needles wrapped in paper. We would arrange them inside a flattened paper then roll the paper around those needles and moisten the two edges of the paper with our saliva to form our cigarette which, now, looked more of a cigar than a cigarette.

When lit, the smoke covered our faces while we laughed and

competed to see who could produce the heaviest smoke. You started with a small cigarette-size wrapper and then progressed to one that was almost five inches long and an inch in diameter. At such a size, the front of the so-called cigarette or cigar was like a fourth of July firecracker. It would burn your eyelashes, the hair above your eyes, it changed the color of your face and smelled like a burning bush.

Smoking it, though, was the easy part. Entering your house after such stupidity was another matter. Once I entered the house, my mother would immediately smell the cigarette and demand an immediate shower, then food but no dessert, to be followed by a stiff punishment from my father when he arrived home from his job.

I was not concerned about my father's punishment as much as my mother being angry at me and physically unable or unwilling to put her hands on me. Her punishment for me was that I felt guilty, and more than punished for my behavior, I felt bad for causing her anguish. She repeatedly warned me not to pursue such an ugly habit. She used to tear up while reprimanding me, which increased my guilt. I could have handled a physical punishment much better than seeing her in such a state.

Then, I had to wait for my father's punishment. Once he entered the house, my mother would immediately inform him about my continued smoking and demand that he immediately punish me.

So, after a long workday, my father, who was anticipating a good, relaxing dinner, would get so angry that he would take it out on me. Being the man of the house, he would demand that I follow him to the bedroom. He would slam the door very strongly to impress my mother of his serious intentions to punish me. But he would, instead, wink at me and with his hands, direct me to go under the thick cover of the bed while loudly proclaiming that he was pulling his belt off to hit me. Instead, he would take his handkerchief from his pocket and throw it at me while I laughed my heart out. While he did this, he would unleash a barrage of insults at me and threaten me with further punishment, including cleaning the yard, among others.

Finally, in a loud voice, he would demand that I leave the room immediately. Opening the door, my father would tell my mother that he had taught me a good lesson. But she would then ask, "Then why is Ghassan laughing?"

And he would say, "I do not have the heart to punish him. He will learn to quit this ugly habit on his own."

Both my parents had such soft, easy-going hearts that we kids always took advantage of no matter where we lived. The best that my father was able to do, as far as punishment, was to kick me in the butt, an activity we call "shallot." No wonder so many of my students told me, years later, that they always took advantage of me because "Dr. B has a soft heart."

My ugly habit of smoking further progressed due to our neighbor, Abu Mo-khayeel (Abu Mo), who owned the only grocery store in the neighborhood. Abu Mo would never finish his entire cigarette. Instead, he would throw it away while still lit. Anticipating this gift, we kids would run after the burning cigarette and smoke the rest of it.

This smoking habit has stayed with me to this day. Yet, I have never been a heavy smoker, thanks to the pain that I feel in my throat when inhaling cigarette smoke. Despite not being an addict of cigarette smoking, on occasion and especially when playing cards with friends or at the casino, I feel the urge to smoke a couple of cigarettes. I do not know why that is. Otherwise, I rarely, if ever, light a cigarette.

As far as drug use and abuse, that was unknown back when I was growing up. I never knew anyone who used drugs and never saw it around my neighborhood. Now, however, drug use and abuse is widespread throughout Israel among its Jewish and Palestinian populations.

I enjoyed visiting my neighbors' homes. Knowing the parents and behaving nicely made me more than welcome. I was always offered cold drinks and popsicles, which were my favorite treat. I was constantly invited to stay for a meal with my friends' families. Sometimes I stayed but other times, I felt shy about doing so.

The funny thing is that despite my social skills, I remain a very shy person. It takes time for me to feel at home due to my focused self-awareness and not wanting to behave in a way that would appear to be cold or lacking in manners. So, many times, I would make excuses to decline these offers to protect myself and preserve my dignity.

Another activity that we did as a neighborhood was to compete against other, far away, neighborhood kids in soccer. For me, this activity was a blessing and a curse, at the same time. My team included my brother and my cousin. As the coach of our team, I was under pressure to treat them like the rest of my teammates. This was hard to do knowing that neither knew how to play or had attempted to learn the game. Instead, they made a joke about our training exercises and would give me a hard time. Yet, I had to coach them equally and pretend that all was good and well.

One incident that still lingers in my memory happened early in the morning as we were preparing the soccer field for an important game with our main competitors' team. After making the necessary chucking of the soccer field's perimeters with white powder, my brother and cousin snuck onto the field while we were taking a break, a few minutes before game time. As a prank, they covered the outlines that we had just defined with brown dirt and pretended they had just arrived to play with the rest of the team.

When the other team showed up, we were all very embarrassed, but the two of them were laughing as if nothing had happened. One of my team members picked up a piece of wood that was laying on the field and stabbed my cousin in the stomach, slightly injuring him.

When the incident was reported to his father and mine, I was severely reprimanded by both. My father took me completely by surprise when he slammed me so hard with his open palm against my right cheek that I fell to the ground. He was ashamed of me not standing up for my cousin against non-family members on my team. In his mind, I was responsible as I had formed the soccer team. This was the only time that my father laid a hand on me. I assume that he was ashamed and angry to do this. I did not know, beforehand, that he had such strength in his hands.

Yet, with his soft heart, my father felt bad about it later. However, rather than apologizing to me, he demanded that my brother either listen to my instructions and respect them or quit the team and apologize to me right away. The seriousness with which he conveyed his message made my brother immediately quit the team and apologize to me for what he and my cousin had done. Finding out that my brother had quit the team, my cousin followed suit, which was a relief to me.

Another childhood experience I recall had to do with my picking and eating pomegranates from our trees. As a young boy, I would sit on the steps of our yard, facing the street, and peel and eat the pomegranates I picked from our trees. Our yard was full of pomegranate trees with hundreds of ripe ones. (I always wondered about the way the seeds of the pomegranate are arranged, which I consider a miracle of nature.)

Photo from 1970 taken in the author's backyard. Clockwise from the left: the author's cousin, Ba'heej; the author's cousin, Walid (Ba'heej's brother); and the author's brother, Habib.

On many occasions, while I sat between my brother and cousin eating the seeds, the most beautiful woman in my neighborhood would look at us as she passed by and say, "Hi, Habibi Ghassan" (which means "Hi, my love Ghassan"). However, she would not say anything to my brother or my cousin. Being jealous of me getting all the attention, they would whack me on my shoulders and ask why she did not say this to them, as well. I would say, "Because both of you are ugly. Do you blame her?"

Another habit, which I now regret, was trespassing into my neighbors' yards and gardens to steal their fruit and nuts. Since our yard was always full of fig and pomegranate trees, my parents always encouraged us to let our friends pick some of the fruit as a welcoming gesture. However, this gesture was not reciprocated by many of the other parents who prohibited their kids from offering this to me. Embarrassed by this gesture, my friends would tell me when their parents were not at home so that we kids could enter their orchard to pick their fruit and nuts. Then, we would run to a hiding place that we designated beforehand to consume them. I have always hated to see fresh fruit and vegetables rotting on the ground.

Sometimes, I will ask the property owners if I can pick up whatever is ripe. Asking for permission has always resulted in welcoming gestures by those who own the trees. Where I live now, in Sierra Madre, there are always lemons and oranges that are not regularly picked.

I also have memories of picking wild anise of which we would cut the long green stems and bring them home for our family's consumption. (I still like to dice the anise stems and mix them with my salad.) We would bundle them, one stem at a time, forming an elongated round bundle of stems, like bundling wheat stems together. To keep them tightly bundled, I used to wrap my anise stems tightly using my father's belt and carry them home under my arm with great joy and pride.

Next to the eastern side of my house stood an empty lot full of large boulders, rocks, and wild grass. My father wanted to purchase it but he was not financially able to do so, therefore, it remained empty until it was covered by numerous houses, later on.

In one of those rocks, we found a deep rounded hole made by nature to nurture our love of baked potatoes. Occasionally, when one of us had money, my friends and I would drop by Um Ya'akoob's grocery store and while the purchase was being made, we would also steal her potatoes. The owner was an elderly lady who we would help when she needed us to lift heavy sacks of onions or potatoes and place them high up on the bench.

Photo from 1970 showing the author's neighborhood. Um Ya'koob's grocery store can be seen on the far right-hand side.

With pockets full of potatoes, we would run toward that rock, fill the bottom of it with dry weeds and sticks found nearby the hole, light them up, and place those potatoes on top of the fire while rotating them. Once they became blackened, we would pick them up and open them up with the steam of fresh baked potato vapor penetrating our noses. We would then apply salt and pepper, which we kept next to the rock hole and eat them. No wonder baking potatoes is still my favorite way of consuming them. On very few occasions, I still bake them that way but without those friends and those memories, they never taste the same.

Early Paid Work Experiences

Not all summer break activities were full of fun. During many of those school breaks, I worked at a flat-repair tire shop to help pay for my books and other school supplies, to relieve my parents of some of their financial burden. We were going through very bad financial difficulties then and my father's income was barely making ends meet.

The tire repair shop was owned by a distant cousin named Saïd ("Abu Jaber"). He would pick me up in his Volkswagen car and drive me to his shop. My job was to fill the repaired tires with pressurized air and measure the air pressure. This was the easy part of it. The difficult part was fixing the flat tires of the Big Rig trucks.

Photo from 1970 showing Abu Jaber on the left side along with the author's uncle, Issa.

Abu Jaber would give me a short hydraulic jack and ask me to place it under a specific location next to the flat tire. Because of my small body size, I would roll under the rig in the filthy dirty yard next to the shop and place that jack under the proper location. Then, I would roll out from beneath the truck and insert the jack handle in its proper location. With Abu Jaber's help, I would crank the jack handle up and down until the tire was at least three inches above the ground. Once it had been lifted, Abu Jaber would use a huge air gun to unlock the nuts so he could remove the tire and fix it.

After it was fixed, he would use the air gun again to tighten the wheel nuts. At that moment, my job was to reverse the motion of the handle and lower the hydraulic jack. Once that was done, I had to roll under the truck and retrieve the hydraulic jack. By then, my clothes would be covered with dirt and smelly tire grease that I encountered while under the rig.

For lunch, Abu Jaber would give me hummus sandwiches and sometimes spam meat, which I hated. After work, he would drive me home again but before I could enter the house, I had to remove my dirty clothes and shoes and place them outside under the staircase. Then, I would immediately take a shower and a nap. My body was always tired and sore, but by working in this way, I made enough money to pay for my school supplies and was allowed to keep whatever was left over for myself. My parents always thanked me for doing this and they never asked me for the rest of the money as they felt that since I had worked for it, I deserved to keep some of it.

During other summer breaks, I worked with my first cousin, Samir, who was an excellent electrician, second to none in fixing gadgets such as radios and tape recorders, among many others. His brother, Salim, sold new electrical gadgets next to Samir's shop. I learned some easy repairs from Samir, but my main job was to help him install all the electrical outlets in newly-built homes. To do so, you needed to chisel a groove, at least 2" by 2" deep, along the walls then lay plastic pipes inside those grooves and plaster them with cement. Once the cement had dried, Samir would insert red, green, and white electrical wires through the pipes that ended at the proper locations of the house's electrical outlets.

Undated photo of the author's cousins. Samir (middle right) and Salim (far right) can be seen sitting with their two other brothers, Saïd (fair left) and Souheil (middle left).

Standing on a ladder and using a hammer and a chisel, I would chisel the solid concrete wall, generating so much dust and small particles that I was covered with it and looked like a white ghost. When my hands got tired, I would sometimes miss the tip of the chisel, which I held in my left hand, when striking it with the hammer in my right hand. On many occasions, I hit my thumb, instead, causing severe pain which I seasoned by cursing the heavens.

This work experience was valuable in that it later helped me in the machining work that I did, which requires steady hands and visual concentration. But the most fun I had working with Samir was when he would hang electrical cords filled with hanging bulbs, high up over a wedding reception area.

This was my golden opportunity to not only help him hang the cords, but also to attend the night's celebration, even though I had not been invited. Seeing men and women dancing, eating, singing, drinking, and joking lifted my spirits. The bands, with their traditional Palestinian folkloric music and song, were at the center of these events and the variety of food served was unbelievable. I ate my fill and danced, sang, and drank (mainly beer with supposedly adult supervision) throughout these wonderful events.

Chapter 5   75

Two photos circa 1970 depicting the author's parents dancing at two of what would be many family weddings.

When Samir and I hung the lights for a family member, the sight of my parents and all my other relatives and guests celebrating increased my love and pride for my Palestinian and Arab heritage, lifting my spirits very high. I have forgotten most of the lyrics to those songs, but of those that I still remember, I enjoy reciting and singing.

Most vivid among my memories is that of my father's dancing. As a folkloric Palestinian dancer, he was the best in our village. Watching him and dancing with my aunts penetrated my heart and soul. Those dancing memories are fuel that ignites my love of Palestine, my parents, and my true love for my family members as it was clearly on display. Those were the days that I will forever cherish as I will never see or experience them again.

After the guests had their fill at the end of these celebrations, those who drank too much would be vomiting at the far edges of the yard. Seeing Palestinians and our Jewish friends vomiting together while laying their hands on top of each other's shoulders and laughing, was a sight to see. Yet, after saying good night to each other, they would drive home in opposite directions following the segregated lives of both brotherly people.

If I could wish for a miracle, it would be to return to those celebrations again. The only thing I have now are vivid memories and some pictures taken during those celebrations. Samir passed away at a very young age in the United States and the open yards where we hung those wires were replaced by modern restaurants but my memories with Samir will always live on forever.

When time permitted, I used to drop by Salim's shop to hear the gossip and check out the newly-displayed electrical gadgets. During those times, we would always purchase homemade popsicles from a shop next door which we would enjoy while watching passing cars, pedestrians and mostly, the beautiful Palestinian women while making comments about them—wishful thinking. Later, both Samir and Salim left with their families to the United States to join their brothers Saïd and Souhail.

Undated photo of the author's uncle, Joseph.

I also worked with my Uncle Joseph, who was a very skilled and gifted carpenter. My work with him was to install the kitchen and book cabinets that he built in his shop then transported to wealthy Israeli homes to be installed. The wealth of the Israelis opened my eyes to their privileged status as the masters of the stolen Palestinian lands. Both the newly-built and abandoned and stolen homes were located on the mountain top of the city of Haifa, which was one of the most beautiful Mediterranean cities. It was the crown that covered the Palestinian mountains. Sadly, most of its indigenous population are no longer able to see that crown shining.

Tragically, it was depopulated by the merciless Israeli Armed Forces using unspeakable war crime methods, including forced sea evacuation on board unsafe boats. They also rolled barrels of crude oil down the mountains and hills where they would explode against the homes below, resulting in death, destruction, and panic. (I was told by many of my relatives that a cousin of ours was caught in this situation. While fleeing her burning home, she picked up her child from her crib and ran toward the sea to board one of those unsafe boats. The boat destination was Lebanon. When she tried to feed her baby, she discovered that, in her panic, she had picked up a pillow rather than her baby, who remained behind in her burning home.)

My uncle's carpentry work was very professional, extremely accurate, and well-built. The owners of those homes to which he sold his cabinets had no reason to criticize him, but I could tell from the way they looked at his work that they were surprised and astonished. Palestinian labor was often demeaned by Israelis as a psychological tool to keep us down. They always insulted our work when things were not done to their satisfaction, calling such labor "Avoda Aravit" or "Arabic work." Rarely did they say "thank you" when it was done satisfactorily, and this put down strategy has become part of the Israeli government's overall psychological warfare against the Palestinians' everyday life.

But what surprised me the most was the lack of generosity the owners of those homes displayed. They never offered us a glass of water or a cup of coffee. Maybe they did not want us to have our lips touching their glasses and cups, or maybe it was sheer ignorance of Palestinians' tradition of hospitality, due to the Israelis racist attitudes and their government's policies, which always encouraged separation and lack of assimilation with non-Jews.

Regardless of which summer job I ended up doing, I learned many work skills that equipped me later in life, especially in my vocational training. Additionally, those summer jobs enriched my social skills when working with people of diverse socio-economic backgrounds. But most of all, I was able to help my parents, financially, which I will never regret.

Chapter 6
Ort Amal Technical High School: Grades 9-11

After completing eighth grade at the hated MAM high school, I listened to my mother's advice and began ninth grade at ORT Amal Vocational High School, located in downtown Nazareth. The impact and the outcome of this vocational training was to last my lifetime. All that I have accomplished in my adult years stemmed directly from my mother's advice to attend this vocational training school. My acceptance of her advice was the manifestation of a very popular Palestinian philosophy, proverb, concept and wisdom, summed up by what is popularly known as "Ridah-Al-Wali-Dayn."

Ridah means "blessing from both God and one's parents" while Wali-Dane means "father and mother." The idea here is that if a sibling listens to the advice of his or her parents, they will always be successful. No parents' advice is meant to have a negative impact; rather, listening to their advice will always bring happiness and success. That is the way I understand that concept.

ORT is a Russian acronym for "Association for Vocational Craft." ORT was and is still the largest vocational educational system in Israel, operating since 1948. The first ORT opened in the city of

Jaffa in 1949. Amal, in Hebrew, means "Work." So, the school is popularly called ORT Amal Technical or "ORT" for short.

The Russian role in Palestine was the spark that inspired the early Zionist colonial settlers in the late 1880's and is still with us today. ⁽⁶⁾ The Russian Orthodox Palestine Society (ROPS for short) influence was clearly displayed throughout Palestine, especially in education and industry. ORT's mission was to educate Israelis, as well as Palestinian/Israeli citizens in the field of machining and welding which was needed to expand the industrial base of the future Israeli economy. Later, most of ROPS' socio-economic, religious, and educational institutions, including the land itself, were confiscated by Israel.

The school's location was at least four downhill miles from my house and almost in the center of canoe-shaped Nazareth. It was close to Nazareth's main vibrant business districts, which included the main bus and taxi stations, restaurants, falafel, and hummus stands, shopping malls, the old Bazaar, pharmacies, souvenir shops, body shops, churches, mosques, and banks.

The school's campus was located ten feet below the surface of the main boulevard, which divided the city's canoe-like shape. To get to my classrooms, I had to take a steep staircase down from the main street where most of Nazareth's hustle and bustle took place.

The mixture of students and teachers was very interesting. The principal, Mr. Hamami, was from a Yemeni Jewish/Arab background. With short black and white hair, a slim body and a beautiful smile, he made things happen. After leaving his electrical shop, my cousin Salim became a teacher at that school. He was among a handful of Palestinian teachers who taught us all the required ORT graduation classes.

Photo from 1968 depicting the author's teachers at ORT Amal Technical. Mr. Hamami can be seen on the far right.

The classes were split between academic and vocational subjects. The academic classes included: Math, Algebra, Physics, Meteorology, History, Government, Arabic, Hebrew, and the English languages. The vocational training included: Blueprint and Precision Measurement Reading; Welding; Drilling; Filing; and my favorite, Engine Lathe and Milling Machines.

What I remember most about the all-male students was the diversity of their political affiliations, religious beliefs, socio-economic backgrounds, and the villages, towns, and cities from where they came. Some were ardent communists, some were capitalists, and others, nationalists. I do not remember any of them belonging to any religious parties, per say, even though we all belonged to either the Christian or the Muslim faith. I still remember that I was the only atheist in my class and said so. Some students were economically privileged, but most were not.

Photo dated April 3, 1965, depicting the author's classmates at ORT Amal Technical. An arrow points to the author.

The communist parties in Israel were then very strong and very active. In Nazareth, the Communist Party published its own newspaper called Al-Etihad, meaning "The Unity," which was distributed by its members and their siblings. Many of my classmates were the sons of very active communist parents. During those years, the cold war between the superpowers: the United States and the Soviet Union, was going through its most dangerous phase. I remember my father, who regularly read the Al-Etihad, trying to explain to me and my siblings the basic ideological differences between communism and capitalism. While he did not join either ideology, he made sure that all of us read the newspaper.

The Communist Party in Nazareth and in other Israeli cities ran for local, and statewide national elections. The most active period during the election time was that of electing the Israeli Parliament or Knesset, which is made up of 120 members who, in turn, elect the prime minister. Both the Parliament and the Prime Minister's Office run Israel's domestic and foreign policies with the increasing influence of the far-right religious parties who won the 2022 election.

This new government under Prime Minister Netanyahu's leadership divided the Israeli society deeper than ever, inflicting national and international condemnation especially toward its brutality toward its Palestinian population on the West Bank and Gaza Strip. Yet, I strongly feel that the real power in the final analysis resides in the Armed Forces leadership, especially the Officers' Corp.

Most of the paper's ideological explanations of Marx, Engels, and Lenin were too hard for me to understand at that age. The ideas about communes were easier for me to understand than class struggle, capital accumulation, surplus value, labor exploitation, or the concept of alienation. One of Israel's early socialist projects was building Kibbutzim or communes to further its so-called egalitarian and socialist programs while stealing and oppressing the native Palestinian population. on whose land those Kibbutzim were erected.

The Kibbutzim were tucked away at the peripheries of the main Palestinian cities, towns and villages rendering them hard to see by the local native population. As a result, newcomers were kept unaware of this land grab. Kibbutzim were also used as military outposts, like that of Spain building their missions on the west coast of the Pacific Ocean, especially in California, as a strategy of oppressing and enslaving the native American population for future profit and greed.

The Kibbutzim were also used as propaganda tools for brainwashing the newly-arriving Jewish refugees who were, at the time, favoring immigrating to the United States. Mostly, they were unaware of their future role of becoming soldiers and by implication, direct oppressors of the indigenous Palestinian population.

My uncle Bishara worked all his life as a machinist at a Kibbutz, located in the city of Affulah at the southern edge of Nazareth. He explained to me that the Kibbutz's members equally divided their labor, income, profit, and other social activities. To make his explanations easier for me to understand, he compared it to the life of a simple Palestinian village where its close-knit inhabitants shared the labor in planting and harvesting their crops. They also shared the same water sources and when harvest time came, they all celebrated at the same time in the center of the village. Whether it was the life at the Kibbutz or the village, I always wished that the Israelis and Palestinians could, one day, emulate such communal living next to one another.

Those years opened my eyes, mind, and conscience to the good, bad, and ugly of Marx's ideology, which was debated a lot among my classmates. All of the students were united on one main issue: that Palestine is for the Palestinians, regardless of their religious affiliations, which included Jews, Christians and Muslims. They further argued that the creation of Israel, guided by its racist Zionist ideology, was strongly supported by the mighty imperialist powers of England, Russia, and later, the United States, for the purpose of serving their own imperialist interests rather than what was best for the Jews or the Arabs.

Most of my classmates strongly believed that the Soviet Union, with its Marxist ideology, would liberate Palestine from the Zionists. This early belief in the Soviet Union's intentions to liberate Palestine was then, as it is now, an illusion and

Undated photo of the author's uncle, Bishara.

deceiving propaganda. No country or any other ideology, then or now, has come to help the Palestinians' quest for liberation—at least not yet.

I do not know why I was so vocal against communism when arguing with my fellow communist students. I always took the stand of capitalism and that of the United States. Of course, I did not know much about the writings of Marx or of Adam Smith. I think that my opinions were influenced by a variety of reasons.

To begin with, I was unaware that I had been brainwashed by the types of movies I was watching at the only theater in Nazareth.

Those movies were either about Agent 007 fighting against the evil communist bad guys, or the American white settlers fighting against the savage American Indians who were always portrayed as committing horrible crimes, including killing innocent white settlers. These settlers were, in turn, portrayed as spreading light and civilization to the savage endogenous American Red Indian territories.

In the case of Agent 007, James Bond was a very good-looking man, sleeping with many beautiful women, driving expensive cars over very well paved streets, eating at the best restaurants, and his two guns never missed. The Russians, on the other hand, were portrayed by those same movies as exactly the opposite. Their agents always lost, they were overweight, evil-minded, and not that good-looking, and were always rejected by western women. The roads on which they traveled were not well-paved and always looked dark, and you never saw the sun shining over the capital of Moscow.

The depiction of the above images was very clear to me: winners against losers, beauty versus ugliness, romance versus rejection, and wealth versus poverty. That is why I chose the winning side of the United States. After all, why should I stand with the Russian losers? I also hated the Indians and loved the cowboys and the pioneers, even as the Israeli/Zionist settlers were treating me as an American Indian, if not worse.

Who could have imagined that, one day, I would be teaching students at California State University, Los Angeles about the power and influence of the media. This especially focused on Hollywood's role in shaping and brainwashing the American people's thinking and attitudes toward the rest of the world and themselves.

During those late adolescent years, ignorance and lack of knowledge about Hollywood's effect on shaping and brainwashing people's attitudes was absent. Thus, my love and respect for the United State and my hate of the indigenous Indian people were on full display.

A second reason that I was so influenced was my mother's strong stand with the United States. She always told me that the United States was the "World's Mother" and without its help, we would be in a much worse situation. "God bless America" was on her lips all the time. She used to show me the pictures imprinted on the gallons of her cooking oil that showed two hand wrists grasping each other with the American flag clearly imprinted on top of both. So, the United States flag and my mother's constant reminder of that picture formed my opinion of the U.S. being the savior of the poor and needy Palestinian refugees.

A third reason was the 1963 Cuban Missile Crisis. As I still remember, most of Nazareth's residents stood with the United States, more so than with the Soviet Union. I remember very well the pictures of President Kennedy being displayed everywhere, especially in the Mom-and-Pop shops. His supporters looked at him as a handsome and charismatic figure and the beauty of his wife, Jacqueline Kennedy, completed the picture.

When I had my hair cut at my cousin's Sami's barber shop, located in the heart of Nazareth Bazaar, President Kennedy's picture was hung in the middle of a huge mirror. Every time he turned the rotating chair where I sat, Kennedy's face stared back at me. But during the Cuban Missile Crisis, most people also began believing in the end of time. I recall that my father left work and came home to enjoy his last meal during the most dangerous weeks of October 1963. I still can hear his voice telling us, "A nuclear war is about to happen and we will all die. Maybe Kennedy will save us and the world from that fate."

I am not sure whether anyone really cared about the Indian savages preventing the Christian whites from their God-given duties of building their economy at the expense of and on the backs and corpses of those indigenous Indians? I did not understand, relate, or see the similarity between the fate of the Native Americans and that of my own people. Both of us were occupied in our own countries when the enemy stole it over the barrel of the gun. Ignorance of the intentions of one's enemies remains the most self-destructive tool in making the birth of new empires possible.

Therefore, when you combine the above reasons, you could easily see why I was defending capitalism with the United States. When later, I began my university education in the United States and began studying its history, my eyes opened and then I began questioning the stand I took at ORT.

Returning to my schooling, for three years my machining skills were second to none. My hands "were golden," as my mother described them, and the work experiences that I gained during summer breaks helped me maintain steady hands, good vision and the lack of serious injuries. The only injury that I had sustained was a tiny shrapnel of steel that flew into my eye while working on the grinding machine. My report card shows a B average on all technology-related classes, such as technology, machining, welding, and iron work. MY worst grade was in the Arabic language because I hated its grammar. My behavior and work ethics were excellent. I missed seven days and never was late to my classes.

Chapter 6   87

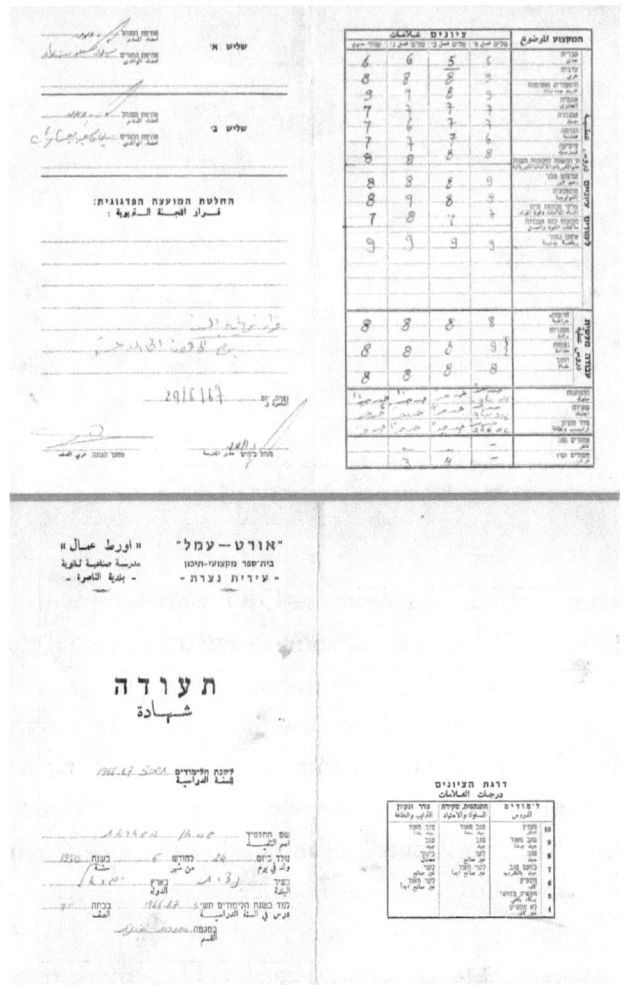

The author's report card for the 1966-1967 school year.

The most memorable events for me at this time were the field trips we took. I still have many black and white pictures that I took with my camera showing my teachers and classmates as very happy. The landscape was full of wildflowers and roses that filled our surroundings. There were trees of all kinds, water springs and very narrow streams dotting the area where we rested for a bite. Singing birds completed that beautiful panorama of Galilee, located at the northern edge of Palestine.

Photo from 1969 depicting one of the many field trips the author took with his class. The beauty of Palestine during spring can be seen.

Unfortunately, the classrooms at ORT were built with very thin metal with many holes in them so it was extremely cold during the winter and very hot during the summer. Yet, those holes were very useful for us students as we could see the women's legs as they stood on the bus platform, which was above our classrooms, as they waited for the arrival of their buses. As we gazed at them, we dreamed of God knows what? I was not one of the students lucky enough to sit by the holes in the outside walls. Teachers always placed me in the middle of the first row; I never understood why.

Our teachers were clever and mean. They used to pick on a gazing student and ask him to repeat the question they had just asked the class. Of course, many of them failed to repeat those questions which would result in loud laughter and punishment. Few of the teachers had any sense of humor; a few others laughed with us and looked the other way.

I had very bad encounters with some of my teachers to the point where I refused to listen to what they were asking me to do or say. They did not record some of my grades, gave me severe grammar corrections in all the languages, posed tough questions for subjects that they did not cover, and silenced my attitudes toward religion with harsh insults and criticism. When the teachers complained to the principal, I would try to explain my point of view and follow whatever he recommended. I trusted Mr. Hamami, as I felt he was a very fair Jewish principal, like my Christian Mother Superior at Don Bosco School.

None of us at school had girlfriends as it violated our traditions and sex was a taboo that was never mentioned unless you were with very close friends and sex jokes were told. Many tried to exaggerate the truth and say they had slept with some girls, as we all had uncontrolled hormones flowing through our veins.

Traditional rules regarding sex before marriage were very strict. I remember walking with a bunch of classmates on our way home from MAM once, when we came across a bunch of schoolgirls walking our way. Trying my luck, I asked a girl named Ameerah (which means "beautiful princess") to give me a kiss. Instead, she punched me in the face and then told her father, who told my father, who gave me the Sha-loot treatment with more insults.

I laughed, even though I was in pain. When my father asked me why I was laughing, I told him, "I would not mind the punishment if, at least, I got the kiss. But to get punished for nothing is not fair," which made him also laugh. Ameerah, was indeed a beautiful princess who refused a kiss from a prince. I still think that she was the loser.

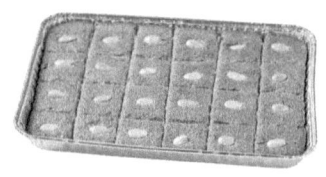

Stock image of harissa.

Above our classrooms there were many sweets and pastry shops owned by Mom-and-Pop businesses. Among the many Palestinian sweets is a dish called "Harissa," which was made by combining semolina and flour. When the mix was ready, the baker spread it evenly in a large pan, one yard in diameter, bordered by at least one inch of trim. When fully baked, they used a very sweet syrup to cover the entire pan.

Due to uneven cooking temperatures, the color of the finished product would vary. At its center, it was reddish and tastier and more expensive for the same size cut than those near the pan's edges. The pieces further away from the center tended to be much darker and on the farthest edges, it was almost burned, dark, dry and tasteless. I always purchased the darkest cuts because it was the least expensive, but it was also embarrassing when others saw me eating it. I looked forward to when I had enough money so I could purchase the center cuts.

The funny thing about this experience is that all of us would run upstairs to purchase Harissa after lunch, and then we would share what we had bought, regardless of its color. So, I always felt equal to my classmates. It also made me realize that I was not the only one who purchased the dark cut.

I forgot about this experience until I ran into a former classmate on my visit to Nazareth in 2010. We spoke about this memory, and I clearly remembered it and laughed my heart out. When I insisted on going back and repeating the same purchasing experience, he told me that the school had moved and the sweet shop owner had passed away so the family sold the business.

After graduation from ORT, many of my classmates left to continue their studies in the Eastern European Bloc [7] countries, such as: Romania, Bulgaria, Czechoslovakia, and of course, the Soviet Union. The communist party, as I understood it, sponsored their education with the promise that, upon their graduation, they would return to Nazareth to help build a more modern vocational educational institution.

Chapter 7
Humor and Teasing as a Way of Communicating

The three years that I spent studying at ORT provided me with the opportunity to learn one more life-coping tool. It sustained the sanity and friendship of myself and other students who had just witnessed a dramatic shift in their socio-economic life due to the Palestinian Nakba.

Like many other people around the world, the Palestinian people used humor and cursing, among many other survival tools, to cope with the sudden, unexpected catastrophe that befell them for the simple reason that they were living in the wrong place and at the wrong time. They were an accident of geography.

ORT was less than a mile away from the center of Nazareth's Bazaar where my father's shoemaking shop was located. His shop was near his brother Aissa's frozen chicken shop and that of uncles Radwan and Ragi's fresh fish shop. Because the shops were located so close to each other, they could see, talk, yell, and cuss at each other all day long.

A photo dated April 10, 1968, of the author with his favorite uncle, Ragi.

At this time, since I was older than when I was attending Kansas Al-Maseeh, I was able to comprehend and observe more elements related to daily Palestinian life and tradition. I began paying more attention to the way humor was used as a communication tool among the population at large and between my father and my uncles.

They did not have phones to communicate with one another, so they reverted to shouting each other's names. Most of the shouting and yelling did not involve business; it mostly involved teasing, insults, cussing, gossip, and fake stories. The main purpose of shouting the name of the other person was to make him peer from his shop and look at the caller whose purpose was to say something that would make him angry. That would then trigger a response of anger and retaliation which was where the real humor took place.

Cussing, in my opinion, is an art form and humor is a gift. I do not know how they managed to mix filthy and disgusting words together to form a sentence. Once one managed to retaliate with harsh insults mixed with cursing, newer—even harsher ones—would instantly be invented by the other. This method of communication was just between the relatives. No one felt insulted or hurt; it just made them laugh even more. Using humor was, for them, a survival tool and a way to deny and escape the pain and humiliation of the Palestinian Nakba. It transformed their deep wounds, pain and hurt into an actual or imagined sense of belonging, survival, and happiness.

No wonder I love humor. A very good joke keeps me going, remembering it again and again, as it keeps me laughing and happy. This love for humor was already inculcated in me long before I arrived in the United States. The following few incidents are a small sample of the many examples of humor being expressed at that time.

One day, I dropped by my father's shop but he was nowhere to be seen, even though his shop was open. I went to ask my other uncles about my father's well-being, but they were missing too and their shops were left open and unattended. So, I went and stood in front of my father's shop waiting for him while watching my uncle's shops. After almost forty-five minutes, they arrived at their shops. Some of them were laughing while others were cursing. Palestinians love to curse. (I always thought that we were, by far, the most cursing people on Earth until I arrived in the United States and found out how wrong I was.)

I then asked my father, "Where have you been?"

He said, "Playing cards at the Bazaar's coffee shop. Your uncles Ragi and Essa lost and they must buy me and your Uncle Radwan's coffee."

I then said, "And the four of you left your shops wide open?"

He said, "Yes, it is very safe here. Who do you think is going to steal damaged shoes, frozen chicken and stinking fish? Besides, we needed a break. It was either take a break for coffee or take a nap in our smelly shops. Which option would you choose?"

Then they began teasing me, asking me to give them the money that I collected selling their stuff. I thought that they were crazy people!

In the middle of the paved Bazaar walkway was a trench almost ten inches deep and almost two feet wide that dissected the two sides of the shops and directed rainwater downward toward the center of Nazareth's main flood zone area. Another purpose of that trench was that it served as a parking lot for donkeys that were used to carrying heavy loads, when needed. All you had to do was ask the owner of the donkey, who stood first in line, to carry whatever you needed to its destination.

The donkeys stood in line regardless of their sex. Males stood behind females and vice versa. So, during their sex drive, which was often, the male donkeys became very horny dangling their organs between their back legs while stroking them back and forth to cool themselves. As I recall, the length of their male organ was at least one foot with a diameter of an inch and half. It was a scene that made people, especially women, uncomfortable.

For my father, this was a golden opportunity to tease my Uncle Radwan. He would stand in front of his shop and yell loudly at Radwan to speak to him. When my uncle Radwan answered the call, my father would tell him that he had a message, and direct him to look at the donkey's dick, which would make him angry.

Immediately, my uncle would launch a counter punch with insulting words that I had never heard from him before. All that my father was able to do was laugh while giving him the middle finger. Then both disappeared inside their shops with further insults to be repeated at some other time in new and different formats.

My uncle Radwan and his brother, Ragi, operated the same fresh fish business until my uncle Ragi decided to open his own fish shop, a few yards away. One day, an elderly lady went shopping at Ragi's fish shop and asked him about the price of one kilogram of a certain type of fish. When he gave the price, she replied that the other fish shop was selling it for one lira less. My uncle Ragi began cursing his brother, calling him a traitor with price gouging and a liar.

In anger, he told this woman, "If you go back to that stinking fish shop and inform the salesman about what I told you about him, I will drop the price by one more lira."

So, the lady went back and told uncle Radwan what his brother, uncle Ragi, had said. My uncle Radwan then told her to go back and tell him that "His fish is old and that he is an ignorant merchant."

When she told that to my uncle Ragi, he knew that she was telling the truth and sold her the fish at half the price—just to piss him off.

During summer break, my cousin Baheeg and I would deliver the lunches that their wives had prepared for them. The four of them used to gather at my father's shop to eat lunch. One day, they opened their lunch containers and were unhappy with what their wives had made for them. I still very vividly remember that my mother, Miriam, had cooked green beans with tomato sauce and rice and my aunt, Hana, had cooked okra with rice on the side. My aunt, Zahrah, had made grape leaves with rice inside, and my aunt, Mouneera, had cooked zucchini with rice inside. The men all began cursing their wives and the rice, wishing they had instead prepared meat, chicken, or fish dishes.

Brushing those lunches aside, they decided to collect some money from each other and send my father to buy fresh cuts of beef, which he brought back and fried with fresh garlic, salt and pepper. In addition to this tasty meal, they began drinking our traditional alcoholic Arak as they gave us boys the lunches to take back to their wives. This was what they wanted.

After that, they took their naps in my father's shop sleeping on mats using customers' shoes as their pillows. They left us boys to watch their shops until their naps were over. When we returned the lunches to their wives, including my mother, we never told them what they said about them. Instead, we just said that they preferred meat rather than rice. Mostly, the women responded, "You never know what men want."

According to my cousin Anees, Abu-Taufeeq, who lived in Temple City near Sierra Madre where I live, one of his uncles had lived with his wife and two children in a large flat built with thick mortar walls. Inside, his wife divided the flat into eating, sleeping, and entertaining areas. As always, the bathroom was a few yards away from the main flat. A large closet and hutch were placed against two walls. The above configurations changed depending on the circumstances that his wife faced.

Her husband used to work in the Negev Desert far away from Nazareth. Those workers used to get paid once a month in cash before going back to their families. One day, he came home after a month's absence. His wife had cooked a delicious meal that he liked a lot. So, he sat with his wife and children on a flat mattress with their food placed on a very low table so that they could reach the food while sitting.

After eating this late lunch, he ordered his wife and children to leave saying, "Barrah" or "get out." Then, he began looking for a hiding place to stash his monthly cash payment. First, he locked the door from the inside and placed a chair and a stool on top of it. He then hid the money inside a box that was on top of the dresser. Then he opened the door and told them, "Fattah," meaning "come in."

His kids and wife came back in and sat around him. But his clever wife knew what he was up to and said to him, "Yesterday, I saw a rat on top of the closet and that rat eats papers." She then asked him to get rid of the rat.

Hearing this, he immediately ordered them "Barrah," so he could climb up on the chair to reach his money in the box. Then, he placed it under the folded beds at the corner of the flat. Now, he called out, "Fattah," to invite them back to sit around him again.

This time, his wife told him that there was going to be a very happy occasion taking place in their neighborhood. Her husband asked, "What does it have to do with us?"

She answered, "The neighbor's son is getting married."

So, he told her, "Okay, great. We will go and do our duty like we have always done during such occasions."

Then, his wife told him that they also asked if they could borrow our beds to accommodate the guests coming from out of town. Getting upset, he now repeated, "Barrah," so he could, again, move his precious money.

After they left, he locked the door again and moved the cash from underneath the bed, placing it on a large plate at the bottom of the dresser. Then he invited them back in by saying, "Fattah."

When they entered, his wife added that, in addition to the beds, the family also asked to borrow their large plates when serving their many guests. He then became very frustrated and suddenly, he jumped up and walked to the dresser and said to his wife, "You knew all along that I got paid."

He gave her all the money he had earned and told her, "You women are always cleverer than us men."

The anticipation of more "Barrah" and "Fattah" made this real-life story very funny, simple, and rich in its symbolism. I will keep remembering it until the last day of my life. It also shows how the roles of women are, in many ways, like other cultures all over the world.

Anees was a very skillful and talented story and joke teller. His mind-boggling descriptions of people's behavior, natural surroundings, old customs, and popular wisdom were outstanding. He even taught my wife how to read the traces that her Arabic coffee leaves behind when they dry forming a strange and unusual background all over the cup. My wife became an expert at this and began reading it as if she knew what she was talking about. To this day, she remembers him when I served that Arabic coffee using a similar cup.

Anees told me many other hilarious jokes and stories that I cherish. Sadly, he left us at an early age. I am sure that Jesus is laughing with him right now. We all miss him.

These humorous incidents are just a sample of the hundreds I have heard. All my uncles have now passed away without any grudges against each other. Their friendship, real love, and closeness to each other remained to the last days of their lives, as strong as ever. My generation needs to keep stories like these alive by remembering them, laughing at their simplistic humor, and the resiliency of coping directly with the pain and suffering of our collective Palestinian Nakba, which inflicted so much pain on all of us.

Foreign Language Classes

In addition to ORT, I attended foreign language classes, three days a week, to learn French, English and German. These classes took place right after my classes at ORT. By that time, my father had already gone home. Therefore, I either walked all the way home or dropped by the taxi station, hoping to share the cost of a ride with others living close to my neighborhood.

When walking home up the exhausting steep hill, I arrive at a fork in the road where one street leads to downtown, the other veers north toward Don Bosco, the third leads west, and the fourth veers northwest toward my house. On my way, I first encountered the house of my aunt Um-Jeries—my uncles Ragi and Radwan's sister. Her house is set high above the street. Now, if she managed to see me walking, she would immediately invite me in for a cup of coffee. I knew that if I accepted that cup of coffee it would lead to a full dinner with her family followed by them giving me a cigarette to smoke. She was a heavy smoker. If I said no to her invitation, she would threaten to throw stones at me downhill. This really scared me so I would immediately accept.

Photo dated June 14, 1970, depicting Um-Jeries with her whole family. Arrows point to Um-Jeries and the author, who can be seen ignoring the camera and eating her delicious cooking instead.

I have never met a person to this day as generous as Um-Jeries. She gave from her heart despite her limited economic means. She raised chickens and collected their eggs. So many invitations ended up with her cooking the whole chicken, with rice and salads accompanied by our traditional Arak alcoholic drinks. Eating, singing, and laughing with her family are some of the most memorable events in my life.

Year later, when she invited me and Lina (my future wife) during our first visit to Nazareth, it was just the three of us. She cooked chicken, again, and fried fish for Lina because she knew that Lina liked fried fish. Um-Jeries insisted that we drink Arak at ten a.m. When Lina declined, she threatened that she would be very sad and mad, so we all complied. But then, you must smoke a cigarette with her and again we complied.

The second house I would encounter was my uncle's Ragi's.

Most of the time, he sat inside the house with his wife. Yet, if he or his wife managed to see me, he would yell for me to join them for a cup of coffee, and he meant it: no dinner, just a cup of coffee with his long stories that he had encountered at work.

My grandparents' home was next, a few yards away from my uncle Ragi's house. My grandparents had a habit of waiting for me at the front of their balcony as they sat on an old beaten wooden bench covered with an even older mattress. They just wanted my company.

Undated photo of the author's grandparents outside their home.

My grandmother always saved me a cup of plain yogurt which I consumed while sitting next to them on a mattress inside their one-room flat, which was used as their bedroom and living space.

My grandfather was the Christian Mukhtar who shared his position equally with that of the Muslim Mukhtar at our destroyed village of Ma' Alool. (A Mukhtar is like that of a mayor.) His stories about his days as the Mukhtar and the pain of seeing his village destroyed by the advancing and brutal Israeli army, opened my heart and mind about our Nakba—even more than ever before. The resiliency by which my family and the Palestinian people, in general, used to survive and thrive despite always being the victims of wars and the orphans of peace, gave me a great deal of pride in my heritage.

My grandfather reminded me of how the Palestinian farmers helped teach the early arriving Jewish settlers to till the land and plant various agricultural crops. He repeatedly emphasized that most of the Palestinian people treated those early Jewish arrivals as semitic brothers and sisters, like our Palestinian Arabs, not realizing that they came to steal Palestine from us by the barrel of the gun. His eyes used to tear up when remembering when he and the Muslim Mukhtar refused to cooperate with the advancing Israeli army, the army destroyed their beloved village of Ma'alool and drove its residents out.

This made me very sad, seeing his eyes tearing up, and very upset at the Arab leaders who, in his opinion, betrayed Arab nationalism and Palestine. He would condemn the western countries, especially England, for its brutal military campaign against the Palestinian people and their leaders, and for giving Palestine on a silver plate to the Zionist settlers. He held firm to his beliefs about the Zionist racist settlers and the United States' policy of full support to Israel's occupation of Palestine, all of which in his mind, greatly contributed to the Palestinian tragic catastrophe Nakba in 1948.

His stories inculcated in me the study of politics, history, human tragedies, and the role of charisma that drew political leaders to it. It opened my eyes to the many historical events that I had not learned about in school and made me proud of his personality and integrity. When he died, which occurred as I was studying in the United States, I was told that he died crying for Palestine and his beloved Ma'alool village. What a man. No wonder I chose political science as my graduate field of study with emphasis on the Charismatic Appeal of Political Leaders.

The defeat of Egypt, Syria, and Jordan during the 1967 Six Day

War at the hands of Israel was largely due to the immense direct military and financial help given to Israel. The United States and its western allies were bent on destroying any nascent and decent Arab charismatic leader with a potential for uniting the Arab world. Israel's role in helping destroy the Egyptian president Gamal Abdul-Nasser was the fulfillment of its duties toward its master's efforts of creating it. This obedient role is still with us today. Israel is no more or less than a vassal state in the service of western imperialism and their hegemonic policies toward the entire region. But most of all, Israel now is the protector of all those coward and corrupted Arab regimes out to destroy any decent rise of Arab unity and nationalism.

The last house that I would encounter was that of my uncle Radwan. I rarely saw him on my way home as it was a little late for his next day's hectic work schedule. Yet, like his wife, he has always encouraged me to drop by early in the morning and pick the freshest tomatoes and cucumbers.

After my uncle Radwan's house, I finally arrived home after taking another uphill street. Most of the time I would find my uncle Aissa sipping coffee with my father on the front stairs facing the road. My uncle Essa's house was almost attached to my house. Indeed, I live in the shadow of all the above memories of people and events. The spirit of their refugee status, woven around our Nakba, has made us thrive to build a more successful life and to live another day so that we could tell our story to the world. Those memories are still chiseled in my heart and mind. They are my joy and sadness at the same time.

Chapter 8
Don Bosco Technical Academy: My Twelfth Grade Saga

At the time of my graduation from ORT Amal in 1968, we were told that the Israeli Department of Education had accredited Don Bosco Vocational Technical School as a full-fledged vocational high school. Therefore, I, along with other ORT graduates, was able to transfer to Don Bosco to complete my high school diploma in Vocational Training. This accreditation was extremely beneficial to our communities, families, and all of us students.

The learning environment at Don Bosco was different from all other learning environments that I had experienced. To begin with, the school was run by European priests, mainly French and Italians. The story goes that in 1859, a group of seventeen young men met with Father Don Bosco in the city of Torino, Italy and began the Salesian Priesthood, known popularly as Don Bosco Priesthood. Its mission was mainly based on the teachings of the Roman Catholic Church with emphasis on strengthening the spirits of the young, guided by reason and faith. Since then, Don Bosco has enlarged its teaching around the world with schools in 131 countries further comprising almost 16,000 Silesians.

Don Bosco Vocational Technical School was strategically located high up on Nazareth's rim overlooking most, if not all, of its downtown area. A very modern paved road made reaching its campus very easy. On its northwestern perimeter, a long and very high thick wall stood with intricate stones that gave it a fortress-like look.

Undated photo of Nazareth with Don Bosco Vocational Technical School located in the top left of the photo. The Church of the Adolescent Jesus is located just to the right of the school.

Behind this wall stood a soccer field which resembled that of MAM, with no grass but instead, hard dirt and many small rocks that inflicted real pain when you fell while playing. Bordering the sidelines of this field were tall weeds filled with sharp needles that poked you severely if you were to slide into them.

Adjacent to its east side was a very small forest that provided needed shade during summer and very good cover when running away from mean priests and bullies or when you were illegally smoking or cutting classes due to bad grades or a stressful day with your teachers. Do not worry; there were NO girls at all who could have made that little forest a very romantic and useful cover. Don Bosco was an all-boys school. To that point, all my schools were boys' schools. What a miserable condition!

This school included a very large complex made up of classrooms, administrative offices, a huge historical Roman Catholic Church, dormitories, the huge soccer field, smaller basketball and tennis areas, agricultural land, and most of all, a modern machine shop led by a French engineer who was its main technical teacher.

Finally, my kindergarten school was part of this Don Bosco complex and was mainly run by nuns. Amazing how history repeats itself! The kindergarten school location was adjacent to the far western end of the soccer field, and I became a frequent visitor to my old Mother Superior. (I liked to remind her of my encounter with her and my teacher at age four.)

Almost fourteen years had passed since seeing my great mentor, Mother Superior, during my kindergarten days. Since that time, I had since visited the school when traveling to Palestine but she was not there. Someone said she had left for France, while others said she died. So have many people who I have loved while I have been living in the United States. This is the price we all pay when leaving our original country; this is a universal rule that you must live with.

The curriculum at Don Bosco was very intense and rigorous. In addition to Arabic and Hebrew, I began studying French, Physics, Electricity, History, Mathematics, Mineralogy, and Religion among my other academic subjects, and this curriculum exhausted me. Yet, the vocational part of it was even harder.

The main machine shop was run by a teacher who was a young French engineer specializing in Precision Machine Shop production. It was a miracle if you got a "B" in his class. I always averaged a "C".

I got better grades in the Production of Machined Parts than in Welding. He trained us to use our eyes as a measuring tool, especially when it came to drilling perfect 90-degree holes and then threading them with a tap holder without using a ninety-degree square.

But the most challenging personal experience I had was navigating my Arab/Palestinian nationalism with the racist European priests. Their behavior became apparent when talking with them about the 1967 Israeli/Arab war, popularly known as the Six Day

War. Their support for Israel, especially its Air Force, was quietly celebrated. They always reminded us of the many Egyptian or Syrian planes that were destroyed by the superior Israeli Air Force. This, of course, included the military support of the European countries, especially that of the United States and France which made that victory possible.

They repeatedly stressed to us students that their religion and culture was far superior to that of the Arabs, even though at least 90% of the students at Don Bosco were Christian Arabs. The continued lack of any sympathy or empathy with the Palestinians was left on the back burner all the time. This was very hurtful and still haunts me.

Here I was, facing students who were already brainwashed by those priests' way before I had arrived. Their obedience to the demands and orders of the school's authority personnel, especially the priests, was followed without question regardless of their fairness. These students took a lot of religious classes mixed with glorified and one-sided European history. Rarely, if ever, was Europe's ugly colonial past in Africa, North and South America, the Far East, or the Middle East ever mentioned. Of course, its destructive impact on the indigenous population, including the Palestinian Nakba, was brushed aside.

Sunday masses displayed many forms of theatrical shows depicting the superior European mass celebration over that of the Eastern Orthodox. I did not care for the way we were told to dress, stand, kneel, make the cross, sing, sway, kiss the back of the hand of the priest, or anything else. Religion was never my priority and I have never believed in it to begin with.

I felt so bad for those students that I began trying to lift their morale by using myself as an example. When teachers and priests began hearing about my conversations with the students, they treated me differently, asking me to do extra, out of class duties such as collecting and sweeping trash and cleaning tables and chairs. They also gave me harsher grades and comments on my exams and homework.

On many occasions, when a student was sent by one of those priests to inform me to report immediately to him, I would refuse—especially if I was playing soccer during break. Instead, I would tell the messenger to go back and inform the priest that he had legs and that he could meet me, himself. I also repeatedly warned my friends and fellow students about the racist attitudes of those priests toward us Palestinians.

This infuriated the priests, who began pressuring the principal, Mr. Dirawi, to punish or expel me from school. As the pressure mounted on the principal, he called me to his office. I began explaining to him my frustration with the racist priests and my love for my Palestinian heritage. Mr. Dirawi tried his best to calm me down. He acknowledged that he was dealing with some racist priests and school policies, but he stressed the need for such teaching institutions to help the students find better and more rewarding jobs, thus helping our communities at large.

Photo of Mr. Dirawi dated 1971. This picture appears on his funerary prayer card, which was handed out at his funeral.

He also told me that he respected my nationalism and in raising students' awareness and understanding of what constitutes racism and discrimination. However, he made it very clear that I needed to calm down or he would expel me as he had a higher authority to answer to, for the wellbeing of the rest of the students.

What was I supposed to do? I was exhausted as the end of the year was approaching, and in no way was I going to disappoint my parents. So, I tamed my fervor and swallowed my pride. By then, the message was out and some of those priests had calmed down, some were reassigned to other schools, and others left the country.

A few days before graduation, I met with Principal Dirawi to express my gratitude and respect. When he asked about my future educational plans, I told him that I was planning to continue my education in the United States, maybe in acting or politics. After I finished explaining my future, he opened his desk drawer and picked up a French journal and shared with me an article that discussed France's need for future mechanical engineers.

He told me that for acting, you need to know people in high places, and politics would eventually lead to teaching. Both choices, he said, could not guarantee me a solid career. He encouraged me to study Mechanical Engineering and pointed out that with my solid vocational education, I would be ahead of the crowd. His prediction of a possible teaching career became a reality fourteen years later.

I thanked him and gave him a big hug and left, never to see him again. He died while I was studying at U.C. Riverside. Being strong-willed, I did not listen to his advice, which later I regretted. But we kept in touch by letters, one of which I still have. It is written in such intricate and flawless Arabic handwriting. What a man!

July 15, 1969, was my last day at Don Bosco. I shared some gifts with my friends and teachers then went home and shaved for the first time, the beard that I was now growing. This activity was extremely important because I had promised myself that I would not shave until I had completed my high school education.

This first-time act was also part of an old tradition that signals the beginning of a man's adulthood. After shaving, I applied cologne and then asked my mom to give me a kiss on my shaved cheeks. (I continued this habit while my mother was alive and now, I ask my wife and daughters to do the honor.

Following her kiss, mother always said, "Na'Aiman Yamah," which means "so beautiful, so loving, so warm," full of a real and pure motherly unconditional love. (I cannot truly capture the meaning of Na'Aiman; the word comes from the "Naim," which means "whispering smooth wind," and "Yamah" is the word we use when calling our mother. So, when my mother used it, I became Yamah for her, one and the same).

I also celebrated my graduation day by going to the movie theater, which cost me all of three dollars, as I quite clearly recall.

LEFT: *photo of the author (far left) and his classmates in front of the Church of the Adolescent Jesus dated June 27, 1969.* RIGHT: *photo of the author (standing, far right) and his classmates in the field near the school dated June 27, 1969.*

The author's report card for the 1968-69 school year.

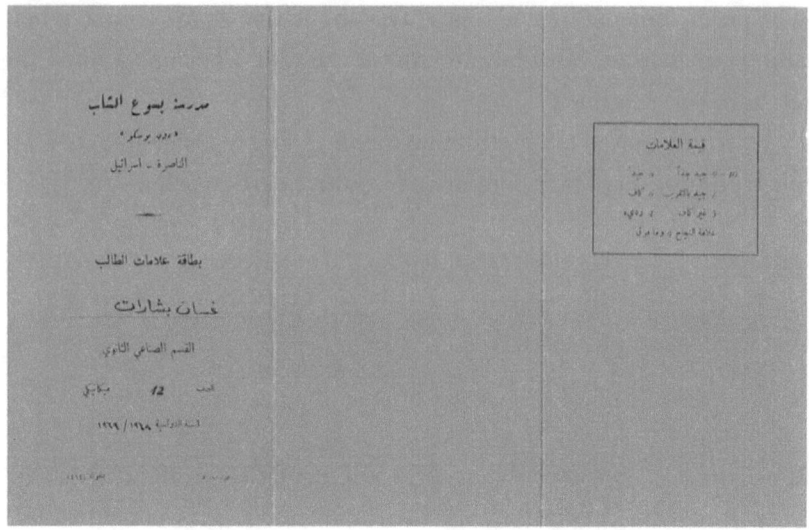

My final twelfth grade report card shows that I was excellent in "behavior" and "work ethic." But, once again, Arabic, Hebrew, and English language classes were my worst grades (barely a C-). I was very surprised that I got an A in religion (wow!) and I also did well in History. Unfortunately, my grades in machining and welding dropped significantly. I attribute that to the harsh grading of our new teacher (a French engineer) who stressed perfection. I was late one day and absent three times throughout the entire twelve grade year.

Chapter 9
A Full-Time Worker and Changing Attitudes

On August 10, 1969, I began working full-time as a welder at the Ford Factory, located high on Nazareth's northeastern parameter. As a fully-grown adult, I now began contributing to my parents' finances. I gave most of my income to my father to relieve my brother, Nabil, from paying his share of the household bills. This way, he could save his money for his planned future marriage. At age nineteen, I began recording in my memoir the number of daily hours I worked, including overtime, and living expenses.

At this factory, my changing attitudes toward what Israel really stood for began to take a dramatic change. I knew then what the Nakba had done to the Palestinian people and came face-to-face with its racism on the faces and actions of the people who I met at that factory, especially my supervisors.

At work, I met many Jewish friends who had immigrated from Arab countries, such as Morocco, Iraq, and Yemen. I also became their welding teacher, following a request to do so by my Turkish-born Israeli supervisor. I was very happy teaching them but what saddened and angered me most was that the salary they were paid was considerably higher than mine. I observed my supervisor's tender and friendly side toward them, but he ignored my teaching efforts. "Thank you" was not on his lips at all. His attitude toward me said, "You must act as being very tough and mean with those inferior Palestinians," even though I was their trainer.

Arrogance makes you stupid and blind. This behavior was very common by most, if not all, of the factory supervisors. Most of them were white Europeans who, along with their parents, were heavily involved in the creation of the illegal Zionist State of Israel. Many had also served in the State's brutal military campaign of killing and oppressing the native Palestinian population during the, so called, "War of Independence."

To this day, I have never understood this: Independence from whom? It cannot be from the Palestinians, could it? Maybe Israel took its independence from the British, the Turks, the Arabs, the Romans, the Persians, the Greeks, the Israelites, the Hittites, the Canaanites, or the Pharaohs of Egypt, to say the least. To my knowledge, no one has ever explained this to me.

While my supervisor behaved one way toward me and the workers, he applied a different standard to the Israeli workers. This same unwritten rule guided most, if not all, of Israel's discriminatory policies toward the Palestinians, then and now. They all followed ambiguous policies and behavior that they deemed non-discriminatory, but to me, they were talking out of two sides of their mouth. I recognized then that discrimination and hatred toward native Palestinians was a deceiving government policy shrouded with fake democracy and full equality.

Despite being treated as a third-class citizen, I always defended my rights and dignity when it came to work-related issues. On many occasions, my supervisor insulted me and told me in Hebrew that my work was "Avoda Arabit," meaning "Arabic work," simply because the welding was not to his satisfaction, even though it was never rejected by the Inspection Department. This racist phrase was repeated all over the place by other supervisors.

But he did not stop there; he demanded an increase in my welded unit production even though I was following the standard production quota that was required from me at the time of being hired. He made it very clear to me that either I increased my production or he would decrease my salary.

I reasoned that my production quota was already at its maximum, therefore, I continued the same production rate while reducing the quality of my work. This resulted in rendering many finished parts to the waste bin. This was my sweet secret and silent revenge; I told no one.

When the completed parts were rejected by the Inspection Department, my supervisor became very angry, launching another racist outburst. I just could not take it anymore and began shouting back at him, accusing him of his discriminatory racist attitude. Hearing the angry exchanges, many workers stopped their work and began clapping their hands in solidarity. I stood my ground by telling him not to use the term "Avoda Arabit" anymore unless he wanted me to call all the rejected parts "Avoda Ivrit," which translates to "Hebrew work." He never responded.

When, on a few occasions, I discussed TIPPTK with my fellow Jewish workers during our lunch break, many of them told me, confidentially, that during their Army training, they were repeatedly instructed by their officers that the Palestinians were the main enemy of the State of Israel. Yet, they wondered about this as we were friends and were now working peacefully together in the same factory.

When I asked them why they left their original Arab countries where they had lived peacefully for so long to immigrate to Israel, the uniform answer was that they were brainwashed by the Zionist propaganda which emphasized the danger of living in an Arab state, the superiority of Zionism over Arab Nationalism, their fear of another Holocaust if they stayed where they were living, that Palestine was empty, and that God had promised it only to his Chosen People, the Jews.

Meanwhile, they began telling me their stories about how happy they were living in their original Arab countries. One of them was a photographer who used to take pictures of Morocco's king at his palace. He wanted to go back there but his Moroccan passport had been confiscated by the Israeli authorities and he lacked the money to purchase a one-way ticket.

An Eastern European man also wanted to go back home but was unable to find enough money to buy the tickets and could not get his family's passports back. A highly-educated Romanian worker told me, "Look at me. I am counting knots and bolts all day with a Master's Degree in Chemistry. They promised me a good job and here I am counting knots and bolts."

The work environment gave impetus to a cascading process of building my negative attitude toward the Israeli/Zionist population and that of the Arab governments, as well. Those happy days when I was helping many elderly Jewish ladies carry their bags to the bus station had dramatically changed due to my disappointment, disillusionment, and hatred toward the Israeli/Zionist State's racist and brutal policies which affected so-called Israeli/Palestinian citizens like me.

To be clear, I never hated or disrespected any Jewish people when it came to their religion, traditions, history, or beliefs. As mentioned earlier, I do not believe in religion, period. My K-12 educational journey was full of religious education of Christianity, Islam, and Judaism. All of them teach peace, love, mercy, justice, equality, and liberty, among many other noble teachings. Thus, I always wished that all the Jews living on this Earth and far beyond could gather in this 10,000 square mile area and practice what Judaism asks them to do. I have no problem with that at all.

My issue is with those who forget what his or her religion and traditions demand, and instead, choose to mix their religion with an ethno-political and racist nationalism by supporting the creation of a sovereign Israeli/Zionist State. When they ignore what that support has done to the indigenous Palestinian population, then I lose my respect for that person. In my mind, once you support the creation of the Israeli/Zionist State, you become part and parcel or an enabler and a participant in the continuation of the Palestinian Nakba. You just cannot have it BOTH ways.

What I experienced at work was the daily hardship that the so-called Israeli/Palestinian citizens face every day, and this deepened my alienation from the total civic life surrounding me. The discriminatory State policies along with all the stories that I heard from my family members, especially my father and grandfather, deepened that alienation.

I recalled my first direct humiliation by Israeli children when, at the tender age of thirteen, I accompanied my father to a doctor's visit in the city of Affulah. My father was wearing his Palestinian headdress when we encountered children on an outing with their teachers. Seeing myself and my father, they began calling us "Filthy Arabs," and "Human Flesh Eaters" among other insulting words. As I tried to answer them back, my father reminded me to be silent as we were in an Israeli city that did not harbor any sympathy or love for the Palestinians.

What saddened and angered me the most was the lack of response from the teachers of these children. Kids all over the world are kids; they do and say many stupid things. But adults are an altogether different matter. Those kids are now in their early sixties, they have already served in the Israeli military machine. Imagine how they have behaved toward the Palestinian populations in the West Bank and Gaza. Just imagine. The chicken comes home to roost; what they have been taught as children, they will practice later and they are doing so every day in the occupied territories and Gaza, mirrored by the ongoing genocide there.

The total segregation between the Israelis and the so-called Israeli citizens further deepened my wounds of alienation. This was augmented by the continued lack of unity among the Arab countries, especially the ruling elite whose financial interest was, by far, more important than taking back the stolen Arab real estate called Palestine.

I could not understand the Western World's support for Israel, especially the United States, which did not acknowledge the Palestinian Nakba as the consequence of such support. The continued infighting between the Palestinian resistance groups triggered my anguish and sadness, to say the least. All of this contributed to my lack of hope for brighter and friendlier relations between and among all the contending forces of this dispirited region. My alienation and sadness reached its worst behavior by the following story that I can never forget.

From its creation in 1948 until the middle of the 1970s, Israel has followed strict martial law policies toward its Palestinian so-called "citizens." During this period, Israel's military practiced very harsh policies in hunting down and killing "Arab infiltrators," as the State called them. Palestinians, on the other hand, called these same people "The Fedayeen" or the "Mujahideen," which refers to a person who is willing to resist and die. Most of them were trying to sneak in or go back to their destroyed villages and towns to retrieve whatever was left.

One very cold winter's night, I heard an Israeli military Jeep whizzing by my house then coming to a screeching halt no more than 100 feet from my house. My house was built on top of a hill overlooking a vast empty landscape with a full view of the city of Haifa, almost twenty miles away. The mission of those soldiers was always to capture or kill Mujahideen while waiting for them inside their military vehicles during the blackness of the night.

Hearing this loud screeching noise, my mother asked me what was happening. I told her that it was a military jeep full of Israeli soldiers trying to capture or kill the Mujahideen. She said nothing. (As an intimidating policy, many Israeli troop drills were conducted on residential streets and in-between residents' homes, as well.)

Then, she rose from her chair and went into the kitchen. A few minutes later, she gave me six cups full of hot tea and asked me to take them to the soldiers to drink. I became so angry. As I previously said to my father a long time ago, "Those soldiers have destroyed your own village of Ma'alool where your own father was its Mukhtar, and you want me to serve them hot tea? Are you nuts? Have you gotten crazy or what?"

Undated photo of the author's mother seen standing in the backyard of their home holding a small coffee pot and cup to serve guests.

Calmly, she told me that she is a mother and thus, knows the feelings of those soldiers' mothers who are right now worrying about their kids not having a warm drink to warm their hearts during such a cold winter's night. "So, please make me happy and take the hot tea out to them," she said.

My mother placed the cups on a tray which I was to carry to the soldiers. However, on my way out, I threw away all the drinks and waited in the cold for a few minutes before returning the tray with the empty cups to my mother, who thanked me for listening to her. This was the first time in my life that I lied to my mother. By doing so, I felt in my own little way that I had avenged myself from my oppressors and stood up for the innocence of the Palestinian people who trusted and welcomed their cousins, the Jews, who would later make them refugees in their own land. I was also remembering her own father's pain in losing his village, Ma'alool.

I just wonder if Israeli mothers feel the same way toward the Palestinian mothers who have lost so many of their children at the hands of the soldiers. Are they telling them to carry hot tea out to them or are they telling them to kill more? I really do not know. Seeing all the brutality of the Israeli Armed Forces on display every day, it was clear that their mothers were not having any sympathy or empathy for the murdered Palestinian mothers' sons and daughters.

In an article that I read in the Los Angeles Times in the September 2021 issue, there was a story about an Israeli soldier who, while eating a sweet cake that his mother had prepared for him during a Jewish holiday, was interrogating and punishing a Palestinian family that included their children. This was while his unit forcefully entered their home looking for God only knows what 'invented excuse'.

Why are their mothers' and fathers' beating hearts not reminding their sons and daughters of their obligation under their own Talmudic teaching to grant mercy and sympathy to others, and instead, are terrorizing the Palestinian villages daily?

This is the difference between my mother's heart and those of the present Israeli soldiers' mothers. My mother's lesson must be remembered and taught at all the Israeli educational institutions with that of my father's instructions for me to carry grocery bags for elderly Jewish women while they were shopping at the Nazareth Bazaar. To this day, and under those circumstances, I strongly feel that I did the right thing, despite betraying my mother's trust.

When I told this story to my kids, they told me that I did not do the right thing and that I should have listened to my mother and served the soldiers hot tea. What a woman my mother was. She has always carried that Palestinian warm and generous beating heart.

Almost fifty years have passed since the incident with the hot tea.

As I continue watching Israel's brutal policies, almost on a daily basis toward the Palestinian people, I am very much convinced that what I did at that age was correct. I have not read, seen, or heard any stories coming out of Israel that resembled the stories of both my father and mother. Until and unless the hearts and minds of the parents of the present Israeli Armed Forces' sons and daughters change and become like the heart and mind of my parents, I expect the daily brutalities of Israel's Armed Forces to increase in intensity.

What has happened to the moral and merciful teachings of the Torah and the Talmud that I learned back at ORT Amal?

Photo in the Los Angeles Times in an article dated November 14, 2023, showing a settler parent hugging his son with a weapon slung over his shoulder. This picture is a study in contrasts: at this same age, the author was helping to carry the grocery bags of elderly Jewish ladies at the bus station, rather than holding a gun.

Meanwhile, the heavy work I was doing at that factory made me realize that you must really work hard to make a living. This made me appreciate the hard work that my father, mother, sisters, and brothers did to keep my family going. Working hard became deeply imprinted on my conscience, a long time ago, when I began working at age ten to help pay for my needed school supplies.

Chapter 10
The Solitude Years: Listening, Reading, and Maturing

While my changing attitudes were deepening in my conscience, I was then living with the rest of my eight siblings and my parents in a new house located above the old one. I do not remember how my father was able to build it. I am sure that he borrowed money and with the help of my four, older siblings: Hana, Nabil, Emil and Hiam, who were working at that time. I also contributed my meager income from my job and with what my father was able to provide, they were able to build this beautiful house.

This house was where all my memories resided until my departure on June 21, 1971. The house was much bigger than the original one with three bedrooms, a kitchen, a bathroom, and a nice spacious shower. Two verandas surrounded the house. One of them overlooked the entire neighborhood where I could see part of upper Nazareth, the homes of my uncles Radwan, Raji, Eissa, Bishara, and Elias. During the night, I could easily see the many lights emanating from far away villages located inside and outside Palestine including the West Bank. My father used to name them for us. Those lights included those shining from the majestic city of Haifa, among many more sights.

This spacious veranda was where my brothers, cousins and uncles used to play their favorite card games. The losers cursed and smoked a lot, while the winners just teased, laughed, and of course, smoked. I was never a participant in these games and I was not allowed to play soccer on this veranda. My mother always warned me not to even think about kicking the ball against its walls.

A few years later, my parents installed strong thick blinds on its two sides converting the veranda into a living space in addition to preventing any rain or cold wind from penetrating its previously open walls.

The other veranda was no more than four feet in width and twenty feet in length and was located at the entrance of the house. To enter the main door of the house from the street, you had to climb a few steps (no more than five as I still remember) that led to the entrance of the veranda and straight to the main door of the house. Unlike the other veranda where playing cards took place, this one was more precious to me.

On most summer days when my father arrived home from work, the first thing he did was to build a fire in his yellow-colored fire pit or as we called it "Kanoon." Our job, if we were home at the time, was to use beat-up cardboard that my father had cut from somewhere and puff at the charcoal that my father had initially let. Once the fire pit was ready, he used to brew his coffee and place it near the Kanoon fire.

Undated photo of the author (left) and his father (center) with the kanoon by the steps where the author's father, uncles, and cousins would sit to drink coffee.

Most of my siblings, cousins, and uncles knew beforehand about "Abu

Nabil's after-work habits." Suddenly and without being invited, many of us used to gather around him expecting a cup of coffee and gossiping. But my real cherished memories were when my uncles Essa, Radwan and Ragi used to gather around my father after they had eaten their early dinners, dressed in their pajamas. My uncle Essa was next door so he would arrive before the rest and sit on the step close to my father who sat on the flat floor of the veranda on a beat-up mattress.

Next in line was my uncle Radwan who sat below my uncle Essa's step, followed by my uncle Ragi and the rest. If we were lucky, we got to sit on the remaining two steps. Once all the steps were filled, we would bring the dinner table's chairs and place them on the veranda and watch those four people in action.

Remember, all four of them had just left the Bazaar where their teasing never stopped. Now, they would bring their unfinished and polished arguments here to tease each other further at my house while sipping their coffees. We, the brothers and cousins who surrounded them, would listen to their jokes, cussing, and arguments while igniting and adding more fuel to the fire, which caused them to cuss more and laugh louder.

I used to love to tease them all and, many times, I was cursed and chased away from them so that I would shut up and stop criticizing and laughing at them. While all this was taking place, my father used to wave his hands to every passing car on our street, inviting them up for a cup of coffee. He didn't know most of these drivers but his generosity knew no limit. I used to feel bad for him at his constant waving to the drivers and so I offered to install a fake hand attached to a chain that you could just move without waving your hands, and that made him laugh.

On very few occasions, my Uncle Jeries, the older brother of my father and Uncle Essa, used to drop by without any notice. I think he missed their jokes and gatherings but he was not part of this bunch, to say the least. My Uncle Jeries used to dress in a full European suit while the rest of the brothers were wearing their pajamas.

The moment he entered, silence took place, and each person offered him the steps that they were sitting on. Of course, my uncle refused as he preferred to sit on a chair. My uncle Jeries did not like cursing or teasing too much. What surprised me the most was the instant silence that would take place when he arrived as their loud voices became whispers. I could vividly see that they were waiting for him to leave as they would tell him that the road leading to his house would soon be filled with wild dogs and coyotes and it would be better for him to leave as soon as possible. By then, it would be close to 7 pm in the summertime.

Undated photo of Uncle Jeries wearing one of his trademark suits.

Knowing their true intentions, he used to tell them, "Ghassan will escort me to the house because his aunt, Wardeh, is waiting for him to share ice cream with her." (Wardeh in Arabic means a "beautiful flower" and she was a very elegant and beautiful lady.)

Undated photo of Wardeh (center), the author's mother (left), and grandmother (far left). On the right side of the photo, the author's sister, Hiam (standing, left side) can be seen with the their cousins, Salweh and Souad. Although none of them smoked, as a joke, the author asked them to pose with cigarettes.

Finally, when watermelon season arrived, my father used to stop a huge truck carrying God only knows how many tons of watermelons to bargain with the driver about buying a lot of them. Our job, as brothers, was to stand six to eight feet away from each other leading to our bedroom. Once my father picked these specific watermelons, then we delivered them to each other in a line. The one who was in the bedroom placed the watermelons under the beds. I am not talking about five but perhaps twenty-five of them. We all loved watermelons!

Although this beautiful house was much larger than the original one, it was still too difficult to accommodate a growing family of nine. Therefore, I decided to move out of the room I shared with my four brothers and into a room that had remained vacant in our original home. Being away from the heavy traffic upstairs gave me more freedom to pursue my appetite for reading all types of books and newspapers and to think about my destiny in life. I was lucky to have my parents' library in our living room where the Taghribat Banu

Hilal book was kept on its beautiful shelves. I remember taking care of this precious book by strengthening its two paper covers with some brown paper that I had cut from a shopping bag I found at home.

Their library contained many history, fiction and nonfiction books about culture and norms, medicine, poetry, and other short stories written in Arabic. A few of them were written in Hebrew, French, and English. The main focal point of the library was the thick Bible that my parents were proud of, but which I hated the most. Those books opened my eyes, heart, and mind about my love of reading and the bug has never stopped since.

While working full-time, I made sure that my mother did not have to walk down the stairs early in the morning to wake me up. Instead, I would get up early and walk up the stairs to greet my mother who had already prepared a fast breakfast and an excellent lunch for me to take to work. She always thanked me for not making her go up and down the stairs, which was hard on her knees.

Having my own room allowed me to have a lot of quiet time after work. On weekends, I began attentively listening to local and international news radio programs, reading in-depth subjects that interested me, and thinking about my future without bothering my family upstairs. We did not have a television at that time and the radio programs that I could get were mainly broadcast from Israel, Jordan, Egypt, and Syria. The main international news was from the British Broadcasting Company, popularly known as the "BBC." Listening to those broadcasts made me more confused than ever.

After a while, I decided that reading a variety of subjects was a better way for me to understand the world around me without bias and conflicting opinions. I did not want someone else to interpret the world for me.

This was the beginning of my education about popular leaders, the Cold War, TIPPTK, the history of Imperialism and its crimes against its victims - the indigenous people, and other interesting topics. I found politics to be a fascinating subject that opened my eyes to the political realities that I was living in as a Palestinian/Arab without a Palestinian country. I had Israeli citizenship, but it denied me my own country and citizenship and separated me from the larger Palestinian community.What a contradictory situation. But at least, I was lucky to have a loving Palestinian family and friends around me, and to be living on my ancestor's Palestinian soil, close to the destroyed Palestinian village of Ma'Alool.

Those two years of solitude made me a different person and I grew up very fast. My political awareness began maturing a lot due to my family's annual visit to Ma'Alool. Listening to the elderly residents of that village describe how the Israeli Army destroyed it made me sick. All around me were the remnants of my parents, grandparents, and the rest of the village's homes, churches, and mosques. But their cultivated fields, water wells and fruit trees had been destroyed and abandoned and the animal herds were stolen by the Army and other surrounding Jewish communities. The fate of Ma'Alool was repeated elsewhere: more than 400 Palestinian villages and towns were destroyed, which amounted to almost half the total number of villages and towns that dotted Palestine before our 1948 Nakba.

Chapter 10   127

CENTER: *photo taken in 1959 of the well that remained running in Ma'Alool after the village's destruction. The author's uncle, Bishara, and his grandmother can be seen in the photo. The other undated photographs depict various picnics taken over the years by the author's family on the rare occasions they were allowed back into the area where Ma'Alool once stood.*

To cover their crimes, the government planted trees with the help of donations coming from right wing and other born-again evangelical Zionist Christian organizations. Ma'alool, thus, became a small forest hiding the crimes that the State of Israel left behind. Seeing my heritage being stolen and destroyed opened my eyes, not only to the TIPPTK but to other tragedies that befall other indigenous communities all over the world.

This included the horrors that the American Indians faced at the hand of the early European conquerors; the unforgiving pain, suffering, and labor exploitation of the African American slaves in the United States; the genocidal policies of the Inquisition in Latin America; and the human brutalities inflicted by the mighty European imperialist powers all over Africa, the Middle East, other Asians countries as well as the more recent Armenian and Jewish holocausts. All this knowledge saddened me and made me begin questioning what made human beings behave in such a way.

My Nakba was just a continuation of the evil and the unjust behavior of all humankind against those who they deemed "lesser humans." This behavior made me lose my faith in humanity's tender heart and wisdom. Otherwise, I reasoned, "how could evil triumph so easily over humanity's goodness? And why is it so easy for the victims to become the victimizers once they are in power?" So far, I haven't found any satisfactory answers nor has anybody else.

My rebelliousness and acts of leadership, which started at an early age, led me to read about popular charismatic leaders in my quiet and lonely room. I read about Churchill, Gandhi, Napoleon, Nasser, Kennedy, Mao, and Stalin, among others. Additionally, I read about the life of Major General Amer, who was the head of the Egyptian Air Force during the 1967 Israeli/Arab war; Major General Rommel of Germany who fought many successful battles in North Africa during WW2; the American Revolutionary War leadership against the tyranny of the British King; and the destructive aftermath of the American Civil War.

I paid special attention to the attrition war between Egypt and Israel that continued after the 1967 War. This attritional war ended in a stalemate. What followed was the signing of the Camp David Peace Accord between Israel and Egypt, sponsored by the United States. This accord took Egypt completely out of its confrontation with Israel. The United States, in turn, paid Egypt $1.4 billion a year to keep Israel's southern front safe and for Egypt to kick the butts of the Soviet Union completely out of Egypt.

Egypt's banner of being "Um-Al-Arroba" meaning "the Arabs' Mother has vanished" and with it, the vanishing of any real Arab efforts to free Palestine. Egypt did not abandon its struggle against Israel because it believed in it but did so because it was clear to its leadership that all other Arab countries have abandoned the struggle to free Palestine due to their conflicting interests and lack of a unified leadership.

The money that the United States paid for Egypt's change of heart could have easily been compensated for by Saudi Arabia and the other Gulf States, thus keeping Egypt's struggle alive, but they refused to do so. Egypt's abandonment of its struggle to free Palestine made it too easy for other Arab States to join President Trump's "The Abraham Accord," which further inspired The United Arab Emirates, Kuwait, Bahrain, Morocco, and very recently Sudan to officially abandon their struggle to free Palestine. This struggle has never been on the minds of those countries' leadership to begin with, thus, there is nothing to lose while becoming an even deeper vassal state to the global hegemonic interests of the United States. The hell with Palestine, period.

On Fridays, I listened to the Egyptian political commentator Hassanein Haykel, who was well-versed in the complex issues and policies of Egypt's foreign relations with the Arab World, Israel, the United States, and the Soviet Union, among others. I trusted his analysis and thus, became a fan of his.

Haykel paid special attention to the Palestinian Nakba and opened my eyes to the rise of Zionism, the roles played by England during its mandated hegemony over Palestine, and the lack of Arab unity in preventing our Nakba. Such analysis with the related subjects that I was reading enriched my knowledge of how and why Palestine was sacrificed on the altar of European self-interests, racist Zionist ideology, the betrayal of some Arab leaders of their nationalism, and the aspirations of the Palestinian people.

Haykel was a very inspiring political analyst and was close to the ruling elite in Egypt including its popular leader Jamal Abdul-Nasser.

The complex issues of the causes and consequences of the Cold War fascinated me a lot, especially the socio-economic and ideological differences between communism and capitalism, i.e., the Soviet Union and the United States. I began to understand the roles played by certain European powers, the nonaligned nations, and the United Nations. I also learned more about the nuclear bomb with its evil and unimagined destructive power, as I read about the fate of Hiroshima and Nagasaki after the United States dropped those bombs in the center of their cities.

During that time, I began to write poetry and play chess, both of which resulted in very limited success. Poetry helped me later to win the heart of my future Italian wife, but chess was hard for me to understand on my own. Additionally, I began taking long walks with my friends, playing soccer again and listening to radio stations broadcasting the World Soccer Cup competitions. I remember the year when Italy defeated Brazil 4-1 and won the 1970 World Cup.

During those solitude years, I read many different subjects: Psychology, Norms and Culture; the Anatomy of the Human Body; The Role of Sex In Shaping The Diversity Of Humans And Animals On Earth; and I began reading English newspapers and magazines. This was the time when I purchased *Playboy* magazine for the first time. (Don't get me wrong. It was just to strengthen my English language skills.)

I also read a very limited number of Shakespeare's works but found it boring and hard to understand. (Of course, it is not, but a clear lack of understanding made it so.) I was not interested in reading novels or non-fiction books, either then or now.

One other thing that fascinated me was the immense competition among the largest oil-producing companies throughout the immense Middle Eastern oil and gas reserves. I learned about the ways those companies prospered by exploiting the resources of those colonized nations, only paying a few cents on the dollar to those "ignorant Arab oil producing countries." This helped understand why the Western countries are so rich.

To keep busy outside of my lonely room, I managed to purchase a camera and soon I began taking pictures of family, friends, Palestinian panoramas, and the remnants of our village, Ma'Alool.

Soon, I fell in love with taking pictures of new-born babies, which led me to want to cuddle them after taking their pictures. This habit of loving babies continues to be part of who I am. I always looked forward to feeding my kids and later, my grandkids, their milk and other food items. What fascinated me about using the bottle of milk was that, while drinking their milk, they would stare at my eyes and I would stare back into theirs, wondering what they were thinking about. This has always brought happy tears.

This habit also led me to start singing folkloric Palestinian songs to them that depicted the suffering during Al Nakba and the horrors that they faced during their "Trail of Tears," evictions and the savage destruction and evacuation of their villages and towns. These songs made me cry a lot while the babies were asleep in my arms.

I also got into the habit of buying lottery tickets. I won five hundred liras, which amounts to almost $100.00, which I shared with my family and friends. (I came very close to winning $50 million dollars in 1987, when the six numbers lined up on two different lines. Then again, when it was up to almost $36 million dollars, when I missed one number in the Super lottery in May 2017. I would always purchase lottery tickets when I found myself, unexpectedly, at a place that sold them.)

During those two years of solitude, I took the time to visit my former schools and kept my teachers and principal aware of my wellbeing. Some of those visits were very memorable, especially when, on my way home, I picked freshly grown anise from Don Bosco's farms without any permission. Once, I was caught by a brotherly and loving priest. He snitched on me by telling my father of my crime. My father reprimanded me and then started laughing as he reminded me of my failed attempt at kissing Ameerah. He was right: I always failed at getting away with illegal activities.

Many of my family members who live in the United States came during those years to visit us back in Palestine/Israel. Among those visitors were my cousins, Sohail and his brother Saïd, who lived in Southern California, and my Uncle Assad and his wife, my Aunt Wardeh, who lived in Ohio. Sohail was newly wedded to a beautiful American lady named Ginger. Coming back to visit us was a big deal that energized the entire family with celebrations taking place to honor them in many homes.

Sohail and Ginger on their wedding day.

Chapter 10   133

Undated photo from the late '60s of the author (center) with his Uncle Assad and Aunt Wardeh.

For those homes to accommodate a big gathering required more tables and chairs, which were carried by me, my brothers, and cousins on our backs, while also grabbing the two edges of the table between the two of us. Carrying them to the house of my Uncle Jeries, the father of both cousins, was difficult as it was far away.

As family members, we felt honored to do such a task as there were no places to rent chairs and tables at that time. I was 20 years old, and my other cousins were older and younger than me. None of us felt ashamed or left out; we did it because our parents asked us to do so, so that the host did not look as if he was unable to accommodate the seating of his guests.

By this time, I had decided to continue my education in the United States where my cousins Saïd and Sohail were already living in Southern California in the city of San Gabriel. Meanwhile, I also attempted to play matchmaker when my friend Joseph asked me if I could arrange a meeting with a family whose daughter, Laurette, he was interested in marrying. I was extremely close to her parents and especially to her brother Gabi. Joseph always told me that I was too mature for my age but that I could create a miracle by uniting them in love, and later, in marriage. When that happened, I would serve as his "Best Man."

This delicate mission needed long advanced planning and patience. By early March in 1971, the efforts of my cousins, who were sponsoring me, came to fruition when all my travel paperwork and tickets were in place. When Laurette's father told me that he needed time to discuss the issue with his wife Gabi and Laurette, I told him that I was leaving very soon. So he promised to let me know as soon as possible. Then I heard nothing.

A photo from 1972 taken in San Gabriel, California, showing the author and his two young cousins, Annan and Ra'aid (sitting front), and his older cousins, Saïd and Sohail (sitting, background).

When the day came for me to leave Nazareth, I apologized to Joseph, who felt sad to see me leave. Later, we lost communication so

I never knew if they got married or not. I really do not know why I didn't think about falling in love or getting married before I left. I think that my education was so much of a priority that love never appealed to me at that time.

I didn't even have enough money to purchase an engagement ring nor build a house or paying pay the rent. The older siblings were way ahead of me. Falling in love at the time was a very dangerous adventure let alone finding a girl who will risk such one.

Despite my learning and growing experiences during my two years of solitude they were not always filled with happy memories. My cousin Saïd, who promised to sponsor me in my attempt to get a Student Visa, did not have the time to do so due to his hectic schedule during his visit back to Palestine. He had previously promised to go with me to the American Embassy in Tel Aviv to complete the paperwork needed for my visa.

I was very dismayed when we were unable to visit the embassy. I felt like my opportunity to move to the United States was over. I was confused, sad, and full of anger. My head, neck and shoulders were still in pain from the effort of carrying all those chairs and tables to accommodate the reception.

However, after he returned to the U.S., he asked his wife, Irma, to help me complete my paperwork. Irma was a real angel with a magnetic smile and grace. She was a Mexican citizen, who my cousin had fallen in love with when he lived in Nazareth, via their letters and phone calls. She left this world at a young age, and I miss her a lot.

After Irma helped me complete my Student Visa paperwork, my cousin Saïd and his brother Sohail officially sponsored me which enabled me to get the Foreign Student Visa to enter the United States. But there was further disappointment in my family relations. My mother left our house to live at her father's house after she got angry with my father. My father always expected my mother to prepare and cook the birds and rabbits that he and his friends hunted

Photo from 1976 with Irma (left) and the author's soon-to-be-bride, Adelina.

and to cook for his friends who he invited to our house. She felt that with all her other household duties that she was physically unable to accommodate this weekly habit.

I supported my mother and told my father, "If you want to eat what you hunt, then cook what you hunt in their houses. No more here. If they come, I will tell them to leave right away, for we only have one mother."

My father became very angry with me but I stood my ground. Then, I went to my grandfather's house and spoke with him and my mother. His advice to his daughter was, "As long as Ghassan and his siblings are standing with you, you should go home to your husband." And so, she did.

My father then asked for a compromise: to allow him to raise a pig in the basement. I told him, "If you take care of him, it is fine with me and the rest of my siblings and my mother."

After a few weeks, my father hated the bad smell, the hard work, and the cost of food for the pig, so he got rid of it. My father continued hunting but ate the kill somewhere else. (My father would soon pay a heavy price for his hunting habit.)

My greatest disappointment, though, came when I resisted an old Arab custom that required my sister, Hiam, to marry my cousin Es'eed, who had reluctantly asked for her hand in marriage. When my sister began presenting her case to my father and uncles, arguing that Es'eed was like her brother as they had been living next to each other for generations, she also stated that she was not ready to get married. But my father and all six of his brothers refused her request and demanded that she marry her cousin. This came from an old tradition that allowed a first cousin priority to get married to his first cousin. According to tradition, she was required to obey this custom regardless of her refusal or lack of real love.

Chapter 10

Two photos from 1970. LEFT: the author's sister, Hiam (left) and their cousin, Adooleh (right). RIGHT: the author's cousin, Es'eed, and the author.

When my sister cried her heart out, I went off the deep end and began cursing my uncles. I warned my father that I would commit a horrible crime against them if they persisted. I argued loudly and clearly that this stupid custom must end now and not later. The rest of my siblings also took my sister's side but none were as confrontational and willing to fight as I was.

But my uncles and my father stood firm and refused my wishes and that of my sister. I then confronted them, promising to stand with my sister no matter what the cost, even if it included going to jail. I also told them that my respect for all of them had vanished.

This face-to-face confrontation made my father so angry that he tried to hit me in the face. I put my hand behind my back and told him to go ahead but he was unable to do so. My father had a very soft heart and he loved us all unconditionally. I told him that the main duty of any parent is to defend their kids' happiness and safety and to love their children, first, before their love for others even if they are brothers and sisters. He did not utter a word while turning his face away from me before leaving me standing alone.

Later, I heard him telling my mother that he had searched his soul and decided that Hiam's happiness was his priority and that he would never agree with his brothers, no matter what. He told my mother that she had given birth to a fighting lion and even though I was driving him crazy, I was right.

Up until the time I left for the United States, my father never directly apologized to me for attempting to hit me, nor did I expect him to. He just smiled at me and passed his fingers through my soft hair, something that he used to do a lot as a tease and as a show of love. He also took me to a Bedouin wedding, my first and last one.

My father did not know that I was listening when he said those things to my mother. That same day, he walked to my Uncle Essa's house and told him that Hiam would choose who she wanted to marry and that his son was like her brother. Thus, his nephew's request to marry her was denied. My Uncle Essa and the rest of my uncles refused to talk to my father for many months until his message became clear. Then, most of them realized that this custom must stop for the sake of their own children.

Photo from 1968 depicting the author's cousin, Walid (left); the author's two brothers, William (center) and Habib (right).

These problems did not stop with Hiam though. My youngest brother, William, began cutting classes and spent his days playing and running away from his educational responsibilities. My parents gave up on him so the task fell on my shoulders. I used to sit down with William after a long workday and try to convince him about the benefits of education as well as the hardship and hurt he was inflicting on my parents.

His excuse was that school was not for him. He was barely ten years old and too stubborn to listen. When I failed to convince him, I started dragging him to school and scolding him in front of his classmates. Additionally, his teachers began keeping him after school as punishment for not completing his homework. This worked and I continued helping him with his schoolwork while rewarding him with a few liras that I was able to save. Many years later, he told me that he wished that I had punished him even more given that having left his education midway had cost him many good jobs.

Chapter 11
The Pain of Departure

On August 11, 1970, I received my official high school diploma which I hung on the wall overlooking our home's dining table. By the end of that year, I had made close to 5000.00 liras ($1,500 dollars). I kept 1,446 liras for myself and gave the rest to my father. (At that time, one dollar was equal to almost four liras.)

At the beginning of 1971, I began preparing for my departure to the United States. I purchased the airline ticket, submitted my resignation at work, and asked my new supervisors to write me letters of recommendation that I could use as a job reference in the United States. When the word of my departure spread throughout the factory, many Jewish and Palestinian workers applauded me on my way out. They shouted that I was their hero and wished me good luck. I will never forget that moment.

I had stopped attending my language classes so there were no more visits to the homes of my family and friends who I loved so much on my way home. The buzz and energy of Nazareth's downtown Bazaar had ended, as well. Leaving meant that I would no longer be able to breathe the fresh air of Palestine and especially that of my destroyed village, Ma'alool.

This would also be the end of my visual panorama of Nazareth and the rest of Palestine, seeing the beauty of its women and the masculinity of its men, the smiling and laughing faces of its children, the beauty of its geography in the way its homes and villages are built, and the smell and look of its vegetables and fruits. I would leave behind the clarity of its lakes, rivers and sea shorelines; the grazing cows on its low-sloping hills and its flat meadows; the beauty of its wildflowers and shrubs; the singing of birds and barking dogs; and its distinct religious shrines depicting the three religions of Judaism, Christianity and Islam. And finally, I would no longer see the remains of its old archeological sites, scattered throughout Palestine, retelling the story of its long history of occupation by many civilizations and empires that enslaved its indigenous people and forbade them from achieving their independence.

I felt a strange feeling of being lost and unable to comprehend or face the reality of leaving my family and Palestine. How was I supposed to face my mother, father and siblings, let alone all others? This deep guilt, shame and sadness felt like a ton of bricks on my shoulders and all my memories rushed back to confuse me without mercy. Day in and day out, I could not look into my parents' eyes. I think they knew my feelings so they just looked the other way or they would change the subject to something that had nothing to do with my departure.

As the day of my departure drew closer, I started spending a lot of time in my room, alone, crying my heart out. The guilty feeling came often, hurting me relentlessly and mercilessly. I didn't understand why I felt this way as I just wanted an education.

I also knew that my parents, like all other parents on this Earth, wanted the best life for their children. My mind kept telling me, that doesn't matter: are you not leaving the ones that gave you life, nourishment and love? How could you do that to them? Have you asked them if getting an education is a good enough reason for you to leave them when they have depended on you for so long? These questions and hundreds more kept me awake all night long. Added to it was this God-damn guilt that prevented me from thinking straight.

Yet, as my day of departure drew closer, I tried my best to put all this negative thinking behind me and began to breathe deeply to regain my trust in myself. My questions then changed as I pondered my own ability to leave and survive in the unknown.

I began asking myself what my values were. Do you have the strength needed to survive in an unknown place? How about finding a decent job that will provide for all your needed expenses, especially tuition and rent? How are you going to keep in touch with your family and friends? How are you going to maintain your inner strength, courage, integrity and sense of humor? These were some of the questions I asked myself.

Undated photo of the author's paternal uncles and aunt, along with his paternal grandmother. This is the only photo the author has depicting all of them in one photo.

My answer to all the above was that I have a solid family who love me; I have deep roots which nourish and sustain my values of ethics and integrity; I can stand tall when faced with life's challenges; and I have always been responsible, loyal and hard-working. I had solid work experience and excellent vocational training, a welcoming extended family in California, and I felt equipped to thrive and successfully complete my education in the

United States, no matter what the cost. All I needed now was the strength to deal with the heavy weight of my emotions of leaving my family and Palestine.

On March 21 of 1971, on the first day of spring, I left behind Palestine, my family, friends, and memories to pursue my education in the United States. I was three months short of my 21st birthday. The hugs, goodbyes, and kisses from my friends and family members were overwhelming. What I most remember though is my mother's face: her physical anguish and sadness needed a master painter to transcend the pain of a mother who was about to let her son go.

It is a universal truth that no mother will let her child leave the nest without knowing that doing so will provide a better life and future for them. That was what was going on in her mind. She knew that I was about to fly away from the nest and embark on an unknown journey. Her lips were trembling and continually saying: "God be with you" as she wrung her hands together. This picture of my mother's agony and pain is still so clear in my memory fifty years later. I believe it is worthy of Michelangelo's ingenious painting skills to capture such an image.

My father, on the other hand, wanted me to leave, not only for my education but for my safety. Among the many deceitful policies that the Israeli government conducted since its illegal creation was in recruiting young Palestinians to serve as informants. My father learned this from a very close Bedouin friend who was serving in the Israeli Armed Forces that the Israeli Shin Bet (an FBI-like entity). He told my father that they were very interested in recruiting young men like me and this concerned and alarmed him as to my safety, so he fully supported my departure as soon as possible. (I did not know this until years later.)

Unlike my mother, my father stared at me with a few tears and told me to keep my head high, to be a good person, to honor our family, and to never forget our Palestinian heritage. He wanted me to stand for good causes and foremost, to complete my education. I was speechless and kept repeating that I would be back with my

Doctorate Degree in hand. Nothing less would be fair to them after they took care of me for over 21 years.

While I physically left Palestine, Palestine has never left me. It is what I am all about and maybe, subconsciously, I chose to study politics to enable me in the future to find a way of bringing real peace and justice to the Palestinians and Jews. To this day, I do not believe that the creation of the sovereign Israeli State is the solution for ending the continuation of the Jewish people's 2000 year-long suffering, nor the suffering of the Palestinian indigenous people that has been going on for at least 10,000 years of recorded history.

My brothers, sisters, and other family members drove me to the airport. At the airport, I found my high school friends, Maroon, Tawfik, Elias and Nader, waiting for me to say goodbye. What a day that was!

Chapter 11 145

Photo page: the top four photos show the party thrown by the author's parents on the night before he left. Bottom left: an undated photo of the author's best friend, Maroon. Bottom right: a photo of the author on the tarmac as he walked to board the plane that would take him to the United States.

After a thorough and humiliating body and luggage search, conducted by the Israeli security personnel (a practice that is only done to non-Jews and mainly Palestinians), I boarded the airplane. I first landed at Athens-Greece airport, then flew to Paris, France, then to New York. From New York, I flew to Los Angeles and arrived on a Monday morning, March 21, 1971, which was the celebration of both spring and my new life.

When I arrived in Los Angeles, I found my cousins, Sohail and Saïd, and my cousin Siham's husband Edward, waiting for me. After an emotional greeting, we all left for Edward's house. There, I met my cousin, Siham, and Sohail's wife Ginger. After dinner, I slept at Edward's house, which was located in the city of San Gabriel, about twenty miles northeast of downtown Los Angeles. I arrived with a single $100 bill in my pocket, and with that, I began my new life in the United States.

Undated photo of Edward and Siham with their children, taken in San Gabriel, California.

So how did Nazareth's years shape my life until March 21, 1971? What sort of a man was I? What values and beliefs did I bring with me? What were the roles played by my family, friends, teachers, and the larger Nazareth socio-economic community that shaped those values? What sort of dreams had Nazareth constructed in my mind about the United States? What contribution to the American people could I provide? Did I have what it took to survive and flourish in this new country and environment? Or was I just following a nostalgic thought that was about to end soon?

These were the questions that surrounded me demanding answers, and many more. My life in the United States was about to test all the above.

Part Two
The Gas Station Years
1971-1975

Chapter 1
First Experiences

A few days after my arrival to the United States, my family began introducing me to their families, friends and workplaces. My cousin, Sohail, took me to meet his wife's family. When he introduced me to his mother-in-law, a beautiful dignified American lady, he said, "This is my cousin Ghassan." She immediately said, "Son, no American is going to be able to pronounce your name correctly. As far as I am concerned, your name is Gus." I laughed and told her "Gus, it is."

From that day on, Gus became my popular name while Ghassan relegated to legal documents and formal introductions. Conversely, most Arab-Americans called me Ghassan and made fun of "Gus," and back home, my family and friends laughed at that name and accused me of becoming Americanized—or worse.

Sohail's mother-in-law's prediction soon became a fact as very few Americans managed to pronounce my name correctly. I tried my best to instruct them on how to use the back of the mouth to pronounce the "GH" sound but failed. Over the years, and especially when I began teaching at the university, college and high school level in greater Los Angeles, my African-American students called "G'hassan," my Hispanic students called me "Gustavo," my Asian students called "Goose," and my Caucasian-American students called me "Hassan." In South Central, most of my high school students called me "Dr. B," "Dr. Bish" or "Dr. Rat." For me, Dr. B sounded best, but take your pick; all were fine with me.

Having people learn my name was just the beginning of my life experiences in the United States. I was completely shocked to see the number of cars being driven, the width and length of the cities' streets and boulevards, and the way two tree lines hugged them on either side. I was overwhelmed by the whizzing trains, the number of gas stations competing for space with food stands, pharmacies, tall buildings, malls, parks, schools, colleges, and universities of all sizes. All of this was a real eye-opener for me. There were different churches everywhere, far outnumbering those in the city of Nazareth. I also noticed fewer mosques and synagogues compared to the number of churches. Then, there was the volume of shops and businesses, which left me confused and in need of assistance.

What amazed me even more was the diversity of the faces of people everywhere in America and the differences in body language between the African-Americans, Hispanics, Asians, American Indians, Europeans, Whites and Arab-American, not counting countless others. Being around such a wide variety of people put me at ease and made me feel like I was a part of this panorama of human diversity. Back home, I was accustomed to seeing only Palestinian, Jewish, and European faces; rarely had I seen African, Asian, or American Indian people.

The clothing that people wore also amazed me as different styles and colors filled the streets. Men with shorts, T-shirts and bare chests walked around if it was no big deal. Women wore even shorter pants, and many did not wear bras. People strode by looking straight ahead without looking at each other. Rarely did I hear anyone shouting at someone else. Most just minded their own business and did not engage in verbal communication.

On the negative side, there was also the smog. I could not see clearly and my eyes began tearing. The smell of fresh air that I grew up with was replaced by the smell of pollution accompanied by deafening traffic noise.

Chapter 2
Working as a Gas Station Attendant

During my first month in America, I slept at Edward's house while my cousin, Saïd, who owned a Shell Gas station in the city of San Gabriel, began teaching me how to operate gas pumps and the safe way to fill cars' gas tanks. I had never owned a car or filled one up before and I also did not know how to drive a car. Initially, I began working for my cousin as a debt of gratitude for his family sponsoring me in getting my Foreign Student Visa. Soon, I learned how to open and close the gas station, how to change engine oil, fix a flat tire, fill tires with the proper air pressure, clean windshields, check the transmission and brake fluid oils, and among other things, change the displayed gas prices on the high advertising board below the gas station's Shell logo.

Seeing that I was a fast learner, Saïd hired me as a full-time gas station attendant with pay of one dollar an hour, which later increased to $1.75. I was happy regardless of how much I worked or got paid as I felt lucky to have family here.

Two photos of the author in his official attendant uniform taken in 1971.

During the early 1970s, being a gas station attendant was not an easy job. Unlike today, where we have self-service stations, there was no hiding behind a thick glass window while the customers pumped their own gas. You were out front waiting for customers to drop by. When a car pulled up, you had to fill their tank, clean all their windows and check under the hood, which meant inspecting the motor, brakes and transmission oil, the water level in the radiator, and the tire pressure.

If the oil level was low, I asked the driver if they wanted me to fill it up. However, if their tires were low, I would fill them up without asking. Cleaning the windows meant satisfying the drivers and getting their approval on how you did. Otherwise, I had to repeat the task one more time. With all these free services being provided, I was lucky if I received a "thank you," let alone a tip. Yet, my early years of working in Nazareth had equipped me with a good work ethic so I "put up or shut up."

One thing that began changing, right away, was my eating habits as I became accustomed to purchasing fast food. My mother was no longer cooking for me, and the fast food restaurants were too close to ignore. Food such as pizza, hamburgers, hot dogs, burritos, and cold cut sandwiches became the norm, especially during my long working hours. Many times, I would be holding a piece of pizza in one hand while filling the gas tank with the other. By the time I finished pumping gas, the pizza tasted more like gasoline than pepperoni. I ate with dirty hands as there was no time to wash them between customers. When a customer pulled in, I had to run out and serve them right away.

We used to say, back home, that eating with dirty hands helped fight bacteria. (This belief was proven to be accurate by much recent research.) Yet, eating with hands soaked with gasoline and dirty engine oil was altogether a different story.

My eating habits became worse over time as the fast-food industry got the best of my diet. My mother was no longer looking after me and my uncle's fast-food was too close to ignore. This was another price I paid for leaving home. If it wasn't for my cousin Saham's cooking, Sohail's barbeques, Saïd's meat frying at the station, and my so-called cooking at the apartment, my diet would have been much worse.

But in the process, I came to know many decent Americans who really cared about my wellbeing. They did not mind my broken English, especially when they had to repeat their requests several times. I always wore a smile when serving the customers and that helped me receive many compliments. One mistake I made, though, was addressing an elderly customer as "Dad." In Palestine, answering "Yes, Dad" was a form of respect to those who are older than you. When I said this to a regular customer who would drop by and ask me to fill up his tank, he got upset and responded with, "I am not your dad."

My broken English sometimes caused me humiliation. When a customer asked me to recommend a good restaurant, I could not differentiate between restaurant and restroom. So, I answered "Yes, let me show it to you." And I took him to the gas station's restroom. Knowing that I was a foreigner, he told me to follow him to his big motor home while I was filling its tank up. He opened his door and pulled out a big, black gun from underneath his seat and told me, "Son, if I did not know that you were a foreigner and did not understand my request, I could have put a bullet in your head. I asked you to recommend a restaurant to eat at, not a restroom to shit."

I kept apologizing to him because he was so angry. I remember he wore a very narrow tipped boot and sounded like he was from the state of Texas. This was one of many incidents that I attribute to misunderstanding the English language.

I hated working during the cold winter days, the holidays and other happy occasions. During winter, no matter how many layers of clothes you put on, you were still working outside running after cars or checking under the hoods. The smell of gasoline and that of filthy engine oil penetrated my clothes and my skin, as well. Many times, I would forget that my hands were dirty with oil and try to warm them by blowing hot air from my mouth into them without realizing that the engine oil had left its marks and smell on my lips and cheeks. What a beautiful kiss that would make!

These incidents reminded me of rolling under the trucks, back in Nazareth, onto dirty and dusty streets to place the hydraulic jack under the flat tire axle. Working on holidays and other happy occasions made my heart cry, yet my mind kept telling me there was no time for this. I needed money and that was what I had chosen to do as my future destiny. So, I brushed the emotions aside and kept working and reminding myself that I was lucky to have a job.

What I hated the most was when a customer would stop their car in an uncovered area at the station when it was raining. I still had to rush out and ask what he or she wanted. They, in return, would ask me for directions as I was getting soaked and shivering from the cold. Depending on the way they asked me and reacted to my accent, I would either give them the right directions or the wrong directions. It didn't matter anyway because my English confused them and my knowledge of locations was even worse. Some wanted specific directions, which made me angry, as I was shivering in the cold and it took longer but they did not seem to care.

I also learned that most customers had no idea about The Israeli/Palestinian People's Tragic Kismet, TIPPTK, and the huge influence American foreign policy had in shaping and maintaining it. When I would tell people I was from Palestine, they would look at me with bewilderment and say, "Pakistan?" Then I would respond, "No, no, I mean the Holy Land."

"Oh, you mean Israel?"

Then I would say, "Yes, but back then, it was Palestine." At that point, most would say, "Oh, just forget it. It is too complicated for me," and drove off.

Friday and Saturday nights were the saddest of all times to work. By eight o'clock at night, I had already worked ten to fourteen hours. Customers would drop by on their way out at night, dressed nicely and seeming happy with their husbands and wives, boyfriends and girlfriends, family members or friends getting together. Here I was, filling up their gas tank with smelly gasoline and dreaming of a time when I would not have to work so hard and be able to have the money to go out, myself. I kept saying to myself, "The day will come, sooner or later. Remember the promise you made to your parents—all the way to getting your Ph.D."

During summer, when young people stopped by on their way to the beach dressed in swimsuits, sometimes the men would tease me while I was cleaning their windows by asking, "Are you enjoying looking at those girls' beautiful legs?" This would make me smile and nod my head, but it would embarrass the girls who would try to slap their boyfriends.

Working late at the gas station made me aware of all the lonely men and women out there. I could understand my loneliness as a foreign student, but I was unable to comprehend the loneliness of American citizens until I began dating those women and listening to their stories. They felt the effects of loneliness, more so on Friday and Saturday nights than the rest of the weekdays because they were working. But on those two nights, I used to receive the most invitations to go out with them. Mostly, I declined their offers because, as the man, I should be the one to invite them out and pay for them, but I knew that I couldn't afford it.

If they insisted, I would accept their offers on the condition that, next time, I would pay. Many of those nights led to friendships or became romantic dates. Some were very generous, others not so. Some wanted to marry me right away because of my accent while others liked my smile or my eyes. Some played games and stole my heart. That is, until I found the right one five years later. Regardless of the situation, I kept my eyes on the prize which was getting an education.

On April 3, 1971, my cousin Sohail left his apartment with his wife and moved into a house that they had purchased. They invited me to move in with them so I did so until August of that year. There, I had my own room which gave me the freedom to study without bothering anybody. For the first time in my life, I began attending Sunday Mass with Sohail and his family without the fear of Father Ghazal or Father Karelus taking attendance, like they did back home at MAM. Attending Mass with them was the way I could show my gratitude in addition to babysitting, taking care of their yard, taking the trash out, watering the yard, and other mundane duties.

What an ironic thing: just 30 feet away from Saïd's gas station where I began working was a Catholic church where most of the Sunday's Masses were celebrated. Here, I was running away from Nazareth's churches while they were still calling to me, 7700 miles away in the city of San Gabriel. The sound of the church bells reminded me that no matter how far away I ran from Jesus of Nazareth, my cousin, would not leave me in peace but instead, kept hunting me down. I told you he is a troublemaker.

Sohail hosted me for four months while Saïd and Edward opened their homes to me for meals and other family celebrations. On August 16, 1971, I moved out of Sohail's home to a one-bedroom apartment located on New Ave Street in East Los Angeles and became fully independent for the first time in my life.

Now, at age 21 and a half, I was alone but not lonely. My Number One priority became surviving and completing my educational mission without depending on anyone. I realized, very quickly, that without money neither independence nor education is possible.

To make money, I needed to get to work, and I needed a car to get me there, but without knowing how to drive, having a car was useless. So, I began taking driving lessons at $6.00 a class. On September 30th, I passed the driving exam and got my first driver's license. Then, I managed to purchase a used 1963 Chevrolet that cost me $275.00 but needed a lot of body work, which was postponed due to lack of money. After I purchased my car, I opened my first checking account with an $855.00 deposit at Bank of America in San Gabriel. What a thrilling experience! Hey, I felt pre-American and pre-rich.

Two photos from 1971. LEFT: the author with Sohail (right) and Sabah (center), another attendant originally from Iraq. RIGHT: The author with his 1963 Chevrolet.

Meanwhile, my hard-working condition continued non-stop. In my loneliness, I continued writing letters to my family and friends while crying my heart out. I know that most of us who leave our loved ones behind cry a lot when writing to them. This habit lasted for two full years and then began easing. Meanwhile, I continued where I had left off before, keeping track of my life by writing down my daily expenses and the number of hours I worked along with any daily activities, the weather conditions, and the main political events of the day.

Some of the activities I listed were: drinking whiskey, visiting Sea World, the Los Angeles County Fair and Zoo, going to Las Vegas, and visiting nightclubs. All of these things filled me with joy and amazement.

I began also subscribing to an Arab newspaper, Al-Islah, to stay informed about the well-being of the Arab-American communities. To further strengthen my English language skills, I subscribed to Time Magazine, and I began reading about the FBI, and also reading the Almanac. The word "Almanac" is an Arabic word which means "the weather." It is an annual publication listing a set of ongoing information about weather forecasts, socio-economic statistics etc. I also applied for a Social Security card, extended my Foreign Student Visa, and celebrated my 22nd birthday. This was the first time in my life that I had celebrated any of my birthdays. Back home, birthdays were not customarily celebrated; it was just another day—if you remembered your birthday at all. (That has since changed and birthdays are now lavishly celebrated back home.)

Best of all, love finally arrived in my life. I began dating Anette, who lived with her Russian mother and grandmother. The three of them were Born Again Christians who lived by the word of the Lord. I was surprised to learn that people from a Communist country were so religious. They did not like me very much, though, because I was a Melkite Roman Catholic and thus, an atheist and a sinner in their eyes.

Two photos from 1971. LEFT: Anette. RIGHT: the author with Anette's grandmother.

Being a Palestinian made my situation even worse. They defended Israel's creation on the grounds that it fulfilled the fundamental biblical prophecy that for the Messiah to come back, Israel and its temple must be rebuilt, thus empowering the Messiah to convert the Jews to the Christian Lord. For them, the Palestinians were a roadblock to the Lord's roadmap and what befell them during Israel's creation and with it their Nakba, was part of the Lord's plan, as well. This is how they justified their love of Israel and the agony of the Palestinians. It was all in the name of the Lord and so it justified their beliefs.

This toxic attitude left me no choice but to leave Anette, even though I had never been intimate with her because I strongly believed that one did not make love to a lady until marriage. I truly believed that real love must come first before love-making. I heard this from many people back home, which sounded old-fashioned, but then, I believed in it.

At this point in time, I was able to sell my old Chevy for $325.00 and purchase a used 1967 Ford Mustang for $550.00. Just like its sister, the Chevy, the Mustang needed a lot of body and engine work which I was unable to complete due to lack of money. The only things that worked perfectly were the heater and the horn.

The author's 1967 Ford Mustang.

When I purchased the Mustang, I was not aware of its popularity among my generation, especially girls. I think that many of them dated me because of the car I drove rather than how they felt about me. It was no surprise that so many romantic nights took place in the back seat of this car while we pretended to watch movies at the drive-in theater on Valley Boulevard in San Gabriel.

I ventured into playing chess, attended an Arab concert featuring the famous Syrian singer Sabah Fakhri, moved to a new apartment with my friend Radwan, who I met while I was purchasing my airline ticket. (Our travel agent arranged for both of us to fly together on the same airplane to Los Angeles.)

Additionally, I began another close relationship with a girl named Carmen, renewed my Work and Study Visa, became interested in watching movies at the theater, crashed my car at the gas station, listened to the Watergate hearings and found five dollars on the street. (These are all listed in my daily records that I so faithfully kept.)

On my 23rd birthday, things went very wrong. That morning, I opened the gas station at 6:00 a.m., like always, and returned to my apartment at 8:00 p.m. to celebrate with friends who had gathered there to surprise me with a huge party. With no time to even take a shower after work, I began drinking beer, then our traditional drink, Arak, then wine, followed by whisky to please my guests who were offering it to me from their glasses. I was extremely tired and hungry and with that combination of alcohol, I began vomiting so violently that nothing remained in my empty stomach. I ended up with alcohol poisoning which caused me to pass out on my bathroom floor and left me with no memory of what happened that night. It was a 23rd birthday nightmare!

Although I had never liked drinking, especially strong drinks like whisky, this incident remains with me to this day. I almost died, and no one was to blame but me. So now, alcohol consumption is kept at its minimum, especially when I am planning to drive.

To save money, I began cooking whatever I knew how to cook and ate alone after my long workday. Yet, when the time came to wash the dishes, numerous times, I was unable to stay awake long enough to do so. Instead, I would fall to the floor of the apartment and crawl to my bed to sleep. Those were the saddest moments of all. At this early stage of my life in Southern California, survival was much harder than I had anticipated. The images that I saw while watching James Bond 007 films back home in Nazareth portrayed America's richness and easy lifestyle. I now realized that this was not true—the realities surrounding me were the exact opposite.

Chapter 3
My Educational Journey

In early 1971, I began charting my educational journey by applying to colleges and universities all around Southern California. To my dismay, most admission offices did not accept my Israeli Don Bosco Technical High School diploma because it did not meet California's high school academic requirements. So, I was required to attend and graduate from an accredited California high school before I could apply to colleges and universities.

On June 31, 1971, I began attending San Gabriel Adult School, three times a week, between 6:00 p.m. and 9:00 p.m. after a hard and long workday. Transportation was the main problem for me as I did not have a car at the time. (I later purchased a car in September 1971.) To get to school, I depended on Sohail, other cousins, friends and my two feet to get to and from school. On the days that I did not have school, I worked at least 15 hours a day, from six in the morning when I opened the gas station until I closed it at 11:00 p.m. On many occasions, when walking to school, I was caught unprepared when it began raining. On June 9, 1972, I graduated with a very high GPA.

I must say that destiny works in very strange ways. Just like my caring principal, Mr. Dirawi, at Don Bosco High School and principal Hamami at ORT High School, I met the principal of San Gabriel Adult School, Mr. Buck. What a caring gentleman!. He recognized my thirst for education early on. When I told him my intention of continuing to the university after graduating from his school, he immediately began helping me by driving me all over Southern California to nearby colleges and universities to meet their deans and department chairs. When introducing me, he was so passionate about his belief in me that he insisted that I deserved a full scholarship saying, "Your scholarship will deliver a great scholar."

Mr. Buck, principal of San Gabriel Adult School, circa 1971.

However, this was to no avail. Despite Mr. Buck's strong recommendation and his appeal for an exception, no institution offered me the scholarship that I so desperately needed. My Foreign Student Visa did not help, and I did not have a California residency at that time. Mr. Buck apologized, often, for not finding me a scholarship and that made me sad. It humbled me and I felt sorry for myself but more so for him.

I have never forgotten those three high school principals who went to bat for me: Mr. Hammami, Mr. Dirawi, and Mr. Buck. I always wished I had a winning lottery ticket so I could establish full scholarships to students, here in Southern California, as well as in

Nazareth. I think that we have always lived with the memories of those who cared about us and shaped our future lives.

Finally, and after many applications, I was admitted to East Los Angeles College and began my first semester on September 12, 1972, at the cost of $350.00. I felt overwhelmed but I was also extremely happy. Finally, my dream was coming through and now there were NO excuses for failure or apologies for dropping out. Life around me was full of temptations that made my head spin fast and in many directions. Those distractions could have easily influenced me to veer away from my main educational mission. But I remembered my promise to my parents and the constant reminder of my father's humiliation at the hands of Father Karelus and that felt like a ton of bricks on my shoulders. This promise kept me focused throughout my educational journey. Education then, as it is now, is my God and my religion.

The author outside East Los Angeles College (ELAC), September 1972.

While going to college, I began looking for a welding and machining job to bolster my income and cope with my increasing tuition costs. I failed to find machining work, so I began to work at Edward's and Sohail's gas stations in addition to Saïd's. My work schedule changed a lot due to my study schedule. I continued to work as much as possible on the weekends, holidays and in between semesters, and that became the norm.

I do not remember how I intermingled with other students at college or with my teachers. My English was still poor and my concentration on my classes and work left me with much less time for leisure. Rather than starting with easy subjects, I began with psychology, statistics, economics, and English. I found it very difficult to understand my subject matter and without close friends, I did not have anyone to help me. I remember placing Arabic/English and English/Arabic dictionaries next to me to try to understand the meaning of many English words that I had never seen or read before. Those dictionaries stayed with me until I completed my education at ELAC.

There were two teachable incidents at ELAC that were worthy of remembering. My history teacher gave me a "C-" at the end of that semester. I went to his office and begged him to change it to a C and, in return, I promised to complete whatever work he needed for that change. He refused and told me that he would give me an incomplete but I must take the class with him all over again, which meant paying for another whole semester. In justifying his decision, he told me, "No professor was kind to me when I faced the same situation, so why should I grant you that request?"

So, having no other choice, I took his class again. This incident made me swear that when I became a teacher, I would NOT follow such a harmful policy. Instead, I would grant the students the opportunity to successfully complete the work they needed with the understanding that the grade would be changed only from "C-" to a "C."

The other teaching incident was much more productive. During my Life Sciences class, we were asked to dissect a frog. When I finished dissecting it, the teacher was stunned at my immaculate and fast work. She told me, "This is the best dissection that I have ever seen since I began teaching at ELAC." She then told me to become a surgeon as I had what it took: steady hands and sharp eyes. Yes, those were the same golden hands that made my mother recommend me to attend a vocational school.

The author with his Life Sciences teacher at ELAC, 1972.

Knowing that attending medical universities required much more money than I had, and having no one to help or understand my need for financial help, doomed this idea in its infancy. I wish now that I had found someone to help me pursue a medical education.

As I began my second year of college, I was distracted by a lot of bad news. During my first year, my 2.4 GPA disappointed me a lot despite all the hardship that college classes required. This poor result forced me to study even harder. I began working fewer hours at the gas stations, which reduced my income, leading to more sleepless nights worrying about paying my bills.

On top of that, two FBI agents suddenly showed up at my door and demanded that I provide them with proper documents showing my educational progress and my Visa updates. At the time of being granted the Foreign Student Visa, I was told that I had to maintain at least a "C" average or I would lose my Visa and be sent home. So, my 2.4 GPA saved the day and made me even more determined to study harder.

Satisfied, both agents left but the fear they instilled in me was very real at the time. Despite such fear, I followed our tradition, back home, and invited them to have a cup of coffee which they refused. (I later found out that entering without a warrant from a judge is unlawful, which I did not know at the time.)

With my disappointing grade point average and the unwanted FBI visit, I was saddened even further when I received the news of the death of my grandfather, the former Mukhtar of our destroyed village, Ma'Alool. This Palestinian man had suffered during his lifetime from the Ottoman occupation, the British and the Israeli's brutal conquest of Palestine. Through it all, he had never wavered in his firm belief that Palestine was stolen on the altar of foreign domination and interests. He repeatedly told me, "When the Jews began arriving in Palestine, we treated them as our semitic cousins, not knowing that they came to take it from us by the force of arms."

He was a great mentor and solid Palestinian nationalist. I was extremely sad and depressed. His death energized me even more to complete my education.

By the end of 1973, I started fearing the worst and began questioning my decision to leave Palestine. Why should I have to go through such a harsh life when I was still able to go back home and try something else? But I could not bear the thought of disappointing my parents and so, I kept going and never looked back.

At the time of my graduation at the end of 1973, my GPA rose to 2.7 and my English began improving a lot. I also began reading the Los Angeles Times, daily, which I still read to this day. My daily entries began alluding to political events more than ever before. Indeed, there was an entry dated March 12th stating that the Peronista Party had won the election in Argentina, almost ten years before choosing Peron as my main charismatic dissertation topic. To this day, I do not know why I mentioned the news about the Peronista Party winning rather than other topics.

After graduating from ELAC, I began attending Cal State University, Los Angeles (CSULA) in the hopes of completing my bachelor's degree in the field of political science. By now, I had made up my mind that the field of political science would be my final destiny. This decision came after a very intense soul-searching due to the following reasons:

TIPPTK had opened my eyes to too many global tragedies caused mainly by wars among contending nations in their quest for political and economic domination. In the Middle East, wars repeatedly took place for as long as recorded history. Deep in my heart, I wanted to contribute somehow to a peaceful and just solution to TIPPTK. Studying political science meant that I could study international relations and comparative politics. Both, in my mind, were the closest field of studies that could assist me in bridging the gap between the Palestinians and the Israeli peoples quest for a just and lasting peace.

During the early '70s, the Cold War was still raging and Political Science departments all over the United States were deeply entrenched in teaching a variety of courses about it to both undergraduate and graduate students. Most of my friends at CSULA's Political Science Department were interested in studying the Cold War with emphasis on both the Soviet Union's and the United States' foreign policy. Others were interested in studying the foreign policy of Western Europe, and much fewer, the Middle, the Far East, Africa, and Latin America.

Thus, I chose Latin America as my area of specialization for a variety of common-sense reasons. I was already surrounded by many Hispanic-American students and friends from many Latin American countries. I got to know them through my gas station years and my education at San Gabriel Adult School, ELAC, and now Cal State. They were my neighbors and fellow American citizens.

I strongly felt that we shared a history and many similar facial similarities. This similarity was steeped in the long history of Arab occupation in Spain that had lasted over 700 years. That long occupation contributed to the mixing of Arab and Spanish blood. With almost 300 years of Spanish occupation of Latin America (minus Brazil), the Spanish DNA also has been mixed with that of local and indigenous Latin American people resulting in many facial similarities.

Additionally, by studying Latin America's history, I could also analyze some of the Arab cultural influences on Latin America and vice versa, especially in language, religion, and food. (I did not know, at that time, that I would be teaching overwhelmingly Hispanic-American students in greater Los Angeles.)

When studying California's history as part of my course work at ELAC, I read a lot about how the indigenous Indian populations living in the northern and southern parts of the Americas were savagely killed by racist European occupiers using the Bible as a justification. As a Palestinian, the Bible was also used as a propaganda machine in justifying the establishment of the State of Israel and that of my Nakba. With the Bible came the invocation of Abraham's promise to Moses that the land of Canaan was theirs, that they were the Chosen People, and that Israel's creation was and is the biggest sign of the coming of a new messiah: Jesus Christ of Nazareth.

Wow, I thought that only the Crusaders had pillaged Palestine, but I did not realize then that the Spanish inquisitors and the kings and queens of other European nations had done the same thing around the world.

Reading Latin American history further introduced me to many charismatic leaders, among them: Simon Bolivar, Fidel Castro, Salvador Allende, Pancho Villa, and Juan Domingo Peron. Charisma has fascinated me since my Nazareth years, and the fact that Latin America has produced many such charismatic leaders created fertile soil for me to choose one of those charismatic leaders as my main dissertation research topic.

I fell in love with the images of the gauchos of the Argentinian Pampas, just like I fell in love with the images of the desert Bedouin of Palestine when visiting their dwellings with my father a long time ago. These similarities made me imagine that, one day, I would be the Palestinian Ambassador in Buenos Aires. Peron's charisma was very similar to that of Nasser of Egypt and thus, he became the focus of my future graduate work.

The lack of other Arab students studying Latin America's politics meant that I would be among the few Palestinian/Arab scholars specializing in Latin America. And I reasoned that this would increase my chances of finding a solid diplomatic career in the Middle East, relative to that of Latin America, especially that of Argentina.

Now that I had made up my mind, I suddenly became very excited when, on January 25, 1974, Los Angeles County initiated a fee-waiver program to foreign students who were holding Foreign Student Visas with the condition that this waiver would only apply if:

Students had been continuously attending three years of college education; students maintained a "C" average and, students had no financial help from any other sources.

I was extremely happy because I met the above requirements and received the proper paperwork from CSULA confirming my qualification. The average tuition for a California resident was around $80.00 a quarter for a maximum of 12 units. At the same time, a foreign student like me was paying close to $500.00 a quarter.

In addition to the fee waiver, the tuition covered the first 12 units, and any additional unit was free of charge.

When I learned that I qualified, it was one of the happiest days of my life and, at that point, the happiest day for me since arriving in the United States. The fee waiver renewed my confidence in moving ahead and removed my fear of lack of money. To state it clearly, the full meaning of this gift, to me, was as if I had won the lottery. It renewed my confidence and at the same time, propelled me to start seriously thinking about visiting my family in Palestine.

On top of that, I received almost $500.00 back from CAULA that I had paid for my first quarter and saved an extra $400.00 when I paid $80.00 instead of $500.00 for the Spring quarter. That quarter began on April 1,1974. With almost $900.00 more money, in addition to whatever I had saved, I purchased a round-trip ticket back to Palestine for $585.00. I left Los Angeles on June 20th, 1974 and returned on August 5th, that same year.

Chapter 4
Home Sweet Home

Upon my arrival, I found my parent's house buzzing with many relatives and friends. Their rooms were all full with people sitting wherever they could find a place. My father hugged me so tight and gave me a kiss then wiped away his tears with his Keffiyeh, which is the traditional head cover. I hugged my mother, who refused to let go. My mother is a very tiny person. I lifted her up while she hugged me and began swinging her left and right. I did not want to let her go except that she was telling me that she was getting dizzy and to stop immediately. As I stopped, she kept hugging me and telling me that she prayed for me every night and she said, "Thank God that you are safe and here."

Some of my family and friends hugged me, some cussed me while their tears were flowing, and others just waved and threw kisses.

The next evening, my father held a huge reception party for me. I think he borrowed some of the money he needed to pay for it. He became the center of attention when he held his rifle up high between his two palms and began dancing to the rhythms of Palestinian music while swinging the rifle to his left and right. As he twisted his slim waist to dance, the party became energized. I had always heard that my father was the best Palestinian folkloric dancer there was. He was no more than 5' 7" tall, weighing around 160 pounds. Yet, his strides were heavy on the ground, walking fast with a fully erect body position and a face that offered the best smile there is.

Photo of the party thrown for the author by his father (center).

My mother also began dancing when she realized that plenty of food had been served and that everyone was taken care of and very happy. I rarely, if ever, saw them both dancing together. What a memory this created for me at that moment!

A few days after my arrival, my family members took me to visit different places. The most memorable ones were in the far northern part of Palestine, adjacent to the Lebanese border, where streams of cold water passed by you. Some other family members took me to visit the beaches that were not yet polluted. And my friends took me to visit our old schools and began reminding me of all the crazy things that we did together.

Yet, the most memorable visit was to the destroyed village of my family, Ma'Alool, where most of my family celebrated my arrival with a huge lunch and dancing. Afterward, they began their yearly tradition of cleaning up the place by weeding around the graves of my ancestors as well as the remaining walls and floors of destroyed homes, churches and mosques.

Everyone pretended that it was my wedding reception by singing the folkloric Arabic and Palestinian songs. What an emotional and everlasting memorable day it was! Sadly, this was the last visit I had while my father and mother were fully healthy.

I could hardly wait to visit downtown Nazareth again. The Bazaar was still buzzing but the roads were more congested with homes and pedestrians and the donkeys had disappeared from the scene. I was happy to see that the homes of my family that I had visited on my way back from work were still intact and their occupants were there waiting for me to visit them before leaving.

Overall, Nazareth's panorama had changed a lot during the last three and a half years. This was due to very cheap labor that suddenly flooded Israel after its 1967 occupation of Gaza and the West Bank. The exploitation of cheap Palestinian labor, and the total dependency of the Palestinian economy on the whims of the Israeli military authority, largely propelled the Israeli economy to new heights. This boom in infrastructure took place all over Israel, including Nazareth.

Nazareth's streets were too congested now and its municipality's infrastructure was in poor condition due to a lack of equal funding from the Israeli states. Additionally, the increasing influx of newly-arriving Aliyah Jews from around the world required more infrastructure projects throughout Israel, which led to the congestion, noise, and air pollution, to say the least.

When the time came to leave, the emotional goodbyes were like my arrival but less intense than my original departure. My immediate family's attitude toward my departure remained the same but I could sense a changing social behavior in that of other family members and few friends. I reasoned that this change was largely due to the problems that a new prosperity brings with it as well as their cost of living and work schedule increases. This quest for material possessions, as I see it, creates competition between family members and close friends that was not there previously and produces tension, arguments, and stress.

Upon my departure, I had to repeat the humiliating experience of having my body and bags searched at the airport. Those in charge of this function acted with total arrogance, lack of respect and manners. You easily could see the difference between their search of Palestinian-Israeli citizens and that of Israeli Jewish citizens.

Chapter 5
Returning Back Home to California

When I finally arrived home to my apartment, late and tired, I found a letter from the Dean's office at Cal State University informing me to see him immediately. I then set up my appointment with him for my second day back. He sat me down and informed me that Los Angeles County had reversed its decision regarding the fee-waiver due to an accounting error. The County had estimated that only about 3,000 foreign students would be eligible. Later, it found out, after receiving all the applications, that there were close to 30,000. This clerical error was causing severe funding problems that compelled them to now terminate all the fee-waivers that were accepted previously, including my fee waiver. The Dean then told me to register again as I needed first to pay back the school for my Spring and Fall quarters of 1974, in addition to the 1975 Winter quarter.

On top of that, I found letters from both my landlord and my car insurance company demanding that I immediately pay for my August rent and car insurance. I needed at least $2,000 to finance all of these requests but all I had saved was enough to pay $80.00 for one quarter and a little extra to buy food. Although I was shaky and speechless, I remembered that I still had almost two full months to work before the start of the next quarter, so I began a relentless search to find the rest of the $2,000 that I now owed.

My thought was to tap into the nationalism and profitability of my Arab friends. After 1973, the price for a barrel of crude oil had risen from $3.00 to almost $35.00 and Saudi Arabia, Kuwait and other Arab governments had begun accumulating huge amounts of profit. So, believing in Arab nationalism, I sat down and wrote two identical letters to be sent to the Saudi and Kuwaiti embassies in Washington D.C. I appeal to them to help me while invoking my Palestinian/Arab heritage as a hopeful gesture. I also asked that $1,000.00 be sent directly to the Foreign Student Affairs Manager at CSULA, promising that I would pay it back once I was back on my feet.

The Saudi Embassy never answered me and the Kuwaiti Embassy responded by apologizing for not being able to help me. However, they noted that they were helping many Palestinians back in Kuwait. I was completely devastated and ashamed, to say the least.

Adding insult to injury, I read an article in the *Los Angeles Times* describing the huge amount of money that a Saudi prince had lost in Las Vegas—two million dollars—in addition to spending $800,00-a-night for his lavish hotel room. I will never forget these two incidents as they hurt my heart. I now realized that the Arab so-called leaders had (and still have) abandoned the Palestinian people and our cause while suppressing their own people from having decent living standards and a real democracy. After that, I began relating this incident to all those who I knew, including my students, despite its humiliating effect on my nationalism. You just cannot hide the bad and shine the good. Integrity means being honest, truthful, and daring.

At that point, I asked to meet with the Foreign Student Affairs Manager, which I was granted. During that meeting, I promised him that I would pay for the two previous quarters at the end of August, and I would pay for the Winter quarter, in time. I said that if I failed to do so, then expelling me would be just and fair.

He agreed to my terms and I left to open and close the gas station again. Additionally, I took a job working as a car rental agent at my cousin Saïd's newly-opened office at LAX, and I asked my family back in Nazareth to help me out with my financing. They managed to send me $1,000 which I was able to repay later. For almost two months, I worked my fingers to the bone. Whether I was sick, hungry or both, it did not matter. I never looked back or complained to anyone.

The author with his cousin, George, working at Payless Rent-a-Car circa 1975.

When I began the 1975 Winter quarter at CSULA in September, I had fulfilled my promise to the Foreign Student Affairs Manager and fully paid for my Winter quarter, rent, and my car insurance. I also began working at my cousin Sameer's gas station, which his brother Saïd owned before Sameer's arrival. Now, I was working at four different places and determined never to quit. Many days, I would work at the gas station, then drive to LAX and work until midnight, while I was also studying and completing my class assignments.

An undated photo of the the author's cousins: Salim (left), Saïd (center), and Samir (right).

As a rental car worker, I was required to pick up customers from the airport and complete their rental contract. When their car was dropped off, I was expected to take the client back to the airport in time for his or her departure. I also had to wash the cars and fill them with gasoline. The only moments that I enjoyed at this job were the moments when my work activities slowed down because all the cars, thanks to those rich Arab students, had been rented and it permitted me to study even more.

During those two months, my car began to give me a lot of mechanical problems, Annett appeared and disappeared again, I dated other girls, and I attended Palestinian National Resistance celebrations. I also took my Uncle Ghattas, the bishop of the Melkite church in Cleveland, Ohio, to visit the Japanese Village in Los Angeles, and completed the reading of a book entitled, *The Balance of Power*.

On September 30, 1975, I began my first day of the Winter quarter at CSULA and with it, the beginning of an amazing year that tested most, if not all, my values of inner strength and integrity with which my life in Nazareth equipped me.

To begin with, my education took center stage; nothing could have clouded my intense concentration on education, including hard work, both at school and with my actual work schedule. Leisure activities were placed on the back burner. I just looked the other way and never felt the urge to get involved in such distracting activities.

To take advantage of paying the max for 12 units and paying no fees, I averaged 20 units a quarter. I studied at work, libraries, friends' homes, cafeterias, parking lots and other places. I sat in the front row of my classes, when possible, and took notes and asked questions—even when my accent made the other students laugh. I always remembered two rules that I learned from the wisdom of the elderly people back home which I applied to these situations: First, I would rather ask a stupid question than make a stupid mistake. And second, that the authentic, Arabian horse might start slow but it always finishes first at the end.

I have always respected my teachers. Respect for my teachers has been present in my genes since a very early age. Teachers are always right: they love you and have your best interests at heart. Parents always stood with teachers, no matter what. Having your parents receive a complaint from your teacher was what we kids most feared. We knew that our parents would punish us and take the side of the teacher. So, I have always raised my hand when asking questions.

I learned at Madrasat Al Mutran(MAM) never to make any remarks when a student asks questions, whether it makes sense or not. I volunteered right away when my professors asked for a topic or for someone to lead a group project. I erased the board before the professor entered the classroom, without being asked to, and I never boasted about it. I made sure to arrive on time and leave when dismissed, paying full attention to the lecture and not being distracted. I never brought food to the classroom or ate in class, and I was always cordial to my classmates.

During this hectic year, I managed to watch many documentaries including, *The Cairo Documentary*, edited by Hassnain Haykel, the famous Egyptian commentator; Japan's Emperor Hirohito; and President Salvador Allende of Chile. (Later, when I wrote my first research paper, I chose Allende's leadership as its main topic.) I also attended the Conference on Palestine, hosted a friend from my former Don Bosco High School, and visited Universal Studios in Universal City.

Because of my extreme dedication, my grades were outstanding.

The only "D" that I received was in Spanish. (Fifteen years later, I ran into my Spanish teacher while I was teaching at CSULA. I stopped her, introduced myself and told her, "You gave me the only 'D' I ever got," to which she answered, "Well, now that you are a professor, take the class again and I might change it to a 'C.' " We laughed, and I declined her offer.

When looking at my final transcripts, it pleased me to see that I earned so many "A" grades as a testimony to my hard work. By the time I graduated with a Bachelor's degree in political science, my GPA was 3.75 and I was placed on the Dean's list for the two years that I attended CSULA: 1975 and 1976.

So, between March 21, 1971, the day I arrived in the USA, and June 1976, the day I graduated with my B.A. from CSULA, five years had elapsed. At 26-years-old, I was at least four years behind a typical U.S. high school graduate when entering their first year of college at age 19. Yet, I wondered if those students were aware of how fortunate they were.

Chapter 6
The Unforeseen Event

Armed with a high GRE score, as well as a GPA score, on March 19, 1976, I was admitted to the University of California, Riverside's Department of Political Science where I attended my first class in the fall quarter of 1976. I was entering uncharted territory which would, again, challenge all my values and beliefs since coming to the United States. It did not take long for those values and beliefs to be tested.

Five main events took place during 1976 that have shaped, and to a very large extent tested my values that have changed the direction of my life in the United States of America. The first was getting to know a female student named Lina at CSULA.

I first met Lina on May 21, 1976, a few weeks before our graduation. Lina was thirteen years old when her family emigrated to the United States from Grimaldi (Cosenza) Southern Italy. Her Italian name was Adelina but she preferred to be called Lina. (This is like me choosing "Gus" instead of Ghassan.)

A photo of Lina taken in 1976.

I saw her for the first time as she entered the cafeteria where I was eating a late lunch with other male foreign students at a table that I called the "United Nations Round Table." We were all students from Latin America, Europe, the Middle East, Africa, the Far East and the United States, which lent the name. We were loud and politics was the main subject we discussed, followed by comments about girls, especially beautiful blondes. That day, I sat on a chair that faced the main cafeteria entrance almost 30 feet away. I recall that Lina entered standing tall. She had black hair, a long neck and wore a lot of makeup. I said nothing but alerted the rest of the lunch-eating-bunch to her beauty, arguing that she needed no makeup. Of course, some objected while others questioned why my face had lit up? I told them to shut up and we all laughed.

When lunch was over, I went to my Comparative Government class where I found Lina sitting in the front row. I said nothing until the class was dismissed. On my way out, I tapped her on her shoulder and when she turned to look at me, I told her, "You are so beautiful; you don't need to wear all that makeup."

She looked at me with a fearsome and surprised look but said nothing, not even "thank you." (I was lucky she did not slap me in the face like Ameerah did a long time ago.) At that time, I thought that I had screwed up in possibly meeting a new girlfriend. But a few weeks later, I found her sitting in the cafeteria with her girlfriends next to our United Nations Round Table. We could hear their conversations as we were eating and gossiping to impress the ladies next to us.

At this critical moment, Lina decided to tell her friends that her car was in the garage, and she needed someone to drive her to the university. When her friend asked her where she lived, she said New Ave. in the city of San Gabriel. I knew that location very well because I was renting a garage on New Ave. that had been converted into a mini living space. I referred to it as my "mansion."

A photo of the author in his "mansion."

So, I stood up and told her, "I would be very happy to drive you to the university because I live very close to you," and she immediately accepted. (I think my line about her being beautiful worked after all.) I then asked her for her address, which she gave me, but she refused to give me her phone number. So, the next morning, I drove to her address, a few blocks away from my "mansion" and knocked on the door. A tall woman with long, uncombed white hair answered the door dressed in a long white sleeping gown. She scared me! She looked like a Halloween ghost. When I asked about Lina, she told me that I was at the wrong house. I apologized and left, thanking whoever was "up there" for this lady not being Lina's mother.

I then looked at the address she had given me again and found that I had made a mistake in reading her house number. I then drove to the correct address and as I parked my car, I saw a woman's face looking at me from the kitchen window as if she was expecting me. When I knocked on the door, Lina opened it and introduced me to her mother, who had already made an espresso coffee and cookies and offered them to me. Wow, what a mother: beautiful, kind and smiling offering me coffee and food on decorated dishes and coffee cups with saucers. There was an entire place setting with a napkin, fork, spoon, and the espresso coffee mug placed on top of a wooden plate in the middle of the table for me to fill up my cup.

Here, in this moment, my mother's face came into my mind with the way she always served her guests on full display. I thanked her and sat down for a quick espresso while Lina excused herself to get ready. When she returned, the first thing I saw was that she was not wearing makeup, for her face showed its natural beauty and I thought "Wow, what a surprise. I won the race and she really thought that she looked more beautiful without makeup." By the way, this I think was my first-time drinking espresso coffee.

This habit of picking her up and giving her a ride to the university continued that entire week. By then, I got to know her father and the rest of her siblings. It was not that difficult to see that we had many similar cultural traits, between her Southern Italian family traditions and those of the Palestinian/Arabs. Although I was still seeing other girls, I began to think that I might want to be closer with her and perhaps, one day, marry her.

An undated photo of Helen (sitting) and her sister.

Suddenly and from nowhere, the image of my friend Helen, who I met at the San Gabriel Adult School, came to haunt me. She had warned me that my dreams of marrying a Bedouin woman after completing my education and returning home were just dreams and nothing more than nostalgia. I had hung over my bed a picture of a beautiful Bedouin woman as a reminder that one day I would end up marrying a Palestinian woman.

Now, I was completely confused. Was Helen correct? Helen, who was the student counselor at San Gabriel High School, was at least 30 years older than me. Did this dignified American lady see in me something that alarmed her about my emotional nationalistic fervor that she had seen before in other foreign students? I didn't know then and I still don't know now. But it scared me and I began questioning my lifelong belief that the mind is always stronger than the heart. Now that my heart was involved, I was feeling that this belief was totally wrong and needed reexamination. At the same time, my mind (or dedication and persistence) had successfully gotten me to where I was now. The earth was shaking beneath my feet and I could not find the correct answer to these questions.

A drawing a Bedouin woman in traditional clothing (source unknown)

Soon, my visits to Lina's house increased as we had more dates and late-night phone calls at the expense of my study hours. I wondered where I was going and what would happen to my grades and work. I began asking my mind to stay focused and win the race against my heart. But I think my mind's "horse" showed an age problem and began slowing down. At one point, while visiting Manhattan Beach with Lina, I told her that if she was serious about our relationship, then I was ready too. Without hesitation, she said that she was very serious.

At that critical moment, I showed her a small notebook that I kept in my pocket. I told her, "This notebook contains all the addresses and phone numbers of all the girls who I have known and dated." She was surprised and wanted to look at it, but I said, "No. Once I toss it into the ocean, it means that I am fully committed to you and I will not tolerate future excuses for mind changes as I believe a commitment is a commitment, so please decide."

She stated that she was committed and that she had made up her mind. I then walked closer to the waves and tossed that book as far as I could. It floated for a few minutes then sank beneath the waves of

Manhattan Beach, and with it went all those relationships I had with other girls. I wished them "good luck." They all were nice, beautiful and decent girls.

At that point, my mind came back to life and I realized that I was getting into a more serious relationship, maybe for life, and I had no time, energy or emotion to spare, not at this critical moment of my life. After that, I immediately informed all the other girls about my final commitment to Lina. All of them appreciated my honesty for not continuing to date them on false pretenses.

Lina and I then began informing our families and friends of our mutual commitment. My visits increased to her home to see her and enjoy her family's company. Her mother's cooking was second to none and her father's barbecued homemade sausages were outstanding. I began making sausages and wine with him in his garage. He purchased all the grapes needed to fill at least four barrels with grape juice. (A barrel makes at least 52 gallons.) This was a lot of wine. We used an old grape machine grinder to crush the grapes with whatever was attached to them, especially spiders. Lina's father laughed and told me, in broken English, "Spiders are good for the fermentation process."

Undated photo of the author's father-in-law, Francesco, under his grapevines near where the wine barrels were stored, taken at his home in San Gabriel.

The sausage-making was another matter. He used to buy at least 70 to 80 pounds of pork shoulders. Then he would remove the excess fat before grinding them. My job was to hand grind them with a grinder older than my grandmother and place the ground meat into a large plastic bin. When all that was done, he would flatten the ground meat evenly in the plastic bin, then he would poke the meat with his index finger. Depending how deep his finger penetrated the meat, he would know how much salt was needed. After salting the pork, he added crushed, dried red peppers, anise, garlic powder, and then poured a full gallon of his homemade wine all over the meat.

After this "easy" job, he used to tell me, "Now, show me your muscles," meaning that I should mix all the ground meat and the spices thoroughly. This was the hardest part of the entire sausage-making process. You really needed strong hands with a lot of manpower. Once the mixing was done, he unlocked the front end of the grinder and replaced it with another attachment that had a long hollow cone. He used a long cleaned up cow's intestine that he purchased from a nearby Italian market which he then inserted into the cone. I would then fill the top of the grinder with the mixed meat and cranked the handle, forcing the meat out through that cone and into the intestine which formed the sausage casing. This is how the sausage was created. After the entire length of the intestine was filled up, he tied the other end to seal it.

Everything was done very simply without measurement. Lina's father used his eyes as a measuring ruler to tie the long intestine into 5-6-inch-long links. When all the meat was finished, he hung the sausages up in his garage, periodically poking them with a fork to let air out. They dried there for at least a week before he barbecued them or used them in other Italian dishes. I just loved making sausages with him while drinking his wine.

At the same time, Lina began trying out different Middle Eastern foods with a Palestinian twist. My family and hers were cooking rivals and with our visits to Middle Eastern restaurants, she became very well-versed in a variety of Middle Eastern dishes that she still loves today. Her favorite dish was the one I am famous for: tabbouleh. This very simple salad-like dish is, in my opinion, one of the most nutritious foods there is.

Soon, my relationship with Lina and her family deepened as my family and hers began extending invitations to each other. These visits cemented our relations and led to Lina and I deciding to get engaged. To do that, I needed the blessing of my mother and father, of course.

LEFT: *The author's father-in-law, Francesco, at their engagement party in 1976.* RIGHT: *The author's mother-in-law, Maria, along with Fr. Pontrelli (the priest who conducted their engagement ceremony), at their engagement party in 1976.*

My mother asked me one question before giving me her blessing: "Did Lina come from a good family, Yama Habibi?" As I explained before, Yama means "my mother" and Habibi means "my love." So, I became a beloved mother to her. (This is hard to explain but it is part of our tradition.)

I answered, "Yes, Yama. She comes from a very good family."

She then said, "Rida Al-Walidain was always with you, Mabrouk." Mabrouk means "blessed happy occasion."

Just one question, that's all she asked. Her intuition as a mother reminded her of the ways that I have always listened to her and my father's requests and advice. She just trusted me, period.

But when it came to my father, well that was another story. The second major test of my values and beliefs during this uncharted journey was when I received devastating news from my family back home that my father had suffered a stroke and lost mobility on his right side. He was unable to talk, walk or communicate in any way, shape or form. This stroke occurred after an unforeseen incident that took place while he was hunting with his close friend in a faraway forest. His friend had just dropped dead in front of my father due to a severe heart attack.

When my father realized that his close friend was dead, not knowing how to drive, he began running in the middle of the day to reach the main highway to report the incident to the authorities. A passing car stopped to pick him up then drove him to the nearest police station where he reported the incident. Thereafter, my father's health condition changed dramatically.

From that exertion, one of the main veins in his head suffered a nerve blockage, preventing it from sending signals to his limbs and that's what caused his sudden, right-side paralysis. His doctor gave him a shot to cool him down, but it was already too late—the damage was done. This is how my family explained it to me. I was not there for him and that was another price I paid for leaving my family and my country behind.

Now what was I to do? This was the man that I loved and respected so much who gave me life, raised me until I could fly from the nest, and believed in my educational abilities. He had once humiliated himself to keep me in school, he had given me his unconditional love, trusted in my decision to leave our family to go to the United States, and taught me manners, self-dignity, humility, rebelliousness, and the meaning of humanity, itself. I was crushed.

 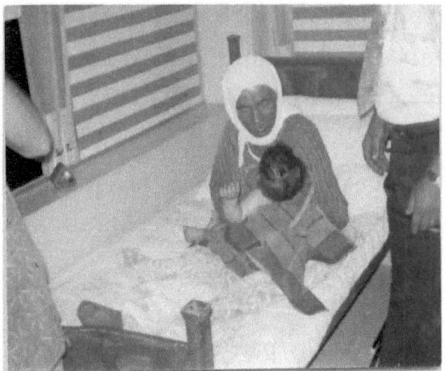

The author's father at his best (circa 1971) and after his stroke (circa 1976).

What hurt me the most was not knowing how he felt about my accomplishments since coming to the United States. I never got a chance to tell him how much my experiences with him meant to me when I was growing up, especially my visits to his shop when he was working at the Bazaar. I also didn't have a chance to tell him about my engagement to Lina, and his approval meant so much to me.

At this point, I had so many regrets and began questioning my decision to leave Palestine. Was it worth it? I was finally free of the burden of my promises to him to complete my education, so why not? I could start looking for more lucrative jobs and thus, enjoy my leisure time and its seductive capitalistic pleasures, just like many of the people who I knew at the time.

But with my broken heart and confused mind, I could not resolve any of the lingering questions I had, knowing deep in my heart that there was nothing I could do to relieve him of his disabilities. I had to swallow my pride and accept the fact that the best way for me to show him and my mother my love and respect was to continue my education in the hopes that I would feel better soon and ride the rough, twisting winds beneath me that felt like broken wings. I still had my mother and now Lina, and for that I was grateful.

So, not having a direct presence with my parents, I asked my father's older brother, my Uncle Jeries, who was living with my cousins Saïd and Sohail to take my father's place in asking Lina's father for her hand in marriage. And that's what happened. We got engaged on October 24, 1976, with both families and friends in attendance but without my parents' presence. Now, there was no turning back.

The author at his engagement party.

Lina also threw me a surprise 26th birthday party at her house and invited many friends, including Professor Bray, who was one of my favorite professors at CSULA. My friend Radwan also threw a huge B.A. graduation party for the three of us: himself, me, and Lina. This was my third test of those values. With those happy events, I truly felt that my dream of completing my Ph.D. was just a matter of time. I was full of happiness, pride, and deeply felt that my promise to my parents was just around the corner and that their Rida-Al-Walidain blessing was still with me guiding my uncharted journey. These happy events and good feelings were the third test of my values and beliefs during this time in my life.

Pictures of Lina flanking a photo taken the day she and the author graduated from California State University, Los Angeles.

But good news does not last long for me. My commitment to Lina began testing these values and beliefs as the fourth challenge. Lina began having kidney problems that required many hospital visits. The outcome was that she needed surgery to remove one of her kidneys. While she was having this surgery at Kaiser Permanente Hospital, I stayed by her side visiting her after my long workdays. At that time, I was working in San Diego, renting cars on the weekends, and it was a three-hour drive. I never made excuses for not going, despite the many jobs I was working while searching for my graduate university campus, car troubles, a constant lack of sleep, and major work problems with my cousins.

Being engaged is a commitment you make to someone you love, and love breaks many hearts as it builds values and beliefs anchored in integrity. You do not turn your back on those you love when unforeseen circumstances happen. As the expression goes, "When the going gets tough, the tough get going."

Now, I was working even harder than before. Driving to San Diego on the weekends to rent cars at my cousin Saïd's new rental office became my fifth job. Commuting between LAX and San Diego and sleeping at the rental office became my norm. During weekdays, I also worked at my cousin's three gas stations. I don't know how I managed to do all this with no mercy to my own body. I just kept my eyes on our upcoming wedding and my Ph.D. goal, which had yet to be fulfilled; both required making as much money as possible. Meanwhile, I began applying to graduate universities, especially those within the UC system, to complete my Ph.D. qualification.

While renting cars, I noticed the two different worlds that exist between Palestinian/Arab foreign students and those of other foreign Arab students. Most of those students came from Saudi Arabia, Kuwait and the Gulf states and were attending, as I recall Northrop University near LAX and my cousin's rental car office. Although none of the students admitted to me what precisely they were studying when I asked, I had a hunch that their education involved some sort of military and vocational training. According to them, their tuition, cost of living and spending money were provided for free by their respective super-rich governments.

They used to rent many cars from me, especially on Friday and Saturday nights. They dressed in fashionable clothes with shaved faces and heavy cologne. They were always in a hurry, claiming that they were late for their parties. I had to slow them down so that they could complete the long, rental contract to drive the rented cars.

Money was never an issue for them. Most carried in cash the amount of my monthly salary, most wore many rings on their fingers while others had expensive Rolex watches and shiny bracelets. I am sure that all this gold was given to them as gifts before they departed from their loved ones' back home.

They spoke to me in their local dialects which I found difficult to understand. The classical Arabic language is very well understood by all Arabs. Yet, because of the diversity and expansiveness of the Arab world, there are also many local dialects. Then there is the added fact that the Arabic language has many words to name and describe objects and subjects.

Despite our similar origins, no one asked me where I came from, how I was coping with life in the United States, whether I was a student, like them, or in need of financial help. There was no sympathy and no empathy whatsoever. I was just a servant behind the counter, no more and no less.

I was sad and angry at that time. Seeing these spoiled students behaving in this way made me sick to my stomach. But I knew that in time, they would also be the ones running the affairs of their governments. Imagine how they would behave toward the rest of the poor Arab population!

The funny thing is that I was deeply involved with my studies, yet on many other occasions, I wished I could be in their shoes. I would say to myself, "Just imagine what it would be like if I did not have to work and instead, could concentrate solely on my education? Better yet, what would it be like if I had the money to go out and enjoy myself or begin arranging for my wedding and future life with Lina without having to count my pennies?"

Then, I would snap out of this dream to face reality: that is, to focus on my education and not let anything cloud my concentration.

Here I was tired after a long workday and thinking about how lucky these students were. Then I would remember that their own government refused to help me with my request for $1,000.00, which was what an average student from their country blew in one week. I kept asking myself, "Isn't the source of their wealth the Arabian crude oil which is found beneath those Arab soil? Why then, is it not shared equally with all the Arab populations?"

I knew the answer then, as I know it now, nothing has changed. You have 23 sovereign Arab governments, most of which were artificially created by former colonial powers that literally drew a line in the sand to form their boundaries. Those same boundaries enslaved them to the mighty dollars of capitalism, the souls of those countries' leaders became corrupted with greed that led them to lose their attachments and responsibilities toward one unifying Arab consciousness. That unity became a pipe dream that forbid the formation of a federal unity like we have in the United States. So, those countries that are floating in oil and the mighty dollar found no need to share their wealth equally with those poor Palestinians and millions of other Arabs like them.

The seeds of their corruption were there to be seen renting cars from me. The termites in their pockets began eating at their consciousness a long time ago and with it is what you see today in the rotten halls of the present Arab government buildings.

My car renting at LAX and San Diego, as well as my other work at the three gas stations came to an abrupt and sudden halt at the end of that year. It began as a complaint about my work performance and integrity at both the gas stations, as well as at LAX. I vehemently objected to this claim and deeply resented the accusation. But my cousin, Saïd, with the acceptance of his brothers, fired me when I challenged them. Thereafter, I lost all my respect for them, as well as my interest in working for them ever again. I had given my all and kept the interest of their businesses always on my mind and in my heart. This fifth test was the hardest of them all.

Soon, I began looking for work somewhere else. It was a heartbreaking situation, but I defended my work ethics, integrity, and dignity as much as I could. Afterward, we continued our family obligations and relationships but with less enthusiasm and much less visitations. I just wanted to distance myself as much as possible from them and concentrate my full attention on my Ph.D. mission and my relationship with Lina.

Part Three
The Transition Years
1975-1979

Chapter 1
The Jump from the Gas Station to the Classroom

This unfortunate situation with my family had resulted in many positive and negative repercussions. On the positive side, it happened at the beginning of my Fall quarter enrollment at U.C. Riverside. Now that I was no longer working, I had more time to fully concentrate on my upper division classes. Soon, the quality of my research improved, my grades went up, and with that, my confidence in my abilities to complete my mission. My overall health improved, especially sleeping; my relationship with Lina blossomed; and I began seriously contemplating the ways that I should approach the topic of my dissertation as well as our marriage.

I began traveling with Lina, visiting many places; getting together with other friends; cooking more; and celebrating holidays, birthdays, weddings, and other happy occasions. This improved our relationship even more. Her father invited us to go with him to Santa Anita Racetrack and he showed me how to bet on horses. That day, I won $250 by using Lina's birthday as my winning numbers as well as my lucky number "11" as the exacta.

My lack of dependency on my cousin's employment forced me to start looking for other jobs. But that inconvenience was countered by the lack of further arguments and counterarguments with them which freed me from further entanglement with the involvement of my family back home. Thus, completing my Ph.D. mission became more urgent than ever.

By the time I paid $865 for the fall quarter, my checking account balance began dwindling and that forced me to look for a cheaper place to rent. I soon found one in the city of San Gabriel that was much smaller than the converted garage that I was renting. It was a very tiny room located ten feet behind the main house. My bed took up almost all the space, leaving only one foot on either side. To get into my bed, I had to climb in from its lower edge. The distance between the bed and the front door was no more than four feet. The bathroom was very tiny and so was the shower. I had to place a flat piece of wood on top of the toilet tank to build a shelf for my coffee pot, beside my tiny electric stove. That was how I brewed my cup of coffee and toasted my bread. Since the shower door was extremely small, I had to squeeze my body sideways to get into it to take a shower, but it worked for me.

Since I needed a bookshelf, I built it by placing two cement blocks on the floor of the room against the far end of the wall. On top of that, I placed a one-foot-wide by five-foot long flat piece of wood to form the shelf. Then, I placed two more cement blocks at the far edges of the flat wood and added another piece of wood on that for my TV. The bookshelf was level and looked good and I was proud of my modifications.

My rental was owned by a couple from Lebanon (Karim and Eptisam Masri) and my relationship and friendship with them was so solid that we remained friends all our lives. A few days after moving in, I was awakened early to a very loud bang outside my room. As I went out to investigate, I found the driver of a trash truck standing next to my car. He asked me if I was the owner of the 1976 Ford Mustang, and I said I was. He then told me that he had accidentally rammed his truck into the back window of my car—which, fortunately, was not shattered but the window frame had a large dent in it and a big hole beneath it. He then told me to call his company's insurance so they could repair the damages or just pay me cash.

When I began getting estimates for the cost of the repairs, I was told it would run around $1,600. I informed the insurance agent that I would accept cash to fix my vehicle rather than fixing the damage. I taped the window's hole over with duct tape and left the dent the way it was and this provided me with money to pay my tuition. I continued to drive my car with the damaged window as if nothing had happened. Welcome to my world of needs over wants. I wanted to fix the car but paying my tuition came first.

Unfortunately, my rental savings did not make a dent in my financial difficulties and soon, I had to pay the winter quarter which almost depleted all of my savings. Now, my quest for finding a job became even more desperate. By the end of that year, I began working for Lina's brother at his Mobil gas station. His gas station was in the city of Duarte, far away from my newly-rented "mansion" and the thought of working at a gas station again haunted me with its smelly and dirty gasoline and oil change smells.

Undated photos of Karim Masri (left) and Lina (center); Eptisam Masri (right).

At the beginning of 1977, I began applying for unemployment benefits from my previous gas station work. These extremely tiny benefits helped in alleviating my financial difficulties but were far less than I had previously been paid. On top of that, my car began giving me a lot of trouble as it needed a new water pump. So, I had no choice but to use my insurance money for that urgent repair. Meanwhile, I left the rest of the needed repairs as they were, and this became a constant reminder of my skills as a foreign student coping with life.

Soon, I began having severe headaches and stomach problems due to my stress over my financial worries. I still had a heavy load of studies and needed to prepare for my first Ph.D. written and oral exams. So, I studied every day for 6 to 16 hours at CSULA's library. The manager at the library was very honored to see a former CSULA graduate student studying for his Ph.D. and gave me unlimited access to a cubicle located on the second floor of the John F. Kennedy library. What a generous and kind man he was!

At the beginning of the spring quarter of 1977, I was informed by the Political Science Department that I was going to receive my Master's degree but needed to repeat one more exam due to an unsatisfactory grade given by one of my professors. I was not surprised as I had in-depth arguments with him over the Israeli Palestinian People's Tragic Kismet (TIPPTK) in which he strongly took the side of Israel. During his lectures, I had been outspoken in my condemnations of Israel's brutal policies toward its Palestinian citizens living in Israel and the Palestinians living on the West Bank and in the Gaza Strip. In his rebuttal, he dismissed my Nakba and argued that it was manufactured by the Palestinians themselves.

Therefore, I rightly assumed that he would give me an unsatisfactory grade. Otherwise, why would he refuse to meet with me so that we could go over the mistakes that he claimed I had made to justify my incomplete grade? Instead, he demanded that I retake the exam, which added more stress, frustration and studying. My Nakba followed me to U.C. Riverside. I did not have any direct proof to justify my hunch but in the end, he did grant me the incomplete. Now, there was nothing left for me to do but take the exam again. This time, with my stellar performance, the professor granted me the passing grade.

With my M.A. diploma finally in hand, my Ph.D. dream became closer to being fulfilled. I was extremely proud of my accomplishments and so was Lina, her family and mine, back home. (This incident with my professor reminded me of the wounds that TIPPTK carries with it thousands of miles away.)

This good news was accompanied by Lina's own news when she began working at the International Bank in downtown Los Angeles. In addition, Lina's elder brother had found me a fulltime machine shop job at Masoneilan, a manufacturer of hydraulic pumps for the U.S. Navy. The company was in the city of El Monte and this job provided me with full benefits, including paid holidays, medical insurance and paid sick days. I had never received such benefits before so it was quite a nice change. Now, all I had to do was inform the unemployment office that I was working, and when I did, my benefits stopped in a few days. Sometimes you win and sometimes you lose. Regardless, I was extremely lucky and content.

Two photos from 1978: on the left, the author's students, whom he invited to Masoneilan on a field trip; on the right, the author in Masoneilan's machine shop. Another photo of the author as a full-time engine lathe machinist at Masoneilan.

With my new job, I began buying tools like micrometers and vernier calipers to help me with my machining production. At $6 an hour and full benefits, I was in heaven! Remember, the last time I stood in front of an engine lathe was 10 years ago. As I had done before, I produced the quality and quantity that made my supervisors very happy. The excellent training that I had received at ORT Amal and Don Bosco Vocational High Schools in Nazareth had equipped me with all the skills I needed to successfully perform my work.

Again, if it was not for my mother's advice to enroll in a vocational school, 15 years earlier, I could not have gotten this job at all. Rida Al-Wale-Dain was on full display. How could I not fulfill my promise to her now that my father was unable to talk, walk or understand?

With my M.A. Degree in Political Science and a full-time job to brag about, I began seriously saving for our wedding. To meet those expenses, I realized that I would need to continue working on weekends at the gas station and asked for extra hours at my new job. This work schedule reduced my concentration on my Ph.D. work so I decided that I would take a leave of absence at the end of the Spring quarter. The Department of Political Science granted me this leave of absence on the condition that I must return within two years or my entire Ph.D. program would be forever canceled. I agreed to this and began devoting all my time to working, saving money, finding more work, and preparing for our marriage.

Chapter 2
Our Wedding

On September 29, 1977, I paid $ 250 to Luminaries, the restaurant that would cater our wedding reception, located across from CSULA. With that reservation in place, we met with Lina's family's priest, Father Martelli, to discuss our wedding arrangements. However, I ran into a major confrontation with the priest at St. Ann's Melkite Church in North Hollywood when we chose the Roman Catholic Cathedral in downtown Los Angeles for our wedding ceremony.

The priest told me that, in our tradition, when a man marries a non-Melkite girl, she must get married at a Melkite church. So, marrying a Melkite man at a Roman Catholic Church was also unacceptable. By doing so, the church would not sign the marriage certificate. I protested and my previous dislike for religion and certain priests reared its ugly head again. I then threatened to convert to Roman Catholicism, Judaism, or Islam if he refused to sign the marriage certificate.

When I realized that he would not budge, I called his superior, the main Melkite Bishop on the East Coast, and explained the situation to him. After a long lecture by him, intended to produce guilt, he made a deal with me. He agreed that we could get married in a Roman Catholic Church, but I was instructed to follow the Melkite traditions that automatically bestow confirmation upon baptism of my male children only. By doing so, my son would avoid the future confirmation, required by the Roman Catholic Church tradition. I agreed to this as if I knew what he was talking about. (I had already figured out that Jesus was a troublemaker and that the priests were his lawyers, twisting his teaching to suit their pockets.)

The planning for our wedding ceremony further intensified at the beginning of 1978 when we began looking for a place to rent. I did not have any money to put a down payment on a house. Meanwhile, Lina's health began deteriorating due to the failure of her first kidney surgery. Thus, my visits to Kaiser, West L.A., for her examinations resumed. These examinations resulted in the determination that for her to keep one healthy kidney she would need the damaged kidney removed. She reluctantly agreed to go through with this.

After her surgery, upon her release from the hospital, we held a big party at her parent's house. As her health began improving, we resumed our wedding planning once more and began looking for a rental place, furniture, appliances, hiring a live band, the wedding invitations and most of all—the menu to be served. We also decided that our honeymoon would be spent visiting Italy and Palestine.

I worked as many hours as the company allowed and never declined any overtime or work on holidays or weekends. I also began looking at additional part-time work as the demand for our wedding expenses began increasing. With more time available, due to my leave of absence from U.C. Riverside, I intensified my political involvement with diverse Palestinian, Arab, and Student Associations, mainly in Southern California. My reading increased, especially of the *Los Angeles Times* daily, and I began subscribing to different political journals, such as: Foreign Affairs, Latin American

Perspectives, Middle Eastern Affairs, the Journal of Palestine Studies, and the Middle East Report.

We decided to get married on my 28th birthday of June 23, 1978, but since it fell on a Friday, we settled on Saturday, June 24th. Our wedding was a very happy event that brought together family members from California, other U.S. states, overseas, and friends, of course.

LEFT: *The happy couple on their wedding day.* RIGHT: *The happy couple with their wedding party.*

After the ceremony, we drove to the Marriott Hotel near LAX to spend the first night of our married life in a very nice room. One of my groom-mates from Pakistan was an employee at that hotel. Knowing that we would be staying there before our flights, he rented the room adjacent to ours, entered our room, and removed all the light bulbs. He turned the bed upside down and then he and our other friends waited for our arrival in the next room.

As we arrived at our room half-drunk and half-asleep, we were unable to turn the lights on and we couldn't see the bed. We stumbled over it and I began cursing the hell out of the Marriott.

Suddenly, I heard loud laughter coming from next door as my friends entered our room and began teasing us. I told them, "You assholes will drive us to the airport in less than four hours." And so, they did. What a first honeymoon night! Nothing took place.

Chapter 3
Our Honeymoon

Our friends fulfilled their promise and drove us to the airport very early on June 25, 1978, and we arrived at Rome's airport very late that day. The next day, we visited the Vatican and other monuments, including the famous ancient Roman Colosseum. I fell in love with Rome's ice cream and its fantastic cold cut sandwiches that were displayed in an array of different shapes and sizes. The beauty of these displays makes you hungry right away. No one comes close to making cold cuts like the Italians.

I also realized how healthy Italians are: very few of its inhabitants are fat or obese as they all walk a lot and drive much less. Rome's transportation system was fantastic but I missed Los Angeles when it came to Rome's streets and roads which are very old, narrow and crowded.

After one week, we flew to Palestine/Israel and landed at Tel Aviv Airport, which now is called Ben Gurion Airport, named after the first Israeli prime minister who played the leading role in establishing the State of Israel, and with it, the creation of the Palestinian Nakba or catastrophe. To this day I just cannot understand how the Israeli population could be so proud of this war criminal and take his name as the first welcoming symbol of the State of Israel. This, even though this airport is built on the confiscated land of the City of Led that his troops destroyed and drove its population out of Palestine all together.

As we entered the security checkpoint, Lina gave them her American passport and they allowed her to exit without any further questions. I was behind her and as she walked away, I called her to wait for me. When they heard me calling her, they asked me how I knew her. I told them we had just gotten married and instantly, the guard grabbed her by her shoulders and told us both to follow him. We were taken to a special interrogation room and kept there for three hours as they went through every item in our suitcases, including our combs and toothpaste tubes, while my family waited to take us home.

That inhumane and humiliating search would make Moses, Jesus, and Muhammed curse the Israeli so-called "security agents." This is part of the Israeli government's psychological warfare against Palestinians. Having both American and Israeli passports and being a citizen of Israel meant nothing either. Lina's association with a Palestinian person immediately made her an enemy of the State. My crime was that I was born a Palestinian, so I was automatically guilty and condemned at birth, end of story. (And again, the U.S. defends Israel as the ONLY democracy in the Middle East. What a lie, for selecting and then neglecting the basic democratic rules enshrined in our constitution, such as equality, humanity, and dignity. Without them, there is no democracy at all.)

Once the search was over, they let us go. As we left the main entrance, I saw my brothers and cousins waiting to drive us home. After greeting each other, we drove to my parents' house which was full to the brim; the emotional outpouring was overwhelming. Family members, friends and classmates were all over the place. For a moment, all eyes turned toward Lina, who was overwhelmed with all this attention.

LEFT: *The happy couple visiting with the author's family during their honeymoon in Nazareth.* RIGHT: *A picture of the party taken during the couple's visit with the author's family during their honeymoon in Nazareth.*

I must confess that I did not write any daily memories during our honeymoon trip which took place between June 25 and August 4, 1978. Therefore, most of my descriptions of the events that took place during our stay in Palestine were from the few memories that I still can vividly remember.

Three important things were on my mind during this visit. First and foremost, was the wellbeing of my parents, mainly my father's deteriorating health condition. Second, was introducing Lina to my Palestinian family, our traditions and heritage. And third, was to visit those places that meant the most to me and played such a vital role in making me who I am.

My father's health was bad. He had no movement on his entire right side. His speech had entirely disappeared and the only sound he could make was "um, um" while placing his fingers on his lips, indicating he wanted a cigarette. That was all that he wanted regardless of who was around him. When he saw me, his body jerked up a little. He raised his eyes up but could not keep his neck straight. Suddenly, his neck dropped down and, with it, his eyes as well.

Dressed in his pajamas with his Palestinian head cover, he was a man in complete despair, unable to do much. And here I was trying to show him my M.A. degree and explain to him what it meant. It was so hard to do! Sitting at the edge of his bed and trying to see his face was all that I wanted. The closer I moved toward him, the more his neck would bend downward. I held my tears for as long as I could until my mother begged me to move away. She was the one who was crying, not for her husband but for me. She had already cried a lot for him and that made her understand the need for others to cry.

Again, I listened to her. This angel of mine came to rescue me from my miserable condition. She knew what was taking place in my heart and mind. She kept telling me, "Remember, you are here to celebrate your wedding with Lina. Your father does not understand anything."

She acknowledged that he had recognized me because, according to the doctors, when he recognized something or someone who he knew before his illness, his body jerked upward for few seconds. That was what he did when he saw me.

I agreed and hearing this made me very happy and relieved a lot of my emotional pain.

My mother's health was also deteriorating as the onslaught of dementia began creeping in. She had lost weight despite being very petite to begin with. Wrinkles had appeared on her face, especially her cheeks. Those wrinkles began covering her angel-like face, the face that said goodbye to me on June 21, 1971. It now showed the losses she had suffered in such a short time.

In addition to me leaving and her husband's physical condition, she also was in pain from my brother Emile leaving Nazareth for the United States. Emile took care of my father while he was there. After he left, my mother was not strong enough to replace his labor, so my remaining brothers decided to move my father to a nearby hospital to be taken care of. This hospital stay triggered a lot of gossip by other family members who did not approve of such a move. I strongly felt that the above four reasons contributed greatly to her sudden deterioration in health.

Despite this, she continued to keep her house extremely clean and neat. She provided coffee to the multitude of visitors and all the sweets that come with it, including cigarettes (it is customary to place a bowl in the middle of the coffee table filled with a variety of cigarette cartons as people in the Middle East smoke a lot. Welcome to our unhealthy habit.)

My family celebrated our marriage with another big party. Many people came, but we did not have the company of my father at the main wedding party. I heard, repeatedly, that without him the wedding party was not the same. He entertained everyone when he was well with his dances as he held his rifle between his two hands and on top of his head. As he moved between the dining tables, guests would sing and clap their hands to the tune of the songs played by the live band. Compared to that, our wedding party was very quiet and boring, to say the least. It was hard for all of us, especially Lina, who never knew her father-in-law or got to dance with him.

I had always wished that my father could meet Lina's father. I could see my father helping him make sausages and wine and accompanying him to the racetrack. After all, my father owned a horse and was an excellent horse rider. Besides that, my father could have shown him how to make hummus and lamb kebab, something that my father-in-law would have truly enjoyed. Just making holiday cookies, alone, could have brought such joy and solid friendship to my mother and Lina's mom. But that dream was never fulfilled because all of them passed away. Only their memories stay alive with me all the time.

During our visit, Lina was always the center of attention. Many of my family members and friends wanted to show her how much they knew about Roman history in Palestine. After all, the Roman Empire had occupied Palestine longer than all the other empires: 637 years in total. On many occasions, I have told Lina that the Italians should have argued that Palestine should fall under their mandate; maybe they could have been more humane to us as compared to the British? I am not sure of that either.

My relatives began telling her the names of the places that they had visited in Italy, including Roman monasteries, churches, schools, orphanages, restaurants, businesses, monuments, streets, forests, mountains, even the cobblestone streets in Jerusalem that carried Roman names. They were competing among themselves to show her their affection for everything Italian, including Italian food, customs, art, and Italian soccer, which, then, dominated the world.

They told her that it was destiny that a Palestinian and an Italian with different backgrounds met and married. I fully believe that there is a truth to that. I told Lina many times, "You have all your family in the United States. What made you fall in love with a financially broken Palestinian foreign student?"

She always says, "Destiny," which is kismet in Arabic, way before my friends believed in it, too.

Many of my relatives had traveled to Italy, as it is only a three-hour, non-stop flight there from Palestine. Some of them were importing Italian marble, clothing, cold cuts, cheese, and other warehouse items. Thus, they were in contact with many Italian businesses and merchants. One thing they hated though were the many dishes of pasta that the Italian restaurants offered on their menus. They used to tell me in secret, with a nudge of humor, "One day we would eat red pasta, then green pasta, followed by white pasta, then black pasta. We were looking for pieces of chicken or beef in it but found none. Since we couldn't speak the language, the only word we knew was pasta."

Those friends and family members drove us crazy with their invitations. Most days, we were invited to lunch and dinner on the same day at two different homes. And if you said "No," you were in deep trouble. Even then, they would insist on breakfast. Believe me, many days we ate breakfast, lunch, and dinner at three different homes.

Besides the invitations, our family and friends took us to visit my old schools, the old Bazaar, and my old neighborhoods. They drove us to the West Bank, where Lina fell in love with Jerusalem and the many Roman monuments, especially the cobblestone streets. She stopped to order a Falafel sandwich topped with tahini. (Tahini is a watery syrup from sesame seed oil mixed with water and lemon juice with an added pinch of salt.) She also purchased cactus fruit from an elderly lady. While the lady was peeling away the skin from the fruit, Lina was consuming it.

Lina and I visited many religious sites: the Church of the Holy Sepulcher, the Dome of the Rock, the Wailing Wall, and the famous Jerusalem Bazaar, among others. We immediately realized the impact of Israel's occupational policies, especially the many soldiers carrying weapons, the many roadblocks, checkpoints, and the constant harassment of ordinary Palestinians going about their daily business. We also visited the cities of Nablus, Jenin, and Bethlehem, among other cities and towns.

This memorable journey was followed by another one that took us to the furthest northern part of Palestine. My Uncle Joseph and my Aunt Salimeh, with their kids, took us to the Northern part of Palestine to visit the City of Banyans where a cold-running stream flows in the middle of the park where we stayed. I remember my aunt placing an oversized watermelon in the water to make it as cold as possible before consuming it. The beauty of this place is just outstanding.

From the northern end of Palestine, we drove a few days to the city of Tiberias where the Sea of Galilee is located. It is not a sea at all but a mid-size lake. It is famous for the miracles that Jesus, according to the Bible, performed when he walked on water. For me, what made that famous was its fish, known as "Samak Sultan Ibraheem" or Sultan Ibrahim or Abraham Fish. When it is fried and you begin eating it hot, you feel that you are in heaven sitting beside the Prophet Abraham (I am just kidding).

My memories of many places that have brought me such joy were disappointing and sad. The Bazaar had changed a lot. My father's shoe shop was no longer a part of the landscape; my Uncle Essa's business had changed and moved out of the Bazaar altogether. My Uncle Ragi's fish business moved far away and instead, he opened a welding shop, and my Uncle Radwan's fish shop was the only one remaining in that section of the Bazaar. My happy years with them, including their teasing and jokes with that of refusing to eat what their wives have cooked for them and sleeping in my father's shop, made me really cry not only then but to this very day.

The new owners and new businesses occupied many of the old guard's locations. The horny donkeys showing their male organs as they waited for cargo were gone, as were the loud voices of merchants. Instead, the old Bazaar became bizarre to me.

Kannisat Al-Massih was still there but its old, open entrance was replaced with an iron gate. My first, second, and third grade classes were moved to a new location and with their removal, my memories of them were also removed. The place was now very quiet with no more soccer competitions between me and Hani, no more fire pits in the classroom and no more Mrs. Rose weaving wool sweaters. Thinking about my favorite back-riding game memories brought tears to my eyes.

I did not try to visit my hated elementary school, MAM, I was told that most of its teachers were no longer there and that Abuna Ghazal had passed away due to lung cancer, and Abuna K. had retired. The unpleasant memories I had at that school made me angry.

ORT Amal Vocational School had moved to a new location and one of my old classmates became its principal. Most of my classmates became teachers at both ORT Amal and Don Bosco. The curriculum at both schools was expanded and many more students were now attending. My favorite Jewish principal, Mr. Hammami, completed his tenure, and my cousin Salim left with his family to the United States.

My favorite and most respected principal at Don Bosco, Mr. Dirawi, had passed away. He had influenced me a lot, especially in my love of our Palestinian heritage and in standing up for what is right. I tried my best to explain to my former classmates, at both ORT and Don Bosco, how lucky we were to attend vocational schools at the time we did, and how my training had helped me find work in the United States when all my hopes of finding a job had disappeared.

Following a request from my former classmates, who are now teaching at Don Bosco, I gave a lecture to their tenth-grade students about the United States' foreign policy. I was very honored to do so. All I remember about that was the students' attentiveness and smart questions.

I was also anxious to visit my family members' homes that I used to stop at on my way home from school, but sadly, they were all gone. Most had built new homes somewhere else and some of my family members had passed away. My grandparents, who I used to enjoy eating yogurt with, were no more. But I will always remember the stories my grandfather told me and his wishes for a peaceful Palestinian and Jewish reconciliation. With his death, that dream had also died.

Nazareth's panorama had changed a lot since I was young. A booming Israeli economy had replaced it with its West Bank and Gaza occupation. This brought about cheaper labor, especially in the construction industry. The booming economy was felt all over Israel and it filtered down to its Palestinian/Israeli citizens. With it, a massive construction boom took place all over Galilee, especially in its capital city of Nazareth. The ownership of cars increased and so did street congestion. The few empty lots at the edges of Nazareth's hills were now full of homes and other businesses.

The bustle and hassle of daily living made people's attitudes to one other more rigid and less friendly. Money-making became more urgent now than ever before and unless you were family or friends, friendly greetings disappeared, replaced by more business-like attitudes. People walked in a hurry, mostly face down, contemplating their daily living and the ever-present competition with others. Capitalism and its lurid quest for more wealth accumulation was evident all over Israel and Nazareth. Drug use and violent gangs mushroomed all over Israel. Mafia-type gangs scared many businesses and forced them to pay royalties if they wanted to stay in business.

The only real friendship that emerged under these circumstances, between the Palestinian and the Israelis, were relations that deal with illicit or mafia-type going ons. So far, statistics show that over 125 Palestinian/Israeli citizens have succumbed to gang violence since the beginning of 2023. The Israeli numbers, I do not know.

The day before we left to go home, my family arranged a picnic at our destroyed village of Ma'Alool. The variety of dishes were outstanding, including the barbecued smell of lamb and chicken. While all this was going on, Lina looked over the remains of my destroyed village and asked questions regarding the homes of my parents and other relatives. She felt angry at the destruction of the churches and the mosque.

My family showed her the destroyed agriculture fields, the old water well, and the barbed wire fences surrounding the main village center. The entire location became a forest and a military security zone filled with military hardware, barking and angry watch dogs, and other unappealing things.

After a long and happy day with family and friends, we left Ma'Alool and began preparing for the next day's long trip home. I had to go through the same emotional goodbyes for the third time and the humiliating airport body and luggage search again. This time, I was aware that I might not see either of my parents again. We then flew back on August 5, 1978, and arrived in Los Angeles later that same day.

Chapter 4
Home Sweet Home

Upon our arrival, Lina's family greeted us with homemade Italian food, then drove us to our apartment where we began sharing our travel experiences during our honeymoon with them. We showed them pictures that we had taken and souvenirs we had purchased.

Soon, I went back to my routine schedule of working eight to ten hours a day, but I also became serious about playing soccer with my friends. This resulted in many injuries, but I kept going. We received many more invitations from some of our family and friends and our social schedule was always busy. Our main efforts centered on furnishing the apartment, paying our bills, and the completion of my dissertation.

My daily newspaper reading continued, and with it, the continued efforts by many members of my family to mend fences with my cousins.

By the end of the year, I managed to get my Green Card, bringing me closer to full citizenship.

I also met the U.C. Riverside's Political Science Department Chair, Dr. Jenkins, to discuss the end of my leave of absence and the start of my Ph.D. program again. He reinstated me immediately in January 1979 and I registered for the 1979 Winter quarter as a full-time student carrying 14 units of upper division classes in Economics, Latin American History, Chinese Foreign Policy, and Concurrent Analysis of Political Science.

Part Four
The Trial Years
1980-1986

Chapter 1
The Start of My Ph.D.

Now that I had become a full-time student, my goal, as always, continued to be the successful completion of all my upper division classes and getting my Ph.D. diploma. Thus, my work at Masoneilan began losing steam. I wanted to continue as a part-time machinist, but my manager refused; he said, "either you work full time or quit."

His decision forced me to leave a beautiful job. Soon, I found a more accommodating machining job at a company named Vacco Industries which lasted only three months. It soon became very clear to me that even with the accommodating work schedule that Vacco provided, I could not successfully fulfill my commitments to my family and studies with a full-time job.

The burden of making money to pay our bills now shifted to Lina, whose job as a manager at a bank required frequent travel to San Francisco for special training on international finance and bank management. So, I became her driver, to and from the airport, as well as her cook.

At the beginning of July 1979, Lina found out that she was pregnant with our first child. This was very happy news, prompting immediate planning of our financial priorities, my research and study schedule, and most of all, the arrival of this treasure.

During this period, many relatives, especially uncles, visited us from Palestine and tried to reconcile my disputes with my Uncle Jeries and his sons. Because he was the eldest brother of my father, by tradition (which I hated), he was to be respected in all his decisions regardless of if they were right or wrong. This screwed-up tradition prompted all who attempted at a fair resolution to take the side of my uncle and his sons. My uncle did not have much choice but to take his son's side in this matter as any other decision would risk the dislike of his sons, who provided him with shelter and a good living standard.

My father by this time was bedridden and unable to do much. The stand that his brothers took, despite his physical condition, made me lose all respect for my uncles. In my mind, they had betrayed their brother by following an old screwed-up custom, and worse, by not standing up for a just compromise. All of them are now dead so I have forgiven them, but I will never forget what they did to me and their bedridden brother.

I try to remember that they always loved me and fulfilled their duties toward me and my family, especially when I left Palestine and when I visited Palestine with my wife. Then, they welcomed us with an open heart and mind. But what changed their attitudes when they arrived here, I will never understand. I am sure though it was following the tradition summed up by the Arabic words "Akhuna Al-Kabeer," meaning "our eldest brother or the Big Brother." That was my Uncle Jeries: their "Akhuna Al- Kabeer," which ensured the conformity of this tradition.

As the pressure of their behavior began mounting on me, it started affecting my health as well as my relations with Lina, prompting further arguments. Lina was not prepared for such an ugly outcome when she entertained and respected my uncles the best way that she could. My continued praise of them as the "best uncles one could find" was not what she was witnessing.

On a few occasions, I began sleeping in hotels around the city of San Gabriel to avoid further arguments that lead nowhere. Yet, despite my increasing study load, Lina's work, Lina's pregnancy, and our further financial difficulties, I stood my ground and refused to apologize. Instead, I reminded them of my hard work and loyalty to them and their businesses and I demanded from my uncle that his sons apologize to me as I had told them "I did not do any harm to anyone," period. I wanted to honor my father who was unable to defend his son. Remembering his stand when it came to marrying his daughter (my sister) to her cousin, my father could have done the same thing and shamed all of his brothers.

The strain of standing firm when I am right has a deep root that goes back as far as I remember—at least to when I was four years old. At this point in my life, I made up my mind that leaving my uncle and cousins behind was the right thing to do so that I could fully concentrate on what was important: my wife, future baby, and my studies.

At U.C. Riverside, I have now begun seriously thinking about the topic of my dissertation. I had always admired strong leadership in personalities in action, including Mahatma Gandhi of India, Jamal Abdul Nasser of Egypt, Salvatore Allende of Chile, Nelson Mandela of South Africa, John F. Kennedy of the United States, Joseph Stalin of the Soviet Union, Mao Tso Tung of China, and Fidel Castro of Cuba. I had also read a lot of books about other strong personalities while living in Nazareth. I, too, had demonstrated my leadership abilities during my life in Nazareth. Specifically, I recalled my roles as a son, student, worker, soccer coach, traditions' challenger, neighborhood inquisitor, and someone who showed courage under stress with my fiery arguments, especially at ORT Amal and Don Bosco's High Schools. Thus, the idea of choosing a strong charismatic leader for my dissertation research topic was already ingrained in me a long time ago.

When I met my future Dissertation Committee Professors, Dr. Chilcote and Dr. Gorton at the Political Science department, and Dr.

Cortes at the History department, I proposed this to them. I wanted to study and research the charismatic dimensions of both Nasser of Egypt, who was already my charismatic hero, and Juan Domingo Peron of Argentina for my final dissertation research topic. Both Dr. Chilcote and Dr. Cortes encouraged me to do so, but Dr. Gurtov advised me to think about taking the emerging Palestinian Liberation Organization (PLO), instead.

A recent photo taken at a restaurant near UC Riverside. The author (center) with Dr. Chilcote (left) and Dr. Cortes (right).

Dr. Gurtov's suggestion was a very powerful one for me, being a Palestinian/Israeli and soon to be an American citizen, with an excellent command of Arabic, Hebrew, and English. I would be in an excellent position to have access to meetings with people in positions of authority on this subject and I could easily read books and documents in three different languages. But the study of the emerging PLO was already widespread and well-known among a wide range of people who were entrenched in Middle Eastern studies: students, diplomats, political science scholars in the Middle East and others.

On the other hand, very few Arab scholars had written about the history of Latin America's politics, traditions, and economy, especially the roles played by its charismatic leaders in shaping the destiny of Latin America's future policies and developments. At the time, I had not heard or read any literature coming from the Arab world. I am sure there were a few, but I did not know of any.

Therefore, I felt that by choosing Nasser, I would still be dealing with the Palestinian/Israeli tragedy as Nasser was deeply involved in fighting Israel as well as pursuing a comprehensive peace plan between the Palestinian leadership and that of Israel. By studying Peron, I reasoned that I would be among the few Palestinian and Arab scholars whose dissertation would mainly focus on the study of the charismatic dimensions of a Latin American leader. In the final analysis, I had to make a hard choice and I chose charisma over the PLO.

When I began my research on both leaders, I was astonished at the amount of literature written and published on both, especially that of Nasser. I was overwhelmed and I knew then that I must drop one of them and concentrate on the other, so Nasser was out and Peron was in. With this decision, I was off and running to research and write my dissertation on Peron and I never looked back.

Chapter 2
The Cubicle at CSULA

My main research work took place at California State University, Los Angeles at the John F. Kennedy Library. The cubicle there that was provided to me became my second home. I had always felt that Cal State was my second home, anyway, for a variety of reasons: I completed my B.A. there; got to know many wonderful local and international students and faculty members there; met my wife, Lina, there; and taught at its department of Political Science for over 25 years.

After grueling study days at U.C. Riverside rather than driving home, I drove straight to the library and stayed there until it closed in the wee hours of the morning. The basement library floor, which I called the "dungeon," became my refuge. I sat at the furthest table possible in a comfortable chair to avoid other students' disruptions and noise. After a while, the number of citations that I gathered on Peron mounted in the hundreds. I did not have a computer or any other technological means to make such research easier on me. Thus, I began writing all those citations by hand using 3" x 5" index cards. This research activity continued until I completed my dissertation at the end of 1986.

By the end of 1979, most of my required Ph.D. upper division classes were successfully completed. I also was hired, in October 1979, as a part-time assistant professor at the Department working under many full-time professors, including Drs. Chilcote, Gurtov and Cortes, among others. My main tasks were to assist students in subject matter, lecture when I was asked to do so by my supervising professor, correct the initial homework and quizzes, but never to give the final grades. Being in such a position, I realized the power I could exert on students' grades and evaluations, which I conducted in a fair and open manner. At the beginning of 1980, the Department officially advanced my Ph.D. candidacy and I became an "ABD" candidate, popularly known as "All But Dissertation."

Chapter 3
The Birth of My First Child

During Lina's pregnancy, we began the happy exercise of choosing the name of this future baby. We decided that if the baby was a male, then I would choose his name, but if it was a female, Lina would choose her name. Knowing that a female was on its way, Lina decided to call her Jennifer. Then came choosing the middle name. Lina used diplomacy when she decided to call her "Miriam," which is my mother's Arabic name for the Virgin Mary. Lina's mother's name was also Mary. Both names referred to the Virgin Mary so the original biblical name of Miriam fit the bill for her middle name, satisfying my mother and Lina's. (A little diplomacy goes a long way.)

Yet, during her very difficult and painful delivery, my wife's Italian hot temper reared its head again, and suddenly, she decided to change the baby's name to Stefania without my consultation. I immediately agreed and began laughing a lot. And so, on January 31, 1980, Stefania was born and I became a father. I called all those who I knew and informed them about Stefania's birth and everyone was extremely happy. What a major change!

The author with Stefania at one-year old.

Stefania was born in the middle of my teaching, writing my perspective, taking a full-load of studies, researching, performing family and household obligations, looking for a job, and being a full-time husband (and then father), as well.

Stefania's sleeping habits were not good; she rarely slept and neither did I. She suffered from severe stomach pain that kept her crying all night, in need of a companion. I helped Lina with all the required needs of nurturing Stefania. I used to tell Lina that the only thing remaining was for me to get pregnant. Feeding, changing diapers, playing, singing, taking her for a stroll to the park and putting her to sleep were some of the duties that I helped with so Lina could concentrate on her work at the bank. She was the main breadwinner then.

All our other household chores fell on my head, as well from shopping, vacuuming, cooking, washing dishes, paying bills to making sure that our cars' maintenance was done in a timely manner. Laundry was the only task that I did not perform. To decrease the pressure on me, Lina's mother came to the rescue. I used to drop Stefania off with her at 6:00 in the morning then drive to UC. Riverside as Lina slept in San Francisco on a weekly basis. Depending on what time I completed my work, research, and studies, I would pick up Stefania, again, and spend the night with her enjoying fatherhood and the hard work that comes with it.

When I cared for her, I frequently sang folkloric Palestinian songs that mothers back home sang to their babies to put them to sleep. While singing those songs, which mainly depicted the suffering of the Palestinians' long history of occupation and especially the Nakba, I used to cry a lot. Sometimes, I would weep while Stefania was drinking her milk. I did the same thing with all of my kids and grandkids, as well. In addition to singing to her, I used to concentrate on her eyes looking at me while she drank her milk from her bottle, wondering what my baby was thinking about. Her gaze at me began changing my belief in God—a God that I never believed in as this father-daughter relationship must have been created by someone we call "God."

So many nights, Stefania's temperature would rise so fast and so high. When calling the doctor during the wee hours of the morning to advise me on what to do with her temperature of 103 or 104 degrees, the doctor would tell me to sit down with her in the bathroom tub filled with warm water to reduce her temperature. Sometimes it worked; at other times, it did not. In addition to not sleeping, the warm water made me sleepy and tired, but not Stefania.

Even so, when morning came, I had to take a shower, dress Stefania, take her to her grandmother's home, then drive straight to UCR, which was 55 miles away. What was on my mind then was passing all my oral Ph.D. exams and getting approval on my prospective. Those tasks drained my energy to the point where, on many occasions when Lina was working in Los Angeles at the bank, I would sleep at friends' apartments near U.C.R. Sleeping close by helped a lot, especially because we were all UCR students studying different majors and hoping to pass the required exams.

My persistent, hard work paid off by the middle of the year when I passed all my required Ph.D. oral and written exams, including Spanish language, and my perspective was finally approved by Dr. Chilcote, the head of my Dissertation Committee. My full-time job, from this point on, was totally devoted to doing more research, writing my dissertation, looking for a full-time job, and caring for my family.

Passing the exams and the prospective required a special celebration which also included Stefania's baptism in June of that year. Many friends and family members from Palestine, Idaho, and Ohio joined us for it. The baptism united all of us again, including my uncle and aunt Jerries and their sons and families, in a large hall with a very beautiful dinner and exchanges of greetings, gifts, and laughter, leaving our dispute behind.

I needed a break from the never-ending pressure and stress. Soon, I learned that my brother Emile was planning his wedding in Virginia. So, I traveled to Virginia to attend his wedding to an American lady in July. Since I learned that traveling on a bus was much cheaper than flying, I booked a ticket on board a Greyhound bus that passed through the entire length of the United States in three days. I will never do that again. On board the bus people were coughing, smoking, babies were crying and adults were cursing and trying to sleep on the bus was a nightmare. I was also surprised at the wide expanse of this country. It made me realize that without the west and east coasts, the U.S. is a rural farming country.

Virginia's humidity, heat, and large mosquitos made my stay very miserable. I could not keep up with the showers I needed to take each day. A few days after the wedding, my brother and his wife took me to visit the historical city of Williamsburg and the wax museum, which I enjoyed.

August 1980: the author (left) with his brother, Emil.

After my brother's wedding, I continued my journey to Ohio on board another Greyhound bus to visit my aunts, uncles, and their families who lived in Cleveland. On December 11, 1989, one of my uncles, Ignatius Ghattas Bisharat, was appointed by Pope John Paul the Second as the Archbishop of the Diocese of Newton for the Melkite Greek Catholic Church in the United States and South America. The City of Nazareth welcomed him back with a huge celebration, including our super proud family, the Bisharats.

My uncle showed me the Melkite Church which he helped to build in Cleveland where we celebrated my arrival and the wedding of my cousin in its beautiful hall. His brother, my Uncle As'ad, then took me to visit Niagara Falls and the surrounding casinos. The Falls are a wonder of the world and a constant reminder of the power and fury of nature. It deserves our respect and protection rather than our destructive policies toward the environment. Of course, I played at the casinos, and they were as stingy as those in Las Vegas. My other uncle, David, the third brother, took me to visit Sea World and soon, I was on my way back to Los Angeles on board the same hated bus. Home sweet home.

A photo taken around the time that the author's uncle, Ignatius Ghattas Bisharat, was appointed by Pope John Paul II as the Archbishop of the Diocese of Newton for the Melkite Greek Catholic Church in the United States and South America.

Upon my return, it became very clear to me that a major change in my life must take place. My marriage seemed shaky, raising a baby was extremely exhausting, my part-time job was not helping, and my research and writing were interrupted too many times. I felt that my life was suspended and aimless. Plus, the burden of fatherhood made me feel guilty and shameful for dropping Stefania off so early at her grandmother's house, exposing her to the weather, especially during those early hours on cold winter days. I felt that her mom should be home with her enjoying motherhood rather than being away at work.

I felt deeply ashamed that I did not have a full-time job that permitted Lina to stay home. Thus, finding a job with decent income became the main task at hand, ahead of my research and writing. Additionally, the apartment we were living in was too small for the three of us and the constant traffic next to our apartment's windows became unbearable, especially for Stefania's sleeping habits. So, we decided to start looking to purchase a house or move to a bigger apartment.

We took a small loan from Lina's father, brother, and the realtor who found us the house. With the savings that we managed to set aside and with further tightening the belt, we raised the down payment and moved into a three-bedroom home in a quiet cul-de-sac in the city of San Gabriel in November of 1982. The cost of our house: $105,000.

This house needed a lot of work, some of which I did, and some which I hired contractors to do. The fact that we had a house away from the noise lifted our spirits and our arguments decreased. Now, Stefania had a bigger yard to play in with other kids in a safe neighborhood.

Chapter 4
Starting at LAUSD: The Machine Shop

I have now begun looking for a full-time job. Just like the dissertation, it also needed extensive research to find one. When reading the *Los Angeles Times*, I found an advertisement for a job search company by the name Haldane that promised high-paying managerial jobs after going through its training program.

Desperate, I contacted the company and began a year-long training that required attending special seminars and classes on how to write an effective resume and cover letters; how to behave during job interviews; the most effective language to use when contacting people over the phone, how to dress, and a strategic job search.

It was not cheap at all. I used to pay $125 a week for such training, which drained my energy as well as our bank account. Yet, these job search methods were successful in getting me to speak with and meet high-level company executives but failed to produce any management job at all.

During the early years of the 1980s, our economy was in a deep recession. Very few companies were hiring from the outside. Most job openings were filled by people who were already working in those companies. On many occasions I came very close to being hired, when suddenly, the executives who promised me the jobs would change their minds at the last minute and call to inform me that they had hired a person from within their companies. The disappointments and broken promises now began affecting my health, especially my breathing along with grinding stress and depression.

Looking at the number of contacts that I made showed, very clearly, the intensity of my job search and the hard work and commitment that I invested to relieve Lina from her work so she could stay home with Stefania. The list that I still have includes the names and ranks of all the top executives at companies in the United States, the Middle East, Latin America, and Europe. These companies were involved in a variety of businesses including: construction, banking, medical, petroleum, insurance, shipping, education, travel, translation, tourism, government, and many other businesses. I met many top executives, chief economists, diplomatic attaches, department chairs, university presidents, doctors, engineers, and consultants.

The amount of travel time was astronomical as I recorded the mileage. I drove for these job interviews plus the time spent on phone calls, mailing resumes, cover letters and thank you notes—it mounted in the hundreds of dollars. This mad job search took me away from my dissertation, Lina, and especially, our baby.

In the end, Haldane was unable to find me a job so I demanded they reimburse me for what I had paid to them. As always, I strongly argued that despite following its program and instructions, Haldane was unable to find me a job—as it had promised when I signed the contract. Haldane used the recession as an excuse, but in the final analysis, they paid me most of what I had spent. (The Haldane training did not go to waste. As we shall see, I used its teaching methodology with my high school students, later on.)

The bright side of this exhaustive and failed job search was the many people who I met when I shifted my energy from finding a high-level paying job in the private sector to that of the public sector. I began seeking public school teaching positions, either in social studies or vocational training.

Two individuals then came to my rescue. First, I met the chairman of the Industrial Department at CSULA. His name was Dr. Phillips Jenkins. Among his department's vocational programs was that of Machine Shop. This was a surprise to me because during my two years as a student, I did not realize that CSULA even had a vocational program, let alone a Machine Shop. I became very interested in teaching in his Machine Shop classes but did not have an immediate opening.

Despite this, Dr. Jenkins later introduced me to a Dr. Bernie Sandoval, who served as the Director of The Manpower Program with the Los Angeles Unified School District. When Dr. Sandoval reviewed my Machine Shop vocational education, training, and work experience, he immediately offered me a full-time, non-tenured Machine Shop teaching position at East Los Angeles Skill Center.

After completing all the needed documents required by the District's job application process, I was hired on April 20, 1983, and began teaching Machine Shop classes between the hours of 1:00 p.m. and 7:00 p.m. This job was another heavenly gift. Imagine, a full-time job with full medical insurance coverage, paid holidays and sick leave and a pension plan to brag about. This job led to more than 28 years of teaching with the District until unforeseen and unfortunate ugly circumstances compelled me to retire in April of 2010. Ridah-Al-wale-Dain came to the rescue, one more time.

At the time, I did not have my Ph.D. diploma yet. My M.A. and the B.A. diplomas in Political Science, which required so much hard work, commitment, perseverance, sacrifice and expense had failed to help me find a decent job. In the middle of it all, the completion of my dissertation hung in the balance constantly reminding me that my mission had yet to be completed.

I turned around to blame somebody but found myself at the center of it all. No one forced me to study Political Science. I chose it on my own with my free will. I was pulled into the vortex and gravity of a never-ending "black hole" called TIPPTK: the Palestinian/Israeli Tragedy. I wanted, so much, to become part of the solution in bridging the gap between the two most tragedy-ridden people on Earth.

With my dream shattered of finding the perfect job, I swallowed my pride and accepted being wedded to a Machine Shop career. What came first was my family and paying my bills. Machine Shop job or not, I wanted Lina to stay with Stefania and I would have, at that point, accepted any other job.

Chapter 5
Teaching at East Los Angeles Skill Center

I was told by the school administrators that the students at East Los Angeles Skill Center were parolees who were given a second chance by the judicial system at putting their lives together. All they had to do was attend and graduate from a vocational school with a degree that would provide them a decent job and income. Failure to do so could mean the loss of such an opportunity and the possible return to Youth Rehabilitation Centers or jail. That was what I was told at the time.

My students at the Skill Center were of Hispanic background with few African American students, but no Caucasians, as I remember. Teaching these students became my destiny and my call. This teaching experience opened my eyes to so many familiar circumstances that I had also experienced and still do. I simply can say without hesitation that I learned much more from my students than they learned from me. Most of them now are in their late 50s and early 60s, but I still have not forgotten my memories of them, which I will cover in later chapters.

I was 33-years old now, and I looked physically very tiny standing next to them. The number of tattoos on their faces, necks, forehead, ears, hands, and fingers left very few uncovered body parts. Because I had not seen many adults with that many tattoos before, I became scared and the students saw this and used to laugh at me.

Yet, when they began explaining what all their tattoos meant, I could fully sympathize with them. Those tattoo symbols were very personal and sentimental reminders of someone or something that they had deeply loved and respected but had lost due to gang or domestic violence, overdoses of drugs or other tragedies. Some symbols were the faces of their girlfriends, parents, and siblings. The artists who completed such work were, in my opinion, extremely gifted. They just needed the right opportunities to excel in art, which could have opened many opportunities for them to safeguard their future. Who knows—East Los Angeles could have in its midst some "rough diamonds" who could be great artists, the likes of Michelangelo or Picasso.

I always respected my students' feelings toward their tattoos but advised, as much as possible, never to retaliate against who did them wrong. When I suggested they leave their gang affiliations they would just laugh at me. So, I strongly advised them to pursue a fair compromise with their adversaries without resorting to violence. I do not know how many of them listened to my suggestions.

Now, I found myself teaching and working in an environment with many dangerous machines, like engine lathes, milling, grinding, drilling, sawing, welding, and other machines. And my students were using very dangerous tools and equipment that could have easily been used as lethal weapons if they chose to do so as steel rods of all sizes were around them all the time. The number of hammers, scribers, chisels, files, and sharp cutting tools were all over the place and easily accessible.

So, I made sure that safety and lack of any injuries were my Number One priority, for me and them. They knew that their safety was job number one and nothing else came before it. When I observed a student not following safety rules, I would shout at him with a very loud voice so that he could hear me while the machines were running.

I wanted so badly to prepare them for future jobs that I invested my time in helping to find them jobs. Thus, in addition to teaching them basic machine shop and welding skills, including the use of machine shop precision-measuring tools, basic mathematics and blueprint reading, I also began preparing them for job interviews, how to write a resume, where to look for job openings, how to dress and the proper use of electronic communications. I was proud of myself for being able to incorporate what I had learned at Haldane in my present job. And on many occasions, I attended workshops and conferences sponsored by local industries who were looking for well-trained, qualified machinists and welders.

Among my students was a very famous boxer whose first name was Oscar. I cannot recall his last name—it may have been "de La Jolla" but I am not sure. He was continually escorted by his bodyguards to my shop. The principal also asked me not to let him work on any dangerous machines to prevent injuries to his hands. Instead, I was told to give him light work in addition to teaching him safety rules, how to use measuring tools, reading blueprint etc. So, mostly, I gave him projects that required the use of files and measuring tools. He told me, many times, that using the files required forward and backward movement that was part of his training as a boxer, as well. I told him, "Do not practice your boxing skills on me or on any other student," and we laughed at this and things went very well.

Here, I was in front of students who were taller and stronger than me and when I got upset with them for not following safety rules, they never got angry at me. They all told me that, at heart, I meant to protect them, and they understood that the angry words I used never carried any racist undertone. They were able to explain to me what constitutes being racist by giving me ample examples of how body movements, facial expressions, and the selection of words used in addressing them conveyed this message. This included inappropriate comments used to describe the clothing they wore, the food they ate, the music they listened to, the zip codes of their neighborhoods, the way they walked and talked, and their customs and heritage.

Their explanations were, to a very large extent, like my own in Israel when I was growing up which I vividly described in Part One of this memoir.

Finally, I felt lucky to have this job and the opportunities that came with it in helping my students who came from troubled and unfortunate pasts. Meanwhile, I kept looking for a different job that could lead me closer to my ultimate career in the local or international political arena, especially my goal to become a future Palestinian ambassador to Argentina.

My teaching job also opened up my eyes to my love of teaching and caring for others, just like I was cared for by my loving family, principals, teachers and community, back home. Thus, I began seriously considering teaching as my future career in addition to my dream job in Buenos Aires.

Despite my shaky satisfaction with this job, it did not last long. After five months of teaching, I was laid off at the end of September 1983 due to lack of funding, among other reasons. I felt sad to leave my students hanging without completing the proper training for finding a decent job in a machine or welding shop.

On top of that, Lina did not quit her job while I was teaching but postponed it until the start of my summer vacation, in the hope that I would sign a new teaching contract with the District, which unfortunately did not materialize. With my job loss, she continued working and my dream of her being home disappeared.

Chapter 6
Where Do I Go From Here?

Now I was back to square one: no job and the extensive job search did not produce anything. On top of that, we were expecting our second child. Therefore, I redoubled my efforts in sending more and more resumes and cover letters to many educational institutions in the hopes of finding a permanent teaching job. These efforts led to being hired as a political science instructor at Compton College. But it only lasted one day as the teacher who I replaced suddenly changed his mind and came back to retake the position that I had been offered. So again, no job. I didn't even get paid for that one day of work.

By October of 1983, I managed to find a machine shop job in the city of El Monte. The shop was owned by a young Armenian man named Henry. The roof of the plant was made out of a thin tin metal that covered all of the machines—kind of an open-air factory without air conditioning. But the heat during hot days was unbearable.

The metal that I used to machine needed a lot of special cooling liquid to cool the cutting tool and the machined parts. Upon touching the hot machined metal, the cooling liquid produced a very nasty vapor that often made me dizzy and smelled worse than the gasoline at my cousin's gas stations. The noise of the other running machines was deafening, and the bathroom was horrible. After two months of working there, I got laid off due to a lack of further work contracts. In a way, it was a blessing in disguise. But now, I was again without a job.

By the end of that year, the Dean at UCR refused to renew my leave of absence, and I was put under severe pressure to write and complete more chapters, or else. So, I withdrew from the next quarter and redoubled my research and writing efforts. By mid-year, I was able to give Dr. Chilcote my first and second chapters with the hopes that they would be approved by the rest of the dissertation committee.

Meanwhile, I never stopped sending out my resumes and attending meetings with top, private companies' executives but to no success. Among those letters, one was sent to Parson Corporation, an engineering and construction company located in Pasadena which was doing extensive business in the Middle East, especially Kuwait and Saudi Arabia. I was surprised when a top executive there granted me a meeting with him. I prepared myself fully, including the purchase of a new blue suit which I was not able to afford without charging it on a credit card.

However, the meeting was a nightmare. At the time, I did not know that he granted me this meeting because of my last name—Bisharat. Bisharat was also the last name of a rich and politically connected family in the ruling Hashemite Dynasty which ruled the State of Jordan. When this man found out, during my interview, that I came from a modest Palestinian family and that I was not affiliated with that Jordanian BISHARAT family, he immediately stood up and told me to leave. On my way out, he said, "You have wasted your time studying political science."

This comment really hurt but I swallowed my pride and said to him, "Were you not using the Bisharat name as a political tool to get you to the king? You say this because you did not get any connections from me to the king. People like you need to study politics before becoming members of corporate America. We can live without you, but you cannot live without us. Thank you anyway." Then I left.

I recall that this executive's office had mahogany covering all of his office's high four walls, as well as the ceiling. His matching mahogany furniture, especially his desk, was worth more than my car. There was a special waitress serving him and his clients who dressed in a white apron. I remember her wheeling a cart full of hard liquor (most of which I had never seen before) and many kinds of fresh fruits and nuts into our meeting.

But I did not get to enjoy one drink, any fruit or nuts, nor did I ask for anything. My Palestinian pride was deeply injured, yet I did not beg for anything. Instead, I fully understood that I was a "useless Bisharat" to him in connecting his company's business with King Hussein Ibn Talal. What could I say? I had the right last name but the wrong Palestinian heritage and identity. The nightmares continued piling up.

His words kept me wondering if I had chosen the wrong field of studies. Maybe he was right. I had not used my political science education yet, and many private and public entities were not in the mood to hire or entertain a political science student without at least a Ph.D. diploma. I did not have any other choice but to brush his words aside and focus on what I had invested in: my family and getting my Ph.D. To cave in and quit was not an option at all.

My lack of results in finding a job led to even more fights with Lina, and the prospect of a divorce became more seductive to the point of trying to hire a lawyer. Fortunately, the lawyer we contacted, for whatever reason, did not show up for his meeting with us at his office.

During all this, I again became a student at Cal State University, Los Angeles and began taking extensive classes to pass the California Education Skills Test (CBEST) exams to get my Social Studies and

Administration credentials completed. My hope was that I would be hired as a Social Studies teacher by the Los Angeles Unified School District. Additionally, I began taking classes to complete my Vocational credential in Machine Shop and Welding as a backup to my plan.

Chapter 7
Luck Talks and Stress Walks

Despite all the unbearable circumstances I endured, many lucky strikes took place during November of 1983. First, I was able to complete the first and second chapters of my dissertation, and second, I was again hired by Dr. Sandoval to write the Machine Shop Teaching Competencies manuals for the entire LAUSD.

During the early years of the 1980s, Congress passed a new legislation called the Job Training and Partnership Act to encourage school districts, nationwide, to teach vocational training to their high school students. This Act became popularly known as (JTPA). My job was to follow the JTPA teaching curricular guidelines and to write teaching competencies manuals, publish them, and then distribute them to all the machine shop teachers throughout the district.

I was provided an office and a person to type what I wrote. Then, I moved to the District's Third Annex in downtown Los Angeles to begin my new research for writing those competencies, in addition to my other research and attending my classes. This research required extensive reading about the history and evolution of Machine Shop technology and the role it played in the manufacturing industry, the variety of machines used, and their proper names, safety rules and measuring tools.

PREFACE

The competencies for Production Machine Shop have been developed in four topic areas as follows:

1) Part One: Principles and Practice of Machine Shop
2) Part Two: Saws, Drills, and Grinders
3) Part Three: The Engine Lathe
4) Part Four: The Milling Machine

Each topic has a number of competencies identified. The competencies are presented as a series of goal statements followed by one or more "indicator" statements. An "indicator" is a performance objective describing an ability, which, upon attainment, will establish competency for the stated goal.

ACKNOWLEDGEMENTS

Appreciation is extended to the Los Angeles Unified School District's Skills Center Coordinators, counselors and instructional staff who have provided their time and cooperation during the research and data collection stages of this project.

Grateful acknowledgement is made of Lucinda Stites, Word Processing Instructor, and her crew of student word processors who have assisted during the production of materials.

The technical information provided in the attached material has been developed form the course text, General Industrial Machine Shop by Harold V. Johnson, Chas. A. Bennett Co., Inc., Peoria, Ill.

Competencies have been written by Gus Bishart with the assistance of Claire Werner as part of the school district's contract with the City of Los Angeles and the State of California.

Bernardo R. Sandoval, Director
Manpower Program Development
December, 1984

Preface and Acknowledgements to the 1984 Machine Shop Teaching Competencies Manual for Los Angeles Unified School District.

Seven months later, I managed to complete this assignment. I wrote over four hundred pages of teaching competency manuals that covered the engine lathe, the milling machine, the drilling machine, and the band sawing machine. Additionally, I covered the safety rules, reading blueprints and the proper use of machine shop measuring tools, among other related subject matters. I gave the final completed teaching competency manuals to Dr. Sandoval who published them and distributed them to all of the district's machine shop teachers.

During my work at the Third Annex, Dr. Sandoval was asked by the Central Office to utilize my teaching experience as a substitute teacher, when needed. Thus, I began subbing at many different high schools throughout the district. This subbing experience introduced me to the ways other teachers conducted their teaching agenda and subject matter. I also began visiting many machine shop teachers to explain to them the teaching manuals in the hopes of better and more successful teaching and training outcomes. Once the teaching competency manuals were published, Dr. Sandoval terminated my position due to lack of further funding, leaving me, again, without a job.

A third strike took place during January of 1984, when I swore allegiance to the flag and became a U.S. citizen. By now, I held dual citizenship of Israel and the United States but not a Palestinian citizenship. What a heartbreaking condition this was for me. I just knew that the ambassadorial dream job in Buenos Aires would never materialize. It was, after all, a dream.

The fourth strike happened when Dr. Sandoval drove me to Locke High School in South Central Los Angeles and showed me the school's machine shop that had been closed for six years. Then, he asked me if I could take over and become a full-time machine shop teacher, which I immediately accepted.

Ridah-Al-wali-Dain struck again as the fifth lucky strike when Mr. Rios, the Industrial Technology Dean at Los Angeles Trade Technical College, who I previously met during my job search, called me during April. The dean told me that he had lost his machine shop teacher, who died unexpectedly, and offered me a part-time machine shop teaching position in his place. Of course, I immediately accepted this, too.

The machine shop at LATTC was a huge one. There were many machines—some that I had worked on before and others that I had not worked on. Scanning the length and width of this machine shop building made me wonder how a high school education had impacted my life and that of my family in the United States. Simple and loving advice from my mother made all of this possible. What a lucky man I was. This part-time job was to last six more years.

Meanwhile, during March of 1984, my wife gave me my sixth lucky strike when she gave birth to our second child, a male. Per our agreement, I got to name him and I called him "Nabil," which means nobility and generosity. I chose this name so that when people address me in the traditional Palestinian way, they would call me "Abu Nabil," the father of Nabil, just as my father was called in Palestine, following the name of his first child, Nabil.

A photo of the author's son, Nabil, taken shortly after his baptism. Stefania (left) is seated next to the author's mother, Miriam (center, holding Nabil), with Maria, the author's mother-in-law, seated on the right.

With two children at home, my wife was now able to quit working and I became the breadwinner. With this seventh lucky strike, I was very happy and content with my life. I now had two jobs, yet the field of machine shop teaching was not what I wanted as a career. But I knew that without such machine shop work, I could have been in a much more desperate situation. So, I swallowed my pride again and kept thinking about the hidden meaning of Ridha-Al-wali-Dane.

Nabil, age two and a half.

Amid more sleepless nights, due to Nabil's lack of sleep, I was still searching for better jobs, writing my dissertation, studying to pass the CBEST exams, and taking classes to complete three other credentials in Vocational Training, Social Studies, and School Administration.

While undergoing this unbearable hard work and stress, I was asked by my former San Gabriel Adult School principal to deliver the main speech to the graduation class of 1984. He told me that he still remembered my hard work and commitment to education and the excellent character and integrity that I displayed during my education at his school. My speech resulted in many thank you's and applause from parents, students, and teachers. This was my eighth lucky strike.

I do not know how I managed all this, but what I know is that the pressure and stress on my health was very evident. I began suffering from a heavy breathing condition, episodes of anger, I tired very quickly, my vision was blurry, I had trouble concentrating and, on top of that, I was continuing to argue with my wife, Lina.

With the arrival of my mother to celebrate Nabil's baptism and to see my first child, Stefania, my previous family problems reared its ugly head again. But Lina and I were overwhelmed with joy at my mother's arrival. I took her to Las Vegas, Disneyland, Universal Studios, and other nearby places. She also visited her sisters in Ohio and her close family members in Idaho.

But my mother's visits with my family here were not that happy at all. The continued arguments and counter arguments made her visit miserable. Seeing her under so much pressure increased my anger and lack of respect for my family here. This second stressor was unlike the other ones as I witnessed her sadness right inside my home and that affected all of my family.

My anger and frustration with my cousins were on again. They did not care how they were treating my mother, despite her husband's stroke; they also did not care about how their behavior affected her health and my family. My mother came here to celebrate a happy occasion, not to be stressed out.

During her stay, I tried to remind her of her advice to me to attend ORT Amal Vocational High School in Nazareth. She remembered her advice and also my reaction at the time, very vividly. I could see tears in her eyes. She kept telling me repeatedly that "no parents on earth give their kids bad advice; all the parents on earth wish the best for their kids to live a better life than theirs." What wisdom, what a loving and caring mother. There is a lot for parents and their kids to learn from such wisdom.

I did not think that she was able to fully understand what benefit her advice provided to me. So, I kept telling her that if it were not for her advice, I could not have what I now had. I thanked her so many times as I held her hands, looking straight into her eyes. What wonderful moments and memories that time created for me.

Chapter 8
The Theft of My First Three Completed Dissertation Chapters

As if I have not seen the worst yet, I found out that just a few days after my mother left for Virginia to visit my brother, someone had broken into my cubicle at Cal State University's library and had stolen all the completed and half-completed chapters of my dissertation. Since everything I did was on paper, I did not have any backup chapters or copies. My documents were my most valuable possessions at that time, as well as the other essential reading materials that I had put time into gathering during my extensive research work at the same library.

I was stunned to say the least. At thirty-four years old, after all the hell and sacrifices I had gone through to do this work, now, it was gone with the wind. I was at a complete breakdown. I mean, how often do you hear of someone having his or her dissertation stolen? Well, I was among the very few. Why me? To this day I do not know.

All that I know is that I went home broken-hearted and told my wife what had happened. She urgently advised me to quit writing the rest of my dissertation. Having earned my Master's degree, she argued that I should be happy and content as she was happy and proud of my achievements. I did not argue much. I pretended that I wanted to use the bathroom, then I closed our bedroom door and went into the bathroom where I began banging on the walls and crying very loudly in the hopes that no one—my wife or kids—could hear me. My cries came from the deepest place in my body and carried very distinct and agonizing sounds as if I were exhaling the last breath in my body.

I took refuge in swearing to decrease my depression and stress. This was a habit that I had carried with me since Nazareth. I cursed all those who lived in heaven, I cursed the moment that I left Palestine behind, and I cursed the miserable working conditions that I was facing at Locke High School. I also cursed the Political Science Department at U.C. Riverside, my Dissertation Committee members, Argentina, Peron, Israel, and the entire world. Cursing calmed me down, and I threw myself on the bed and slept.

The next day, I reported the theft of my dissertation to the library manager and began an extensive trash can search throughout the campus. I checked every dumpster and every trash container, but I found nothing. I also asked for help from the campus newspaper printing manager to print an ad offering a $50 reward to whoever found and returned my briefcase with all my work—no questions asked. The ad ran in the newspaper, but there were no phone calls and I never got my briefcase or my work back.

The only question that was left was. What do I do?

First, I decided that nothing would stop me from continuing my mission. I had already invested so much of my life into this mission and I could not quit now. I was never a quitter, and I wasn't about to start now. The promises that I made to my parents were chiseled into my mind, deeper than in granite. My promise had deep roots, long nurtured by my Palestinian heritage and expressed by the daily living experiences in Nazareth of my family members, friends, neighbors, and those in the surrounding environment.

Second, I now have two, growing children whose early life I had missed due to my work and studies. What was I supposed to tell them if they asked me why I did not finish my dissertation after wasting all that time researching and writing, rather than spending time with them? What if they asked me why the time that I spent with them was not as valuable as working on my dissertation?

I realized, very quickly, that I had an obligation and duty to complete the task of finishing my dissertation—as much for myself as for their sake.

And what about my parents and my wife who had stood with me this far? How about my committee members and other professors and friends who were encouraging me all the time to keep on going? What about my students who I told daily about the value of getting an education, for them to keep moving forward and to complete the highest educational degree possible? These were some of my most heartbreaking questions.

Third, I hired a friend to type and save all my work going forward at a cost of $1,800. This enabled me to keep as many copies as possible in case another theft took place. I kept copies in the trunk of my car and Lina's, at my in-law's house, at my office at Locke, and at my office at Cal State. Despite all of these precautions, a second break-in took place in my cubicle in December of that same year. After reporting the second break-in, the manager granted me a different cubicle on another library floor.

This second break-in made me realize that someone was after my research. Could it be that the two of us were working on the same topic? Could it be that someone did not like me and wished me ill? Or was someone planning to integrate my special chapter on Evita Peron into his or her script for the upcoming 1991 production of the movie, *Do not cry for me Argentina*, which made Evita the central theme of the movie?

While I never got any answers, I continued to check different Latin American journals to see if any article contained my research material, but to no avail. After ten years, I abandoned this practice.

Fourth, I resorted to whatever fresh memories I still had in rewriting the three, completed chapters as well as the other, half-finished ones. I gathered whatever relevant materials I still had and those that I had left at the offices of my committee members. This exercise opened my eyes to ways that I could improve what I had previously written by doubling down on my research to find new books, citations and documents related to Peron.

I do not know where all of this energy came from. All I can remember is that my research and writing gathered steam due to continued pressure by the Department to make solid progress in completing more chapters. I was racing against time, giving it my full commitment, and spending countless hours after work, during weekends and holidays to devote to this. That sacrifice meant that I missed countless celebratory events, such as: birthdays, weddings, trips, and other family gatherings. I would console myself, "Now, my dissertation comes first and soon, I will be able to enjoy all these happy events. I am still young and there are many more happy events in store for me."

There were days that I did not see my family at all. I would leave our home at 5:30 a.m. to teach at Locke High School and for two days at LATTC. Once the teaching hours were over, I would get something to eat on my way to the library. Usually, at the famous Mexican restaurant by the name of El Tepeyac, located in East Los Angeles. Then, I would resume my studies at the library until it closed at midnight. By the time I arrived home and got ready for bed, it was already 1:00 a.m., and I would have to get up again at 5:30 a.m. that day and repeat the routine all over again. The few hours that I slept were compensated for and energized by drinking a lot of coffee early in the morning, eating cold cut sandwiches for so called "breakfast," and if I was lucky, eating whatever leftovers that my wife had left in the refrigerator.

By the end of 1985, I had completed five out of seven chapters of my dissertation. The committee members were very happy with my progress and wished me the best. I felt great and began seeing the light at the end of the tunnel.

Additionally, I began teaching summer classes at Carson High School for an extra paycheck between the hours of 8:00 a.m. and

12:00 noon. This summer teaching schedule allowed me to study at least eight hours a day for six straight weeks.

I also started teaching Saturdays at the Regional Occupational Program known as "ROP," that the district had newly begun. I could not refuse any extra money, now that my family was growing, and with it, having bills to pay.

The happy news of my writing progress extended even further when Dr. Hopper, the Chair of the Political Science Department at Cal State University, Los Angeles, called me and offered me one class to teach during the Fall quarter of 1985. The subject was United States Foreign Policy. I was in heaven and immediately accepted the offer.

So now I was working full-time at Locke High School, part-time at LATTC, Cal State, the ROP program, plus summer classes with the District. Added to that was my still unfinished CBEST exam preparation, the classes taken to complete three credentials mentioned above, my continued job search, my unfinished dissertation, and my family responsibilities. How much could a human body take?

It was a mad dash for survival. I enjoyed the few soccer games that I watched Stefania play, I was happy about the extra money coming in, the progress of my dissertation and teaching Political Science at the university level. All of that energized me and helped me to continue what I was doing. Wow, for the first time in my life, I was actually teaching Politics in addition to Machine Shop studies.

But, as always, happiness does not last long for me. By the end of the year, I was separated from Cal State and lost that employment. I had to sign a separation document, which I used to call the "divorce document." This separation freed up a lot of my time for my research and writing work and I also had time off for the holidays from my other two jobs. At that point, ten-to-fifteen-hour workdays were normal, so with the extra time, my progress increased a lot.

When Christmas vacation was over and I returned to my normal teaching hours at Locke High School and the college, I began experiencing a lot of medical problems and stress. This was directly caused by violence against me by many of my students. During those days, Locke High School was a "war zone." Most days, you would see police helicopters, ambulances, police cruisers, and campus security guards on campus. The student fights that broke out every day were normal.

This was caused by a diversity of inner-city gangs on campus. Crack and cocaine use was widespread, which devastated the neighborhoods in South Central L.A. Later, I learned that most of the drugs were left at the edge of the railroads by the CIA and other elements to create instability to adult Hispanic and African American men and women.

As all of these things were happening in my life, I began calling in sick to give myself a break from such a violent atmosphere. But rather than stay home and relax, I chose to go to the library and study even more. At the end of January of 1986, my two kids started having high fevers again so our visits to the hospital and their doctors increased a lot. The chair of the Industrial Department at Locke began giving me a hard time again. This time, the principal threatened to interview another teacher for my job. This really scared me and added more stress to my marriage leading to more fights and arguments with my wife.

Financially, I found that the loss of income from Cal State had affected our spending a lot. So, we decided to take out a loan on our house in the hopes that I would soon finish my dissertation and Cal State would hire me back. The loan relieved a lot of pressure for me and so, I was able to concentrate and work harder.

With Spring break coming, I spent more of my free time at the library and was able to complete more chapters on time. I also passed the CBEST exam and made great progress toward completing my other credentials.

Chapter 9
Completing My Educational Mission

On September 15, 1986, my committee members signed the documents completing my dissertation, and it was conferred on December 13, 1986. This was one of the happiest days of my life. Wow, I had finally fulfilled what I had promised my parents and myself. It is hard to explain or describe that feeling but, on my way home later that day, driving on the I-60 freeway, just before exiting the 57 freeway north, I gazed at the lights of the city below me and cried like a baby. I had stopped at this same location many times before and dreamed that one day I would complete my dissertation, like those other students at UCR who I had felt so happy for. Now, today was MY day.

This happy occasion was followed by another one when the Adult School principal at Locke High School offered me a class to teach, two days a week for three hours between 3:30 p.m. and 6:30 p.m. at the Machine Shop. I accepted his offer and now had two principles to deal with: the day and night principals.

During this time, Lina and I managed to buy a new Mazda Sedan and I began looking to purchase my graduation ring, which I promised myself a long time before to buy when I completed my

Ph.D. So, I had not purchased a ring when I completed high school, my Bachelor of Arts Degree or my Master's degree. It was either going to be my Ph.D. ring or no ring at all.

I now decided to go back to Palestine to visit my family again. On December 12, 1986, I left Los Angeles carrying a copy of my finished dissertation. Upon my arrival, I was greeted, as always, with a celebration so my family could express their pride in my having completed my Ph.D. and teaching at a university, as well.

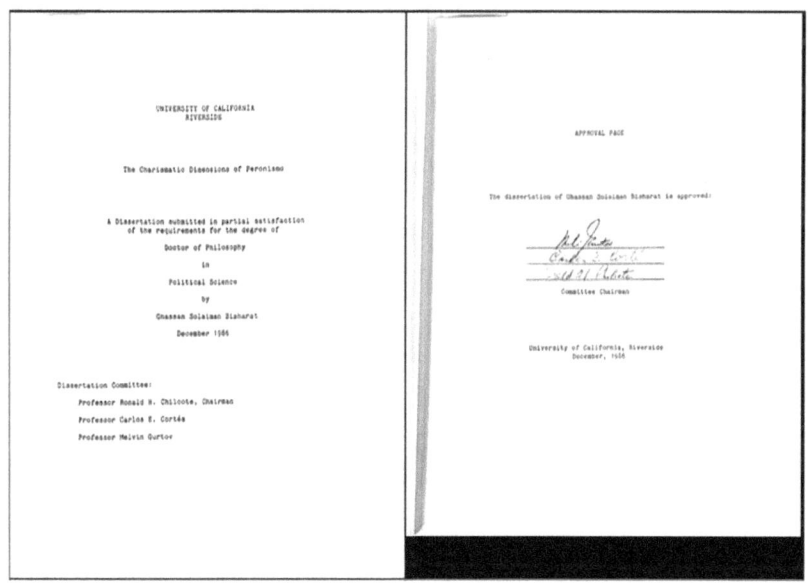

The Title and Approval pages of the author's Dissertation.

I gave my mother a copy of my dissertation with pride. Of course, she was unable to understand what it was and just looked at it. Dementia has taken its toll while my father was incapacitated. Neither of them understood what I had accomplished in fulfilling my promise to them, a long time ago. It took me by surprise as I was unable to fully comprehend what had happened. I began questioning whether my sacrifices had been worth it as my sadness and dismay was overwhelming. But what could I have done? This was my kismet and I had to accept it.

While there, I visited my father several times at the hospital that became his residence. Since I was asked to deliver a speech to the 12th grade graduates at Don Bosco Technical College, I had to revisit my memories of the past, friends, and family. This trip took my mind away from the stress I was constantly under in Los Angeles, yet I did not enjoy it much because of my parents' medical conditions.

Undated photo of the author's aunt, Na'Ameh.

During that trip, I also got sick with a nasty virus that kept me inactive at my mother's house for most of my stay. It was a miserable illness that required many doctor's visits to our home because I was unable to travel much.

But on the positive times, I got to celebrate Christmas with my family for the first time since I left them fifteen years earlier. My Aunt Na' Ameh gave me a farewell dinner, and then I left Palestine on December 29th, arriving back to Los Angeles on December 30th with enough time to celebrate New Year's Eve with my family.

Although my Doctor of Philosophy Degree in International Relations and Comparative Politics was conferred on December 13, 1986, we had to wait for the official graduation ceremony that took place at U.C.R. on June 14, 1987. Meanwhile, we began preparing for that day. I depended on Lina to choose my cap and gown as well as the color of the stone for my golden graduation ring. She fitted me with the right sizes of the cap, gown, and the ring. I insisted that the color of the stone for my ring be as red as possible. To me, red has always represented struggle, revolution, change, suffering, sacrifices, and love. A garnet was the choice closest to my color and I accepted it for my graduation ring.

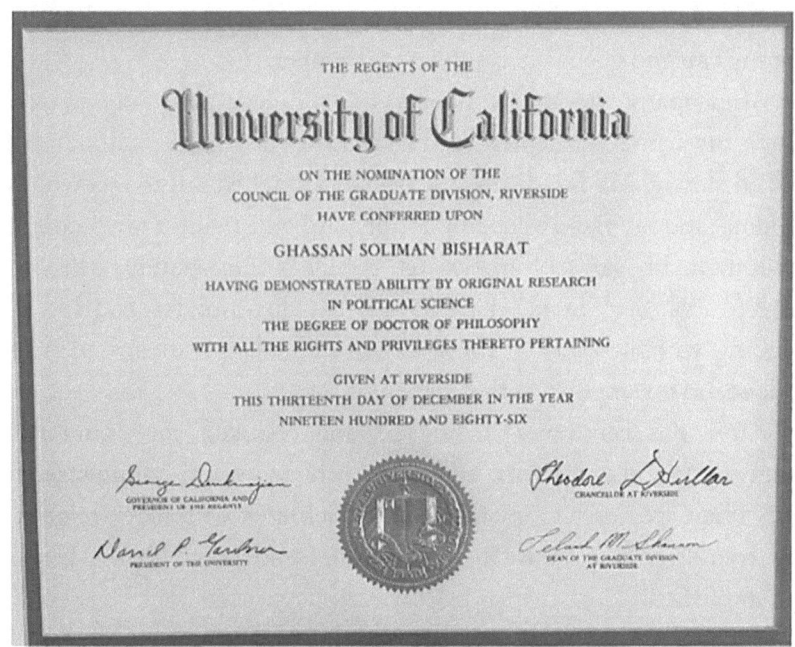

The author's diploma and graduation ring.

As I waited for that day to come, I was very nervous. While driving for the last time to U.C.R., my mind wandered, and the playback tape of my educational experience came to haunt me. I kept my tears of joy in check so that no one driving with me could see them, especially the kids. It seemed to take forever to park my car and walk toward the green, flat lawn. But then, the kids began running all around, and I had to chase them as Lina called to me to slow down so that my cap and gown stayed clean and proper.

After many graduate's names were called, my time arrived. When my name was called to the stand, I was very emotional and walked slowly. My hand shook a little as I reached out to receive my diploma, and my family cheered loudly and whistled for me. Looking out at them, I began sobbing because the faces of my parents were not there to look back at me. I truly felt that this diploma had lost its meaning without them. I know it was difficult for anyone to truly understand my anguish at that second.

After the ceremony, I hugged and thanked my committee members, friends, relatives, and other professors and administrative staff. Then, we drove to my house and celebrated with many relatives and friends. My promise to my parents had been kept. Mission Accomplished.

Graduation Day. TOP: *the author and Lina.* MIDDLE: *the author with his in-laws.* BOTTOM: *Nabil and Stefania wearing the author's cap and gown.*

Now that my educational mission had been completed, my job search mission was going nowhere. I was exhausted seeking a full-time tenured teaching position and I finally decided not to keep wasting my energy on illusive jobs. I just accepted my fate and became more relaxed as I focused on my family. My job then became routine: full-time at Locke High School and part-time at Cal State University. I swallowed my pride and felt lucky to have both jobs.

As I turned my attention to my kids, I started getting more involved in their after-school activities, including their sports and music training, and watching all their games, especially soccer. Most of their games took place on either Saturdays or Sundays and I enjoyed them a lot. After the games, we would all go out as a family for dinner.

On October 14, 1993, I received the bad news that my father had passed away. I could not attend his memorial though because the Department Chair at Cal State refused to let me leave as we were in the middle of a new quarter. So, instead, I left for Nazareth to celebrate the tradition of his mass which was observed forty days after his death.

Unlike my father, I was able to attend my mother's funeral when she passed away on March 12, 2008, but then, I did not attend her forty-day mass celebration. They both passed away without knowing that I had fulfilled my promise to them, and they never got to read my dissertation. What a tragedy that I did not get their acceptance of my promise fulfilled. I have had to live with this knowledge since that time and that regret will stay with me until the end when I am six feet under.

But there was a happy incident that took place in the country of Jordan. On August 13, 2004, I visited my family for the fifth time since leaving Nazareth on March 21, 1971. Unlike other visits, this one was memorable for a different reason: My cousins: Eseed, Walid and Baheeg had arranged a trip to the country of Jordan with a bus they rented from the Jordanian Ministry of Tourism. Joining us cousins were my brothers: Nabil, Habib, and William with their wives. Lina did not accompany me.

From left: the author with his cousin Walid (1968); the author's cousin, Bheeg (1970); the author's cousin, Eseed (1970).

We first drove to the Jordanian border and then we needed to go through the Israeli border check point where everything went well. When we entered the Jordanian side, the driver of the bus was waiting for us. He drove us to our Hilton Hotel downtown in the capital city of Amman where we stayed for two days, toured the city and ate at its many restaurants and shawarma stands.

On our way back to the border though, the bus broke down and we had to wait for a new bus that the Ministry of Tourism promised to send us within two hours. The weather was very hot so when we exited the bus, we began looking for a place to sit. We found a house under construction with an empty garage that had a one-foot-thick concrete wall and we sat there to wait for our new bus.

A few minutes later, a car stopped, and a beautiful woman got out. She asked us what we were doing sitting in her neighbors' garage. When we explained our situation, she immediately invited us to her house. We all hesitated as to what we should do while she walked toward her house. A few minutes later her father appeared and insisted that we at least have a cup of coffee with his family.

As we entered the house, we were greeted by at least fifteen other people, including children sitting under a huge grapevine shade. Suddenly, his wife appeared and asked us what we were doing in Jordan. When my cousins explained to her that they were welcoming me back from America and that I was a professor at a university, she insisted on sitting next to me.

I was very much taken when she began asking me very sophisticated and knowledgeable questions about the American government and its foreign policy. She told me that her two sons were studying in France and that she was very proud of my accomplishment and hoped that her two sons would follow suit. Now, both her and her husband began insisting that we join them for dinner, but we had to decline fearing that the bus might arrive, and no one would be there. (Our bus driver had joined us at this family's house.)

To compromise, they insisted that we pick as many apples as possible from their trees, which we did. On our way out, we realized that many other people had come to see us as word of our encounter spread around the neighborhood. One of those people was a woman who was pregnant with a son. She asked what my name was, and I told her "Ghassan." She immediately told me, with a nudge from her husband, that she would name her son Ghassan. Then, we both became very emotional but could not hug because of our tradition.

I am telling this story not to glorify myself but to validate what I have always believed, and that is that as Arabs, we are all the same and hospitality is in our blood. We were all Christians with some having the cross hung from their necks. But our hosts were all Muslims. We did not know each other and yet, we were treated as family, brothers, and sisters. We were in the middle of a village far away from both the Palestinian and the Jordanian borders, but these villagers mirrored our Arab traditions and pride, something that had been lost and ignored by the ruling elite, kings, and princes of present-day Arab countries. I believe they should and must be ashamed for not uniting as a big Arab family without artificial borders and religious divisions.

This incident took place almost twenty years ago, but it still has meaning for me. Since then, I have asked my cousins when they visit Jordan again to drop by and thank that family and see how Ghassan is doing. My Cousin Eseed, who arranged that trip, passed away a year ago. What a loss. We all miss him.

Now I have two grown up men named after me. Gustavo who lived in South-Central Los Angeles, and Ghassan who lived in a village located in the Arab country of Jordan. One is having Mexican American heritage and the other an Arab Jordanian heritage. Both are separated by 7,700 miles. Who knows if I will one day meet one of them, or both? All I know is that I think of them all the time.

Of course, getting my Ph.D. ended up being only the first step, the first pillar in building my life. I continued teaching for another sixteen years. A whole career unfolded for me, thereafter, and while I have always taken pride in knowing that the promise made to my parents to complete my Ph.D. was fulfilled, a new honor soon arose: to continue to teach my students, and through them, building a life and career dedicated to education and the belief that no matter where we come from, there is value in living a life well-spent. In that way, the twin pillars of my life—my love for my parents and my love for education—were built.

Part Five
A Life Well-Spent
1986-2010 and Beyond

Chapter 1
Reflections on My Everlasting Teaching Memories

When I arrived in the United States on March 21, 1971, I was three months short of my twenty-first birthday. Thus, I was considered by the U.S social-ranking standards to be an adult. My adolescent years were spent learning the art of machine shop production and welding. I never imagined that one day I would live in the United States of America and be a machine shop and welding teacher at a high school and at a college. Nor did I ever imagine becoming a professor in political science. My destiny, or kismet (as we call it back home) was to become an educator in this foreign land and especially in the greater Los Angeles Basin.

This is an amazing destiny, an unbelievable kismet. This is what my mother predicted when I married my wife. She said, "Lina is your kismet." After all, I was a Palestinian/Israeli/Arab foreign student, and she was an Italian-born citizen as well as an American one. We met at the same American university taking the same class in the same classroom and at the same time. That IS kismet.

I have always reminded my wife that the Romans occupied Palestine the longest, among the many other foreign occupiers, almost 630 years. Therefore, the League of Nations should have given Italy the mandate over Palestine following the first world war and not England. Maybe The Israeli/Palestinian People's Tragic Kismet could have been avoided altogether' no one knows. But Palestine's tragic kismet turned out the other way. It was mandated to the Queen of England whose country's long history of continued colonial racist and oppressive policies toward the indigenous populations that its empire had conquered have continued in Palestine, as well. England's mandatory power planted the seeds and greatly contributed to this tragedy, as well as to my life's destiny.

From 1972, when I began attending East Los Angeles College, until I completed my Ph.D. in 1986 at U.C. Riverside, 14 years had elapsed studying political science. Add to that, 28 years, part-time, teaching political science at the university level, and 20 years, full-time, teaching social studies at the high school level, and you can see that my educational life was immersed in the jungle of politics. That's in addition to the other 10 years of teaching machine shop and welding.

Setting aside my teaching years at U.C. Riverside, Cal State University and Los Angeles Trade Technical College, one of the most difficult parts of writing this memoir was reliving cherished memories of my high school students. They showed so much promise but struggled to overcome the injustices of living in the wealthiest country in the world while being denied a fair shot at getting ahead.

During the early years of the 1980s, most of my students were incredibly kind, generous, loving, and gifted young men and women. Yet, the society in which they lived, often treated them as 3rd class citizens and branded them "thugs," "gangbangers," "scum," "losers," "addicts," "looters," "rapists," or worse. This often was for no other reason than the color of their skin, the clothes they wore, the music they listened to, the food they ate, and the zip codes in which they lived. It was hard to teach them that the Founding Fathers' fundamental vision and mission in writing our unfinished

Constitution was to build a fair and just society, as many of them lived in a society that was anything but.

My experiences as an adolescent high school student, back home, deeply connected me with my adolescent South Central and East L.A. students and their daily struggles with discrimination and injustice, albeit, in a different way than I did as a Palestinian/Israeli/Arab 3rd class citizen. I also struggled at that tender age and as an adult here in the United States, with all kinds of assumptions being made about me by ordinary American citizens based on my name, faith, looks, heritage, accent, politics, and my feelings about America and its role in the world.

Some of those assumptions were half-true but the overwhelming majority were flat out wrong. I, too, grew up in a place where I was deemed a 3rd class (if not a 5th class) citizen by most who viewed me with mistrust and inferiority. Those same citizens had, themselves, just recently paid a very heavy price at the hands of another government that had treated them the same as they treated me. How could those who were victimized so quickly forget their own painful experiences and become the victimizers of other people, just as powerless as they used to be?

The simple truth is that I felt connected to my students because I, too, experienced the kind of injustices and struggles they faced. I, too, often questioned how our U.S. government could turn a blind eye toward Israel's treatment of its own victims: the Palestinians. How could they not see its racism, bigotry, injustice, xenophobia, and the cruelty that "democracy for some" imposes on its minorities of brothers and sisters? I questioned this as I was teaching the American Constitution, which strongly condemned these practices. This contradiction drove me crazy, made me angry, sad, and confused—to say the least.

The unsparing and capricious treatment of non-white minorities by America's government is not surprising. It is rooted in the history of colonial racist settler's policies toward the native indigenous people and has continued since then. This same body legalized and otherwise protected, state laws infused with malice against Native Americans, African American, Hispanic Americans, Asian Americans, Arab Americans and other minorities, like me. Most of my students' backgrounds hailed from the above minorities. In this way, I always felt a real sense of shared history and solidarity with them, a history of "majority rules over minority" mentality, winners over losers, might over right, and out of sight, out of mind.

I wanted, so badly, to use all my joyful and painful educational experiences in the United States and in Palestine as a tool to help them succeed in their future educational journeys. This tool included giving them unconditional free and from the heart lifelong lessons that I had painfully learned and utilized to complete my journey, so that they could complete theirs, as well. I know that I influenced many of them to successfully pursue higher education, as I was told this by many of them when they visited me during their university's semester breaks, but I also knew that I did not reach all of them.

That said, the reality is that I paid a heavy price in accomplishing this after leaving Palestine. I finished my education, fulfilled my promise to my parents, built a wonderful family, and lived in a wonderful part of the world. But I often struggle with this reality, not knowing how many of my former students succeeded in their struggles to complete their education and build a better life for themselves and their families. And I wondered how many of them failed, when we all started from the same unfortunate socio-economic hardships.

Chapter 2
Frustration of Love

The saddest moments of my high school teaching experiences were not when I was assaulted or called all kinds of derogatory names by some of my students, but when I gave them their final semester grades while explaining the reasons for arriving at such grades.

The amount of uncompleted homework, quizzes, projects, midterms, and finals was overwhelming. The amount of valuable time they lost for studying due to on-campus fighting, ditching, detentions, suspensions, truancy, and absenteeism was devastating. My constant reminders to them that not completing their work and missing classes would lead to failing grades were repeatedly ignored. This persisted even when I wrote the names of those students in danger of failing on board and advised them to see me as soon as possible. My repeated reminders went in one ear and out the other. This continued to take place for at least a month before their final grades were processed. My reminding, begging, and pleading never stopped.

The ease with which they excused themselves for missing valuable study time was astonishing. Most of the notes I received, supposedly written by their parents to excuse them, were fake and the dean's office often looked the other way. Missing and cutting classes was not a big deal at all, it seemed.

But when they received a failing grade, these same students stressed the fact that they did attend my classes, most of the time, and deserved a better grade. I was also accused of not recording the work that they had completed.

The twelfth graders were, by far, the most hostile and confrontational toward me. To listen to their grievances, I would stop my lectures and ask them to cool down and stop what they were doing so that I could discuss with them the reasons for their grades. I had very few students who achieved A's and B's and many with C's, D's, and F's out of 30-35 students per class. The grades, per class, roughly broke down as follows: 1-2 A's, 3-5 B's, 6-8 C's, and the rest D's or F's.

My process was: First, I would show them the grades that I had recorded and demand they show me their completed assignments that they said I did not record. Of course, nothing was ever provided. I did this all day long with all my five periods of classes.

I also asked many questions with the intention of finding out the reasons for their lack of work at home and at school. I also intended to have the few high-achieving students share with their classmates how they studied to help them achieve the same results. I reasoned that at least the failed students could feel at ease with their friends and might listen to them with an open mind rather than listening to me.

When the students with better grades were asked to explain their studying habits to the other students, the common theme most shared was: "My parents will kick my ass if I fail; I work in a group with other students; I study hard, stay away from trouble, attend school regularly, and I listen to my teachers."

Meanwhile, most of the failing students would either laugh at them, mumble a few comments under their breath, refuse to pay attention, or lay their heads on their desks as if they were sleeping.

Those among them who did speak had their own way of looking

at things. They would say that as their teacher, I was a white boy who didn't understand the hundreds of years of discrimination against the brown and black-colored people in such a racist society; that there was liberty and justice for some but not them; that they did not have parents at home; that most teachers did not care about them and many were racist; and that working hard at school would not change the bullying of gangs, the use of drugs and violence in South Central LA. Here and there you would hear someone say, "Why should I get good grades? I might not live until graduation."

Soon, silence replaced these discussions and sadness filled the air and looking nowhere became the norm. Suddenly, I felt defeated in my attempts at provoking further discussions. I felt I had failed at bridging the gap between those with good and not so good grades, and I became the focal point of my students. I was being challenged by them and my first thought was, "How am I supposed to respond?"

Meanwhile and without even thinking, the recorded experiences of my childhood, adolescence and adult life began rolling backward. Imprinted on that tape was the stand I took at age four against that teacher who discriminated against me. I recall walking to school at that young age, working under big rig trucks with dirt all over me so that I could help my parents pay for my education. I recalled my father's humiliation at the hands of the priest at my school who wanted to force me to leave. I remembered hearing and seeing very young Israeli school children calling me and my father "filthy Arabs" and accusing us of having tails between our legs (like the devil), without any intervention by their adult teachers.

I thought about the military units exercising their drills among Palestinian homes, including in my Haret El-Keroom neighborhood, the constant whizz of the defining supersonic military airplanes' aftershock noise over Nazareth, and the destroyed remains of my village. I remembered the racist attitudes of the European "so called" priests, and the way the arrogant rich people looked down at me and my uncle as we built their library's book cases in their newly-built homes on stolen Palestinian land. I thought about the constant ID inspections by the racist Israeli Armed Forces, the constant humiliation of the Palestinian people by an intolerant and xenophobic society supported by so-called European and American democracies. And finally, my gas station years, my ongoing struggle to complete my Ph.D. diploma and raise a family among my many challenges. I thought to myself how lucky my students were compared to my life's journey.

These cascading memories took place as I looked straight at them, reminding them that despite what they were experiencing in their harsh and racist lives, they were still much luckier than me in not having to go through what I had in my harsh, racist past growing up in Palestine.

I kept reminding them how lucky they were in having a free education, transportation, and meals. I continued to remind them about the importance of their heritage, of the respect their parents and their school would have for them if they achieved this great accomplishment that their ancestors had left behind. I told them that if they completed their education, it would be an asset and a shield that no one could take away from them; that they could use their education to resist ignorance, intolerance, poverty, violence, and racism in the United States and work toward positive changes in their socio-economic conditions.

I also offered to provide my students with an extra 45-minute tutorial before the start of first period, and I devoted my lunchtime to help them complete whatever assignments they still needed to turn in for their final grade. I would ask them in a frustrated tone, "What else do you want me to do? Take advantage of these offers. You will not find another Dr. B tomorrow at your colleges and universities who will love you and care for your future like me."

I pointed out to them that during my teaching years at Locke, Jordan, Narbonne, and King/Drew High Schools, I noticed that most teachers, counselors, and staff worked hard, cared a lot, and loved them as much as I did. At the same time, I emphasized that while a tiny minority of teachers were racist, most teachers were the bridge that made their crossing, from high school to university, much easier to navigate. Thus, they had no excuse to not work hard and avoid a failing grade.

Suddenly, as if from nowhere, I started breathing hard and I began crying in front of my students as I tried to hide my face with my palms. I still do not know where those tears came from or why. Was it because I had a weak personality? That I failed in my teaching practices? Was it from too much pain or pressure from my previous life experiences? Was the pain that I had sustained due to so many students' violence which resulted in so many injuries and surgeries? Or was it from my real and unconditional love for them?

I just wanted so badly to inculcate in them my love of higher education, the endurance it required to achieve this goal, and the rewards that a higher education would offer them.

My frustration not only stemmed from my concerns for their successful high school graduation, but from my worry about their future success in higher education at their colleges and universities. This concern had to do with my own struggle as a foreign student in navigating the jungles and trenches of higher education. Since then, I had learned how difficult the requirement was to successfully complete it. After all, I was simultaneously teaching late afternoon classes at Cal State University and Los Angeles Trade Technical College.

I tried my best to utilize my lifelong educational experience, wisdom, and common sense to draw the best lessons possible for my students to use in their pursuit of higher education and in their social life. I do not know how many of my lessons achieved my objectives. All I know is that I gave them my best teaching skills while also showing them respect and unconditional love and care. That is all that we teachers can do.

Chapter 3
To My Students, My Endless Love to You All

The fact that I have dedicated this memoir to my family, the American People, to my kids and grandkids, and to my South Central and East Los Angeles students remains the driving force and the bedrock for my work here. I shared many of my experiences with my inner-city students in the Greater Los Angeles area, especially those in East Los Angeles and South-Central Los Angeles. Those memories have enriched, strengthened, and tested, most if not all the values that I came with when I arrived in the United States on March 21, 1971. Without those memories, I could never have written my memoir to begin with.

My full-time high school teaching career with the Los Angeles Unified School District began at East Los Angeles Skill Center (ELASC) in 1981 and ended at King/Drew Magnet High School in 2010. This teaching journey reflected and mirrored my enduring painful and joyful life experiences here in the United States, in Palestine/Israel, or the Holy Land. I would rather call it The Tragic Land.

Despite the tremendous difficulties that these teaching experiences have inflicted on my body and soul, including direct assaults by my students that have resulted in many injuries and surgeries, those memories have outweighed and surpassed all the pain of those assaults and surgeries, some of which I will endure for the rest of my life.

The following stories and events are but a handful of such enduring memories that are chiseled in my mind and conscience with everlasting love and care of my teaching relationships. These all took place at a specific time in the history of the United States.

Some of these stories and events are more elaborate in my memoir than others. I did not know then that I would be writing about them later in life. All these stories and events are equally important to me, none are less so than the others. They also reflect in real time the main historical and socio-economic changes that Los Angeles was going through at that time. In a way, these memories covered history in the making.

And so, let us begin, though I must admit that from the outset that I do not have many pictures to substantiate the content that follows. I never expected to write a memoir then, and so I ask the reader to use your imagination as describe the events below.

East Los Angeles Skill Center (ELASC): 1981-1982

Lunch With the Bunch

Most of my students at ELASC were of Hispanic American background. As I was told at the time by the school authorities, most if not all my students, were parolees who were given a last chance by the courts to rehabilitate themselves by successfully completing their education at ELASC or facing going back to jail. As a vocational class the machine shop and welding training were a path to finding better jobs and careers that could help them leave drug use and gang lives behind.

I looked very tiny among them. They were much taller, heavier, muscular, and hardened than me. Tattoos covered every inch of their exposed bodies: fingers, necks, elbows, cheeks, foreheads, ears, noses, chests, arms and legs, to say the least. Because I had not seen many people covered with tattoos, and because I was brainwashed to believe that these images depicted symbols of gangs, drug users and violence, I was scared to be among them.

My own prejudices were in full display. The machine shop was full of deadly tools and equipment. What if they attacked me or began fighting with each other? Who would come to my rescue? I was on my guard all the time not knowing if I would go home alive that day. Soon, all my fears disappeared when I began having lunch with them, rather than with the rest of the teachers inside the faculty lounge.

At lunch time, most of them brought food from home. I was not that familiar with their home-made cooking. Sometimes, they offered me some of it, but most of the time I refused because I did not want to use my position as their teacher to take advantage of their generosity and leave them with less food to be consumed. I knew, deep in my heart, that they needed the food more than I did and I felt that it was not fair or ethical to eat their food. I had experienced poverty too, so I used many excuses to decline their offers.

Instead, I insisted on sharing my food with them. But they also declined. Their excuses varied but the common one was that the quantities of my food would not fill a quarter of one of my students' stomachs—which would make us all laugh.

On many occasions and without my knowledge, my students would pool their money to send a student to purchase Mexican food from King Taco, a fast-food restaurant. This place became popular all over Los Angeles but during those early years of the 1980s, it wasn't that well known.

Upon the food's arrival, the students would spread the food out and invite me to eat with them by separating my portion from theirs. It then allowed them to say that it was from them, and thus, I could not refuse. By opening my food bag, I found true love and never-ending generosity. I mean, how could you consume during barely 35 minutes of a lunch break, two filled-to-the-rim chicken burritos plus four tacos and a large soda, then run a machine shop?

I tried my best to finish as much as possible and the rest insisted that I should take it home with me. They used to repeat this invitation at least once a week. When I insisted on paying, they always refused. The back-and-forth conversations became a learning lesson about my background. These included stories of the way I grew up, the poverty that I had endured, the work that I did at an early age, traditions that I practiced, the teachers I encountered, the racism that I experienced at the hands of a foreign priest, the Israeli's policies toward the Palestinians, the bad things that I did and did not do, etc.

By doing so, they also shared with me the reasons that caused them to commit the crimes of which they were accused. At the bottom of it all was a lack of family support and understanding of what they were experiencing as children of newly arrived immigrants. Not only did they have to get used to the racist attitudes of the society surrounding them, but they also had to deal with their socio-economic conditions of poverty and neglect. How would a father and mother understand the impacts of these dismal socio-economic conditions on the lives of their own children, when both had to go to work? Additionally, both had to be vigilant of the well-being of their other children while, themselves, enduring constant intimidation at the hands of the immigration officials, police, gangs, and drug pushers.

Therefore, my students grew up in a vacuum that lacked parental understanding of what they were experiencing, and a lack of early intervention programs aimed at preventing teenagers from doing harmful things to themselves and their surrounding neighborhoods. This vacuum was filled by their associations with brothers and sisters that shared the same feelings, forming gangs that gave them respect, safety and belonging.

The attraction of drugs in bringing a lot of cash and easy profit pulled them further into buying, using, and selling them, as well. The competition among the gangs for higher profits ignited turf wars that resulted in injuries and killings that eventually made parental supervision much harder and deeply lowered their educational performances.

At least that was what I was told by them and understood at the time; what caused them to commit crimes. In sharing my life experience with them, the one thing that they teased me about a lot was not having a girlfriend and not making love until the age of twenty-four. My god, they just loved it. They cracked jokes about me and then they started gossiping about this or that student not having a girlfriend—just like me—as they kept bragging about their machismo.

I just laughed my heart out and when I could not stop them, I used to threaten them with a bad grade. However, they knew that I would never do that and thus the teasing continued. I must admit, when a stranger appeared, they would stop immediately and become obeying and serious students. Do you believe that?

The taste of those burritos and tacos were not like the ones that I was used to. When I ate Taco Bells' tacos, my hands were almost always immersed in the smell of gasoline and dirty engine oil, I couldn't even taste them. But eating King Tacos with clean hands, it was a whole different experience. The flavors differed and this new experience made me a Mexican food lover. I strongly feel that if it were not for those students' generosity in sharing their King Taco's food with me, I would not be as strong an advocate for Mexican food as I am today.

Sadly, those lunch times did not last long. At the end of the semester, I was informed that the lack of funding for vocational training had declined, and my shop would be closing. Not only did this sudden closure affect the lack of proper machine shop training for my students, but it also stopped me from conducting further contact with the industries around the neighborhood that could have offered my students decent jobs. My hope was to help them get out of the harmful cycle of gangs, drugs, and violence. So, leaving them behind made me angry and sad.

I was not able to find them jobs, I lost the most amazing, loving, caring and generous friends and students that I had had at that point, and I swore never to eat at King Taco again, and I never did. Despite my fear of my students who were parolees, I was still alive with no injuries or surgeries. I felt very safe among them, and my fear of tattooed men and gang members greatly changed for the better. I truly was lucky to be among them.

Javier

Javier was a student who had the most beautiful laugh that one could ever hear. It came from a big heart and deep lungs. He was not as strong and big as the rest of his classmates. We bonded very fast, and his laughter connected me even deeper with him. It brought back those memories of the old Nazareth Bazaar and listening to my dad and uncle teasing each other. I somehow had a hunch that he was the one behind purchasing my food.

Despite such a demeanor, Javier's facial expressions showed a sad family social life. I did not know what he was going through at the time. He was also on his guard all the time and kept his personal feelings and fears to himself. I related to that as I had also been that way at MAM High School when I feared those priests and mean teachers and kept this fear to myself, away from my parents and my other siblings.

Javier fell in love with the bus driver who drove my students from their homes to ELASC. Most of the students began teasing him and asking him about his romantic time with his girlfriend. I had to intervene a lot and stop them from this childlike teasing.

When he decided to marry his girlfriend, Javier asked me to be his Best Man and was surprised when I accepted his offer. He then alerted me to the danger of driving to his neighborhood. I told him, "Whatever it takes I will be there."

I met his girlfriend only once as she descended from the bus and ran toward me and gave me a big hug with a few tears rolling down her beautiful cheeks.

A few days before his marriage, the principal asked me to meet with him. As I entered his office, he told me to sit down and listen. He then told me that he knew that Javier had asked me to be his Best Man, then he stopped and looked me straight in the eyes and told me that Javier was dead. He was shot by a rival gang member with six bullets entering his tiny upper body.

I became speechless and could not move. My tears said it all. What a heartbreaking moment: Javier was no more. Losing your students to gangs, drug use and violence is one of the hardest and everlasting traumas that most of us inner-city school teachers go through. I wished it on NO ONE.

Later, when I began teaching at other schools. I experienced the loss of nine more of my students to that same fate. The trauma of such a loss is still with me haunting me. I think of them all, all the time. My tears are my companion now instead of Javier's laughter. What a loss.

The Boxer

One of my students was a very well-known boxer who later became a professional fighter. I forgot his full name; all I remember is that they called him "Oscar" or "Caesar De La Hoya," yet, I might be totally wrong. The principal told me that this student would always be accompanied by two bodyguards and that I should train him on either welding or machine shop machines and guarantee his safety, God forbid an injury should occur. What did he do that made him a student of mine, I will never know.

When the boxer began his education, he paid full attention to my overall machine shop and welding instructions. There were many machining and welding projects that I required my other students to finish. But with him, I gave him projects that did not require working on machines, and instead, used files and measuring tools for completing his projects.

After outlining the parameters of the project, he was to tighten the metal piece on the vise and begin filing. While standing on his feet, he held the file securely with his hands and began stroking the file forward and backward against the tightly held metal piece until reaching the marked and proper measurement. By doing so, he was able to improve not only his filing skills but also his standing balance, feet firm on the ground. He also enhanced his visual reading of the blueprint outlines and the intensity and power of his file's strokes while remaining a distance from the other students' filing projects.

The boxer was not a part of the lunch bunch I broke bread with. I did not pay much attention to where or with whom he ate. All that I remember is that he was a very disciplined and serious student. His work was above average, and he showed respect to the rest of the students that was remarkable. He also was very humble and always respected my instructions and common sense. On many occasions, the principal thanked me for my patience and for my accommodation with him. But I treated him just like all my other students with respect and love.

When the shop was finally closed, I did not know if he had enlisted in another machine shop or not. I have not seen him nor heard from him since. Yet, many years later, I heard that he became the champion of his boxing weight on the national stage and became a hero and a symbol of pride for his entire East Los Angeles neighborhood.

I do not know how much of my machine shop training contributed to his success. All I know for sure is that the filing skills he learned equipped him with some of those skills that contributed to his becoming a boxing champion.

Many years later, I began reading about a man by the name Father Greg Boyle who became the founder of "Homeboy Industries" specializing in gang rehabilitation programs that could change the path of gang members to pursue higher education and vocational training.

I began from instinct contributing to this organization without ever meeting him. I just knew that he was doing what I wanted to do at ELASC: keeping my students away from drugs and gangs by finding them jobs. What destiny. In a very recent article published on July 16th, 2023, Father Boyle's loving and caring efforts bear many fruits. Among them is the story of Jessi Fernandez who was a former gang member and had very recently graduated from U.C. Berkley. It took a loving and caring effort to create such a miracle. We need many more organizations such as Homeboy Industries.

Locke High School: 1985-1995

Following the closure of the machine shop at East Los Angeles Skill Center, and after completing the Machine Shop Teaching Competencies Manuals that Dr. Sandoval had entrusted me with, I began teaching full-time at Locke High School in the heart of South-Central Los Angeles. Most of my students were African American, and the rest were Hispanics.

LEFT: a photo of one of the author's best students at Locke High School, Nelson. RIGHT: a photo of the author with his colleagues at Locke High School.

The building that housed the entire vocational program was located at the far southern end of the campus. In addition to my machine shop, there were: Print, Wood, Auto, Upholstery, Electronics and Body Shops. Locke was very lucky to have all these vocational training shops, yet the Electronics, Upholstery and the Body Shops were all closed before I arrived. Yet, their original machines, equipment and tools were still intact and looking for teachers to utilize them again. But none was there. A very sad situation.

All the shops had doors that opened to an elongated east/west hallway with two main secured entrances. The Wood and the Auto Shops had their own parking spaces and safety exits, as well. The Print and Machine Shops opened toward a huge parking lot on the southern edge of the campus. Only students who had special permission could enter the shops using the parking lot entrances. The hallways were unlocked at seven in the morning and before and after the nutrition and lunch breaks. The entire campus was surrounded by a high, 10' chain link fence as an additional safety feature.

The neighborhood that surrounded Locke High School was inflicted with severe poverty, deteriorating infrastructures, and debilitating social conditions. Many warring gang factions dominated the scene. Among the many gang names that I still remember were the Crips, the Bloods, the Grapes, the Safflos, and the Eighteenth Street gangs.

Additionally, the neighborhoods were facing a sharp rise in the use of crack cocaine, among many other drugs. The socio-economic conditions were the same as those of ELASC's neighborhood, if not worse. Therefore, safety for our students was, by far, the most important job for all of Locke's teachers, administrators, and staff.

East Los Angeles Skill Center had equipped me with dealing with such a harsh environment. All I wished for, at that time, was to not lose another "Javier."

The Chain Link Fence

In addition to my regular Machine Shop and Welding teaching and training assignments, the principal had asked me to go around the campus parameters to inspect the chain link fences for any open cuts that were illegally made by people from outside or students from inside campus and then tie them up. The principal's intent was that, by closing the gaps and cuts in the fence, it would increase the overall safety of the campus and decrease the problems with intruders from the outside. Those open cuts were used by students to ditch their classes, bring in food from home, arrange fights, meet girlfriends, show up for a free meal, watch on-campus games, and to buy and sell drugs, among other things.

Many of my students in the First Period classes would arrive late. Therefore, I asked those who came on time to help me out with fixing the fence. Having fewer students made it easier for me to supervise them while walking with them around the campus looking for cuts in the fences.

Armed with C-clamps, groove joint pliers, and diagonal cutters, we placed the two sides of the cut fence against each other. Then, using the C-clamp, we tightened it around the joint edges just like sawing a cut in a piece of clothes without needles. We repeated this task, repeatedly, until the full cut opening was repaired as good as possible.

Depending on how long the cut was in the fence, we tried our best to complete as many cuts as possible before the end of the First Period. Then, we ran as fast as possible to the faraway Machine Shop location so that my students could get to their Second Period classes on time as I prepared for mine.

This task was not safe at all. Any outsiders who used those cuts to enter and exit could get angry and harm us. Being at the far edge of the campus near the surrounding inner-city streets could easily have invited retaliation against me or my students. Those cuts were extremely important to the intruders.

The funny and mysterious thing was, the second day after we

fixed them, there they were again. I reasoned that because the location of those cuts was near the far end of the campus which housed the agriculture area, the intruders felt safe in cutting the fence. The vegetable plants, tall trees and weeds provided added invisibility to them as they damaged the fences that we had just repaired.

Soon, I discovered that I was completely wrong. The same students who pretended to help me out by closing those cuts, were using the diagonal cutters to cut back the area that we closed the day before. When I discovered their ploy, they laughed at me and told me to my face that those cuts were useful to them for a variety of reasons. Their list included: bringing food from home, escaping the campus' security personnel (especially the assistant principal), purchasing hamburgers from across the street, committing illegal acts, meeting their girlfriends, ... and God's know what. Of course, they never mentioned smuggling in and out drugs and weapons. That was for me to guess.

What to do? I demanded they return the tools that I gave them. Of course, they insisted that they did not have them anymore or that they had already given them back to me. Therefore, I asked the principal to allow me to use different students from different periods, to which he agreed. And so, I began sharing with the other students the same task.

When I ended up with the same results, I informed the principal that this was an impossible task because it was not safe. I also said that I was not teaching them the skills they needed or doing them any favors. The campus area was too large for me to monitor, and the fence was too high, wide and long. So, he agreed to bring this practice to an end.

My First Period students did not leave me in peace though. They kept telling me that the cuts in the fence were increasing and that they wanted to help me close them again. I told them that the game was over and that they needed to attend First Period or fail the class.

Other teachers came up with other ideas for the fence problem, including applying grease all over the fence's cuts and at the far, top edges of the fence to prevent scaling it. When students went home in dirty clothes, they were unable to withstand their parents' anger. When the world spread among students, climbing, and cutting the fence decreased for a while until the students began using gloves and other clothes that they threw away before going home or entering the school. Those students were brilliant at what they wanted and desired.

The Stranger

One day, while I was watching my students enter my class after their nutrition break, a young person who I did not know or had seen before entered my class and said to me: "Gus, can I go home through your class's back door?"

I told him "You know that it is illegal to do so, but you must wait until the end of nutrition."

He said, "Okay" and sat in one of the front row seats while I continued watching my students enter my class. From the way he looked, I think that he was no more than 17 years old and close to five feet and a few inches tall. He was dressed in jeans and a white T-shirt with a white towel hanging on both sides of his shoulders. He was, as I recall, a very athletic and well-built young man.

He sat for a few minutes and before hearing the ringing of the bell that signaled the end of nutrition, he rose from his chair, turned around, and came straight at me with a closed boxer-like fist and punched me straight in my left eye. My glasses flew toward the ceiling, and my body hit the wall as I fell on my buttocks and lost consciousness. As I was told later, he fled and jumped the fence then ran toward the neighborhood, never to be seen or heard from again.

The panicked students called the Wood Shop teacher, Mr. Anderson, who ran toward me and lifted me up. He placed me on the same seat that the young man who had attacked me had sat in. Mr. Anderson immediately called the front office and soon the assistant principal and the security personnel surrounded me. They advised me to leave immediately and get checked out at the nearest hospital, which was White Memorial Hospital.

The funny thing is that no one volunteered to drive me to the hospital. I had to drive myself while I was in pain with a severe head and lower back ache. Even stranger was that the doctor who examined me took an x-ray and told me that there was no indication of a major fracture and that I should go back to my classroom and continue that day's work, which I did.

I did not know my rights as a full-time teacher at that point. I could have demanded an ambulance to drive me to the hospital and gone home instead of going back to work that same day. Also, the school administration personnel did not give me the proper documents to open a Workers Compensation case to cover my future medical treatment or to compensate me for loss of work, pain, and suffering.

This incident took place during the 1986-1987 school year and a few days before completing my dissertation. Since then, I have seen numerous eye doctors, taken numerous x-rays, MRIs, and CAT scans. One of the most comprehensive eye exams I took was at The Doheny Center. The doctor concluded that I have sustained a very thin fracture and that during its healing process, it trapped a blood vein between the surrounding bones. This helped explain why I still have needle-like pain in my left eye and severe headaches to this day.

I am constantly reminded of this incident when, out of nowhere, the pain in my left eye becomes so sharp that it is like someone poking it with a needle. The pain lasts for a few seconds then disappears until the next episode. This constant pain reminds me of that young man's vicious attack, the way my glasses flew off me, and the way my body fell on the floor of the Machine Shop.

Neither the principal, nor any person from the district's administrative staff ever visited me or asked how I was. I reasoned then that because such attacks happened so frequently in South Central, counseling the victims became a burden and a waste of time.

The saddest part of it was hearing from so many friends and relatives, "How could I have a Ph.D. and teach in such a dangerous place, not even in my field of study?"

What few of them knew then was the amount of time and effort that I had invested in finding a job in my field of study without any success. They also did not know how lucky I was to have this teaching job and to teach the most amazing students on Earth.

Salt and Pepper

Salt and Pepper were the names that I used to call a student of mine whose first name I have always forgotten. His last name was Pepper, which was easy for me to remember. So, "Salt" became his first name. He always made light of it and laughed at the way I pronounced my first name "Ghassan." Yet, he always threatened his fellow students not to call him what I called him.

Pepper was a very tall and heavy young man; he overshadowed me. I think he was at least six feet plus a few more inches tall. Pepper always told me that he was my "bodyguard."

One day, while I was talking to Mr. Anderson in the hallway during lunchtime, Pepper tried to play a game on me. He slowly approached me from behind and with his two, strong hands surrounding my ribs, he lifted me up in the air causing severe pain to my rib cage. I screamed for him to stop. What he did not realize was that his hands were around my rib cage rather than my stomach. When he jerked me up, he separated my ribs on both sides. Because he was so tall, he misjudged the distance between my stomach and my rib cage.

Seeing me in such pain, Pepper began apologizing and blaming himself. I told him not to worry about what he did as I knew he had not intended to harm me. I said, "After all, you are my bodyguard" and we both laughed even though I was still in pain.

Later that night, I could not sleep. The next day, I called in sick and went to my doctor who took an x-ray and found that several ribs were separated causing all this pain. The doctor gave me pain killers and told me that time would heal it, then advised me to take the pills as needed. It took at least a year from that incident for the pain to go away.

That year was Hell on Earth. I managed to sleep only on my back but with extreme difficulty and pain. Pepper made sure that I was okay. During my teaching days, he always felt bad about the whole incident. What a terrific, sincere, and loving student he was. To make me even happier, he purchased salt and pepper shakers and gave them to me as a memory of that incident. I placed them on top of my desk. However, after a few months, they disappeared without a trace. I do not know how or even when. Then, I told Pepper not to purchase new ones anymore.

Even amid such a troubled world, Pepper and countless other students like him, kept me going. They made up for all the other violent acts done to me by other students.

Flapper

Flapper was another student in my Machine Shop class. I do not remember his first or last name, at all. He told me not to call him his real name but rather, his alias of "Flapper." He felt so proud of this name because the name given to him by his "homeboys" meant that he belonged to their gang.

He always told me that if there was one allegiance that he was willing to sacrifice his life for, it would be for his homeboys. He was covered with tattoos, just like most of my students at East Los Angeles Skill Center. He was a fast-talking and fast-walking student without one ounce of fat. He was slim and trim and no more than five feet and a few inches tall.

When I would get angry with him about his grades, he always answered, "Watch your health, Gus. There's no need to have a heart attack disciplining me for my grades. I do not deserve that much attention. I will be killed before graduating from your class."

He strongly felt so and that is why he never completed the required projects—only the ones he liked. Other teachers told me that he rarely returned his homework to them. In my class, though, he felt at home because he was able to work with his hands and complete the projects that he liked.

Flapper had a girlfriend that he loved a lot. She was also covered with tattoos. She was his size and always happy and smiling. She did not take any machine shop classes, but she always met Flapper at the end of the school day, outside my Machine Shop door that faced the parking lot. This way, they could jump the fence and go home avoiding the main front gate for fear of being attacked.

One day, during Back to School Night, when teachers stayed late between 6:00 and 8:00 p.m. to meet the parents of their students and discuss their progress or lack thereof, I stayed in my machine shop with only Flapper and his girlfriend to keep me company. We all stood outside the class door, next to my car, which was parked a few feet from it. Suddenly, a car that was going south on Avalon Street alongside the far end of the parking lot started slowing down and stopped for a few minutes. Then, a person sitting in the passenger seat began lowering his glass window and started shooting in the direction of Flapper and his girlfriend.

They stood no more than four feet away from me. While the bullets hit the steel wall of the machine shop, Flapper jumped on top of his girlfriend and dove under my car as I stood there wondering what was going on. Suddenly, something fell in front of me that looked like a damaged bullet, and immediately, I ran inside the machine shop as that car drove away.

Then, I ran outside again, fearing that Flapper and his girlfriend had been hit only to find them safe and hugging each other under the car. I told them to stand up immediately and to get inside the machine shop. As we caught our breath, I called the front office for immediate assistance and was told that the police were on their way. But no police showed up because most of the students had gone home a long time ago.

I then told Flapper and his girlfriend, "You must go home right away because I have to walk to the administration building to get the schedule for tonight's event."

Flapper was extremely agitated, as was his girlfriend. They both began cursing and blaming a rival gang for attempting to kill them. Then, they both hugged me and began crying while apologizing and repeatedly telling me that "I could have been killed because of their gang activities."

Wow, what an observation? They were conscious of the bad results of such an affiliation, yet they could not leave their gangs. But deep inside, their tears said it all. They might look tough from the outside, but they were soft and gentle from within. You could not know this unless you were with them and felt the pain of their wounded souls.

What could I have done? I hugged them tightly for I knew that they loved me and were conscious of me getting hurt. I did not know if I would see them again. Deep in my heart, I knew that Flapper and his home boys would retaliate no matter what the price would be. You just cannot lay low and show your weaknesses when you live that lifestyle; you must muster your courage and retaliate.

That was the last day I saw them. I do not know what happened to them. I can only guess that either they were killed, found a different school, or perhaps, as always happened, they dropped out of school and committed themselves to their homeboys' gang and drug life.

The Two Brothers

During Summer break, I was given an extra teaching assignment for only four hours a day over a six-week duration. The main difference between the regular teaching school year and this assignment was that I could choose the students who I decided to enroll in my class, rather than the usual method of the counseling staff deciding this.

On one of those summer teaching assignments, two brothers came to register for the class. One of them clearly appeared older than the other. So, when I began explaining to them the required work that was needed to successfully complete this summer Machine Shop and Welding Coursework, the older brother said that his younger brother was the one registering. He added that he would only be present with him every day so that he could complete the program and graduate without dropping out.

When I asked for more information about what he meant by "making sure he does not fail," he told me that his brother had done many bad things when he joined a gang. When he stood with his younger brother in court, he promised the judge that if he granted permission for his brother to attend vocational school, that he would personally supervise him and attend school with him to make sure that he did not drop out and rejoin his former gang.

The judge had agreed that the older brother could provide supervision to his brother during summer school, so I thanked him and told him how noble and loving he was to do this. Both brothers then became fully committed to completing the summer program with my other students. The older brother repeatedly promised me that his younger brother would never misbehave or give me a hard time. I also pointed out that I had the other students' safety in mind too.

On the second day of teaching this class, a young child, no more than 10-12 years old, entered the shop without permission and without being detected. Then, he began turning on different machines. At that point, I saw him and as I was afraid that he might hurt himself, I told him to stop messing with the machines and to leave. But he refused to leave and then began cursing at me. So, I threatened to call security and have him removed at that point. This did not deter him at all. Finding no other solution, I took him by the hand and dragged him out of my classroom and shut the door.

While the door was closing, he began threatening me very loudly, saying that his uncle would come and teach me a lesson. I was so agitated that I replied without thinking, saying, "Tell your uncle that I work between 8-12 every day." And that was that. I never heard from him or his uncle again.

Going back to the two brothers, the older brother was true to his word: his younger brother made magnificent progress, he followed the safety rules and was respectful to me, his brother, and the rest of the students. I made sure not to ask the older brother about what his brother had done as I felt it was none of my business and furthermore, it would be an intrusion into their personal lives.

On the last day of class, I always brought fresh doughnuts from a bakery next to my house to celebrate the end of the program. After most of the other students had left and only the two brothers remained with me, I was ready to close my shop. Suddenly, the older brother told me that he wanted to show me something. He asked me to follow him to his brother's steel locker where students keep their projects, their tools and their books. That's what I thought he was going to show me—his brother's finished projects.

Instead, he pulled out a fully loaded black pistol. I was completely shocked, to say the least. This was the first time in my life that I saw a fully loaded gun up close. I immediately reprimanded him and told him that he had broken the most important safety rule of the district, as well as mine and the rest of the world.

While I was very angry about this, he asked me to listen to why he brought the gun to my class. I told him that he better have a very good reason. Then he reminded me about the child who had come in and threatened to call his uncle to teach me a lesson. I told him that I didn't know why he took this threat so seriously. He then told me that in their neighborhood, such a threat always means retaliation. He had brought this gun in to protect me. He said, "Dr. Bisharat, we brought the gun and were willing to 'smoke his uncle' for you." I asked what he meant by that, and they both laughed and explained that they would kill him for me. This was the slang expression for assassinating someone.

With tears in my eyes, I acknowledged what they said, "You were willing to kill somebody on my behalf?"

The older brother told me, "You are not just somebody; you have no racist drop of blood in your veins. You taught the class with respect, love and discipline to the benefit of us all, not yourself." Then, they both began crying and gave me a warm and strong body hug before leaving my machine shop. I have not heard from them since.

This reaffirms my faith in my students. I have always believed that what all these forgotten and neglected students needed most was just love that was free of stereotyping and racism. Reflecting on my own childhood and adulthood in Palestine, I suffered from racism by foreign priests, Israeli managers at the factory where I worked in Palestine, and from the way the Israeli government treats their victims, the Palestinians. The last thing on my mind was to imitate them and repeat their racist behavior toward my students who I looked at as my brothers, sisters, friends, and family. Do not cry for me, Palestine.

Just think for a moment about what happened in my classroom. And yet, all we hear on the news about gangs, especially those in South Central Los Angeles, is bad news. There is stereotyping going on all the time about their horrible, criminal, and inhumane acts, which we are led to believe is the result of their bad genes. The widespread belief is that there is nothing you can do to rehabilitate them, period. Yet, these same students have so much love to give back to all their communities if we just hear their cries, feel their pain, respect their heritage and most of all, give them the proper, equal opportunities that are given to others.

No local, state, or national policies will succeed in stopping drug use and gang affiliations that always lead to violence, until we experience what they experience: live with them in their own trenches and hear the beats of their hearts, the suffering of their wounded pride, the lack of decent parental supervision, the break-ups of their families and the pain of poverty, racism and neglect.

Only then, will we be able to stem the tide of inner cities' violence. If you want to change the world for the better, go home and love your family and neighborhood first.

Martin Luther King Hospital

Among the many dangerous machines in the shop was the milling machine. For me, milling machines were the second most popular machine after the engine lathe. As with any other machine, you could cut the metal either manually or automatically. If you were manually cutting metal, you were in control of all of the machine's functions but once you engaged the automatic function, then the machine took over and you had to be ready to stop it once an unsafe condition arose.

One day, a student was using the milling machine to complete one of many projects that all my students had to complete to pass the course. During his work, most of the machines were humming and all the students were engaged and focused on what they were doing. As I have repeatedly mentioned, safety was always my number one concern.

This student was cutting a groove on a flat piece of metal. The milling tool was half an inch wide with a radius of two inches. According to the blueprint of his project, he was to mill a groove half an inch in width, one inch in depth, and four inches in length. Once he had set all the required measurements and tightened the metal piece in the machine's vise, he set the machine to the proper speed and feed. Now, all he had to do was push the start key and let the machine automatically do its job.

But then a problem occurred with the machine overheating. If you are milling without the proper cooling system, it will result in the overheating of both the milling tool and the machined piece of metal. Overheating damages the cutting tool's sharp edges and requires it to be replaced, as it is now flawed. The bad thing about the coolant is that it evaporates upon touching the heated metal surface, producing white vapor that prevents the machinist from seeing properly. Additionally, the coolant keeps the milling particles that are cut attached to each other adding more difficulty in keeping the surfaces clean while cutting. To give the machinist better visual control, those particles must be constantly removed. Since this machine was not equipped with an air gun to constantly blow those particles away, most machinists would use either a brush or a rag to remove those annoying particles.

In this case, my student used a small rag to clear the path of the milling tool from those cut particles. But the milling tool got caught on the rag he was using and pulled it in. Rather than letting go, my student tried to pull it out, hoping to free the rag from the milling tool. Instead, slowly but surely, his hand ended up too close to the milling tool and it cut off the tip of his index finger.

When he began screaming, I ran toward him and with the blood gushing out, the first thing I did was stop the machine. Then, I called the front office and within a few minutes the ambulance was there. Meanwhile, I applied pressure to the student's finger to prevent further loss of blood.

The principal sent a teacher over to cover my class and promised me that he would meet me at the hospital to relieve me so that I could go home. The ambulance then took him to the hospital, and I followed the ambulance to Martin Luther King Hospital to treat my student's wounded finger.

I stayed with my student until midnight as neither the principal nor the assistant principal came to relieve me. Only when his grandmother showed up was I able to go home. By then, my student was feeling much better and on his way to a complete recovery. Both he and his grandmother thanked me for keeping him company and for the love and care that I showed him.

I was not surprised as to why neither the principal nor his assistant showed up; they just did not care. I was with him and that was all that mattered. But what surprised me the most was what I saw as I was waiting in the hallway of the hospital while my student was being treated. I saw so many injured people, mainly young people. Most of their injuries were the result of gunshots and knife stabbings due to gang violence, gang revenge, and turf wars.

In addition to bloody injuries, the hallways were filled to the brim with people who had overdosed on drugs, especially crack cocaine, and heroin. In many ways, it was a war zone. I kept thinking that one day, I might also end up at this same hospital as a result of another violent attack. I was amazed at the heroic job that those doctors and nurses were doing; these people deserve all the medals of honor that our nation can bestow on good citizens.

If anyone wants to visually see the effects of poverty and the result of socio/economic decay, what I saw that night would be a good lesson. What remained for me to do was to speak to his doctor and nurses and thank them for a job well done. I asked his doctor if it was okay for my student to continue the rest of his academic year without further working on machines. The doctor said that he could, but he also repeated that he was not to work on machines for a while.

Suddenly, reality set in. It was midnight and I was there, in the middle of South Central Los Angeles, where gangs rule at that hour. I still needed to get myself home and drive at least 40 miles to do so. As a further thank you to me, my student's grandmother pleaded with the hospital's people in their front office to call for a police escort to accompany me until I entered the 110 Freeway going north.

Shortly after, a police cruiser showed up and the officer told me to follow him until I safely entered the freeway. This incident further opened my eyes to the existence of two very real worlds that exist in the Los Angeles neighborhoods, as well as the entire nation.

I, for one, did not know that South Central even existed when I entered the United States. My work circumstances and destiny sent me there to discover a hidden diamond in the rough waiting for me to discover its hidden beauty and shining colors.

Despite all that I did for my student, I did not receive even a thank you from the principal or the superintendent of the school district. I guess I shouldn't have been surprised about that.

Mother Fuckers, Stop Right Now

I do not exactly remember why I left school later than usual that day. I only remember that it was a summer's day between 6:00 and 7:00 p.m. By that time, I thought I knew all of Locke's neighborhood roads that led to the entrance of the 110 Freeway going north. But this thought was to be tested in a very surprising way.

I still do not know why I ended up on a dead-end road. The street was narrow, and homes surrounded it on both sides making it difficult to make a U-turn to reverse the car to get out of there.

Without any notice, a group of five to seven young men began approaching my car while I was trying to back up. To avoid running them over, I stopped the car a few feet away from them. I could see that most of them were carrying baseball bats. Suddenly, they began banging on my car with their bats. At first, slowly, then with stronger bangs, followed by one of them sitting on top of the hood and another on top of my car's roof.

While the banging on the car continued, I lowered my car window and tried to explain to them that I was the Machine Shop teacher at Locke High School which was their home school, but that didn't get any response. Now, I knew deep in my heart that this was the end of me and my car.

With the increasing sound of baseball bats striking my car, I raised my voice louder thinking that they did not hear me the first time. I told them that I was a teacher. Suddenly, I heard a very strong voice coming from the back of the pack shouting, "Mother Fuckers, stop right now. Do not hurt Dr. Bisharat, Gus."

At this command, they all stopped and the two who were on top of my car jumped to the ground. A young man approached my window and asked me if I remembered him. I felt so relieved that I said, "Yes, I remember you. You were the one who helped me clean up the shop when I asked the students to help. Yet, I forgot your name."

He laughed and told me that I had always said to my students that "It is easier for me to remember faces but not names," which was true.

Then, without even thinking about it, I got mad at him and asked why he had dropped out. I said, "I am still mad at you and will not forgive you for that. Remember what your mom told me when you decided to drop?"

He said, "No."

I told him that she had asked me to "kick his ass." When I said this, his friends all began laughing. Like a stupid man, I had allowed my teaching instinct to take over without realizing that my life was in his hands. Why did I do that? I still do not know.

What followed was even more shocking to me. He was still standing outside my driver's door and with a loud voice, he told the rest of his friends, "This teacher does not have one ounce of racism in his blood. He loved us equally and always told us about the vital contributions of the African Civilization and the immense contribution of African Americans in this country, especially Martin Luther King. I saw him crying, begging us to study hard and to respect our heritage, neighborhood, and families. Do you understand, assholes? He is a very good man, yet I hated him because he was disciplining all of us but with love. He was the only person who could get mad at me, and I did not answer back because he always meant well."

You just could see tears in his eyes. He finally told them to move away, and he put his head inside my door to tell me, "Although I pretended not to listen to you, I always listened very carefully so I could distinguish those racist teachers, who are still at Locke, from those who really wanted to teach us from their hearts. You were one of them. I love you, Gus, and I will always remember you. Just back up and turn right on the next street and the freeway entrance will be in front of you."

What could I say? I am still crying as I remember this, 40 years later. This young man literally saved my life. I am 100% sure that if it were not for him, I would have been killed a long time ago.

Tell me how can we judge gang members? I do not know. All of them have hearts of rough diamonds. They just need society to polish those diamonds and the brilliant colors will appear: clear, innocent, and waiting to be seen.

I am still impressed that he remembered my actions, my tears, my discipline policies, getting mad at my students for not studying, and for the jokes I made. He was observing me while I was doing my job and I didn't even know that. I am sure that he did that with all his teachers. Yet, I still do not know why he dropped out of school.

The Taggers—Look Up—110 Freeway

There were many students in almost every period who prided themselves on being a part of the taggers' family. They were very peaceful and meant no harm to anyone. They were smart but lazy. What was always on their mind was tagging things like books, walls, tools, machines, money, seating, my desk, my chair, my briefcase, my notebook, pencils, measuring tools—especially the rulers, and many other things. All the tagging activities took place inside my classroom. The campus grounds were also full of tags, especially the walls, hallways, bathrooms, cafeteria tables and chairs. Tagging was another accepted mode of entry for those who were living in this neighborhood.

As expected, tagging was competitive, resulting in other taggers writing over or around the tags. Each tagger had their own colors, style, letters, and campus locations. Gang members would respond when they were either praised or put down by the tagger's network. Always elusive, taggers were hardly noticed and as a result, often escaped the wrath of gangs who performed the same ritual but with different messages.

Teachers, administrators, staff, security personnel, cafeteria workers, custodians and the community at large hated tagging, period. By far, the people who most hated the taggers were security personnel and the assistant principal whose main task was to catch at least some of them. Teachers and other administrative personnel just observed and reported the locations that were tagged.

Inside my classroom, I was unable to catch them with their hands in the cookie jar. They always outsmarted me and found ways of deflecting my attention so they could keep on tagging. They laughed at me when I showed my frustration with them, but to no avail. I could sense who was tagging but without solid proof, I always avoided the guessing game.

With constant pleading and begging, the tagging activities in the machine shop declined but never stopped. Unless you caught the student in the act, you just could not expel them on a hunch. You also could not send them to the Dean's office, call their parents, or send them to the detention center. If you did so, you would just mess up their learning progress, which would undoubtedly, lead to them ditching your class or dropping out altogether.

Instead, I indirectly threatened those who I thought were the taggers, but I made sure not to alienate them by saying, "Why don't you take more Art classes to really show your talent in how you manipulate letters, colors and words?"

Most of them did not listen, of course. Then, they began tagging my desk, chair and even the drawers of my desk. They opened it and tagged the inside edges of the drawer and around the keyhole. They opened my briefcase that I only used for my students at Cal State University and tagged it from the inside.

Believe it or not, they never stole anything from my drawers or my briefcase. They were decent and good kids. In many respects, I preferred them over the troublemakers and the disruptive ones who did not tag.

They also resorted to drawing sketches of my glasses, bald head, thin hair, and belly fat. They also made fun of my accent and the way I used to cuss, especially saying "Bull Shit." These sketches were given to me as a gift when I told them the machine shop would be closing. It was the way they conveyed their love to me.

Some examples of the Taggers' work, including sketches of the author.

Sketch of the author by Danny Boy.

Chapter 3   315

Sketch of the author.

Sketch of the author.

Before the end of my career at Locke High, they told me that they had a surprise for me to read while I was driving the next day going south on the 110 freeway. To my astonishment, they somehow managed to tag my name, "Gus," in huge letters above the freeway beneath the Martin Luther King Boulevard crossing bridge. Each letter and comma reflected the four colors of the Palestinian flag: red, black, green, and white. My name stretched at least ten feet in length and three feet in height. They chose Martin Luther King Street because of my constant reminders about his great legacy.

When I got to my class that day, I was very angry with them, but they kept laughing at me, asking me how I knew it was them. But they promised to remove it within 24 hours, which they did. What broke my heart was when they told me, "This was the best way to say goodbye and that we love you."

Just think of what it takes to tag my name above one of the busiest freeways in the nation. They risked major injuries, falls, or even an arrest by police. What could have happened if another gang or taggers were there and challenged them? Fights could have broken out resulting in injuries. And yet, they did this to honor me.

How could you measure that? Who could have imagined taggers with such big hearts? What could I have done? Could I still get mad at them or try to understand the reasons that drove them to neglect their education and worship tagging? Why was no one there to recognize their talents at an early age and direct them to the right educational institutions that specialized in arts and calligraphy such as the Self-Help Graphics & Art organization centered on Chicanx and Latinx art in Los Angeles? I did not hear of it at the time, I just recently read about it in an article published by the *Los Angeles Times* on August 23, 2023.

I can only speculate that their families and counselors at their schools did not know about such an organization, nor did they pay much attention to their talent either. Taggers were not appreciated but rather they were demeaned. I only know that at the time I wished they were studying at the right institutions that could have appreciated such talent. My heart was in the right place.

Scene From a Hollywood Movie

Over the years, I have watched a lot of Hollywood movies, not only for entertainment but also to enhance and strengthen my "Decoding Media Messages" class that I was teaching at Cal State University Los Angeles.

Decoding the ideological messages that Hollywood movies were portraying was one of my favorite lectures at the University. Whether the ideological messages were liberal, conservative, revolutionary, socialist, communist, radical or centrist was the challenge that I posed to my students. This activity generated great discussions and high blood pressure.

Many of those movies depicted scenes that portrayed many elements from these diverse ideologies, including the scenes of two rival gangs facing each other while driving head-on toward them with windows open carrying guns aimed at each other. Greed and the quest of power was always at the base of these scenes which mirrored the radical conservative messages.

These same scenes were now carried out by live gangs in a poverty-stricken place in front of my Machine Shop classroom. These scenes resembled a real Hollywood movie, which in my mind and in this situation, portrayed liberal messages where poverty and neglect were at the base of it all.

When I heard the screeching of car tires near my shop, I opened one of the back doors next to my desk, facing the parking lot. What I saw has never left my mind. Two cars were coming straight at each other with both drivers' hands protruding from the driver's window as they fired at each other.

Missing each other many times, they kept driving around each other in a circle, repeating the same task, repeatedly. Meanwhile, they were edging ever closer to my machine shop's back doors near where I was standing. Immediately, my students saw what was happening as they were cutting metal pieces next to the other door facing the same parking lot. They quickly shut the door and rushed toward me screaming loudly, "Dr. Bisharat, are you stupid to keep looking outside? Shut your door right now and move us to the hallway," which I immediately did.

I was stunned, they were right. For one moment, I was thinking about the "Decoding Media Messages" class that I was teaching at Cal State University, and this distracted my attention from my Number One rule that is the safety of my students and placed me in a position where I could have been killed or severely injured.

Yes, for a moment I was "stupid" and my students were completely right. Their quick thinking about my safety mirrored the way they behaved in rushing toward me screaming at the top of their lungs to shut my door and move inside the hallway. Again, those inner-city students came to my rescue. How could I forget them?

The firing continued for a few more minutes until a police siren was heard approaching. Then, the two cars fled the scene using the open gate of the parking lot that was supposed to be always locked by Locke' security personnel. The police arrived too late just as a police helicopter hovered over the parking lot.

This incident reminded me of Flapper's near shooting. I was very lucky to avoid injury both times. Had the hands of those shooters veered a degree or two in either direction, I could have been shot.

Thinking about what I was teaching at Cal State University immediately came to my mind. The socio-economic conditions are always at the base of society's behavior. If all those gang members were provided with an early intervention program geared toward providing them with good paying jobs, and with it, a decent living standard, they would have no need to join a gang. But then, daily, we are being robbed by very wealthy corporations whose aim is to further enrich their shareholders while government officials look the other way. Maybe that is why there is no money to help these inner-city kids.

Rushing For Help— A Meniscus Tear

The safety of my students was my Number One job for me. I had developed safety exams for every machine, tool and equipment that the students used in the machine shop. Students first had to pass the Safety Test before they could work on the shop's equipment and machines. I repeated the safety rules every day and in every period. To fully complete their projects, some machines needed to be held very tightly in a vise grip while students performed tasks such as filing, drilling, sawing, cutting, welding and tapping, among others. All the vices were held securely on a large work bench that was covered by a thick sheet to prevent damaging the wood surface upon which the thick metal sheet was bolted.

Beneath the bench's metal sheet were many of the lockers in which students kept their projects. These lockers had different keys which I gave to my students so that they could keep their personal belongings and projects safe. I repeatedly emphasized that for safety reasons the doors of these lockers needed to be kept closed to avoid injury to students' knees from hitting the sharp corner edge of the lockers' doors.

One day, as the machine shop was humming, I observed a student trying to cut a piece of round hollow metal with his steel cutting saw. He was a little heavy and, in a rush, to finish the cutting. Using his strong body and hands, he was adding a lot of cutting pressure while stroking the saw forward and backward. This caused his forward strokes to suddenly cut the piece while also pulling his upper body toward the vise, injuring him.

I immediately yelled very loudly for him to stop, but he was unable to hear me because of the machines' noise. So, I rushed to stop him without realizing that the drawer of his locker was open, and I struck the sharp corner of it with my right knee. As I raised my knee up to relieve the immense pain, I then struck the top of my knee, again, against the bench edge above the locker. I felt the impact of these double hits immediately when I could not walk more than a few steps.

After consulting with my doctors and getting an x-ray and an MRI, I was told that I had torn my meniscus, and this led to two surgeries to correct it. By going to the gym and getting physical therapy, I was able to improve the healing and the pain in my knee declined. But I still cannot run, squat, bend, carry heavy objects, climb stairs or walk on uneven surfaces, this many years later.

The treating doctors recommended that I would need to place a pillow between my legs when I went to sleep for the pain to subside, and that this might need to be done for the rest of my life to avoid my knees touching each other. Now, all these years later, my pillow has become my constant companion.

Had that student followed the safety rules by keeping that locker's door closed, this incident could have been avoided. In preventing his injury, I paid the ultimate price. Yet, I was never angry at him as he continued apologizing to me and feeling bad that I was on crutches. Again, my knee injuries reminded me of what Salt and Pepper did to my ribs.

These incidents came with my teaching job, and I have no complaints and no regrets. I am just happy that I was able to stop him from getting hurt. The pillow I use every night reminds me of my happy teaching years in South Central, Los Angeles and the beautiful faces of my students—even as I continue my physical therapy and workouts at the gym to keep my knee strong and functional.

They Dared to Speak

During the 1989 school year, while I was teaching my Third Period class, I saw a sleepy student who was very sick and smelled bad. I asked his friends why he was sleeping in class, smelling so bad, and wearing dirty clothes. His friends told me that I needed to understand his social situation.

I then asked them what they meant. They said, "Unless you let us tell you what we see when people use drugs, then you will not understand why he is in such a situation."

I immediately stopped teaching the class and asked them if they were willing to share their stories with me—to which they agreed.

I wrote down the following stories, word for word, while they were describing what they experienced, without any edits. I still have the same yellow pad that I used to write what you are about to read. I keep it as a reminder of the struggles that our students in South Central, Los Angeles went through every day just to attend their classes. It is something that we, as a community, must be proud of.

Student #1: "The people who I saw using drugs acted very funny and were running in the street. The man got undressed and started throwing himself on the street. He smelled very bad. I think he has not taken a bath in three weeks. I think he did not wash the clothes; that's why they were dirty and smelly. He was scratching himself all over. This scene scared me and I told myself that in no way will I use drugs."

Student #2: "What surprised me was the way they acted—they were sparking." Sparking, according to this student, is an act that follows PCP intake. "People start looking at the ground and for any white color to lift and taste. They act crazy. Men and woman are willing to do anything to get drugs, including sex: all kinds of it. As it is, it made me sick to see it happening on the open public streets. So, I will not use drugs so that I will not be sexually abused."

Student #3: "What surprised me was the way they acted. Before starting to use drugs, they appeared grouchy, looked like they did not sleep for two days, and looked sick. After taking the drugs, they looked paranoid, their eyes were very wide, staring nowhere. Then they began feeling as if they had a lot of money. They felt the need to continue using drugs to feel energetic and hyper. I asked the man, "Why are you continuing with drug use?" He answered, "I am looking for my first high," and therefore, I think that he will continue looking for that first high for a long time. I felt sorry for him and decided not to use drugs."

Student #4: "My friend used drugs for a long period of time. He said that when he stopped, he felt sick and needed more drugs. He looked at the drug as medicine and his mother was on drugs too; she never loved those who loved her. She spent their County checks on drugs. She neglected him. That is why he used to come to school looking dirty and sleeping. Please understand that when you see a dirty student at school, think that someone is not there to take care of him. This problem that my friend is facing opened my eyes to the effect of drugs. I will never use a drug. I will never let my child be like that at all."

Student #5: "I saw a person using cocaine in a pipe. His eyes became red, and his face began sweating. He started walking very fast and tried to steal from people to buy more drugs. He became paranoid, especially from the police. This scared me a lot. I will never use drugs in my life."

Student #6: "I saw a man under the influence of drugs at around 8 o'clock at night. I saw a man who began running and taking his clothes off. He started running between alleys and cars. People saw him and began shouting. He was hit by a car and did not feel the impact, yet he pretended to be dead when the police and the fire trucks arrived. The police had a lot of difficulties handcuffing him. This incident opened my eyes. It scared the hell out of me. I will never use drugs. The man is just too much."

Student #7: "There is a substance called 'Sherm' or PCP. A Sherm stick looks like a cigarette that is dipped into a Sherm bottle. Then the Sherm stick is lit and smoked like a cigarette. Under its influence the man fell on the ground. Then the police took him away. He looked like a zombie or someone from outer space. Man, I was really scared. I will never use drugs." (According to this student, a Sherm stick is sold by its length: about an inch costs $10, three inches costs $15, and the cost for a Sherm bottle, which is two inches in length and one inch in diameter, costs $700.)

During lunchtime, I sat and began writing the following comments after hearing and writing the, above, sad stories:

1. Students are daily exposed to the evil of drugs. In addition to coping with gangs and family problems, they also must survive the effects of drug abuse. Thus, their educational performance is greatly tied to their coping skills. They do need our utmost attention.
2. I have also learned that our students are smarter than we might think. The openness with which they spoke and acted showed their self confidence in avoiding drugs at all costs.
3. Students related their experiences to each other. The ones who were reluctant to share their experiences then became motivated and began talking. The support and understanding they showed toward each other's feelings moved me a lot.
4. I became more aware of their problems and more understanding of their feelings by hearing about this. This helped me change my teaching approach and methods. I think a lot about my methods now, more than I ever did before.
5. The federal, state, and local governments must do a better job in stopping the drug flow on our streets. The punishment for those who are selling drugs must be harsher, and most important, the money allocated for education or drug prevention must be increased.

6. Unless we, as a people, become more politically involved, I see a dark future concerning the continued use of drugs.

Disciplinary Showmanship

As I began my full-time Machine Shop teaching at Locke High School, I got to know Mr. Kemp, the Auto Shop teacher, who taught for many years prior to my arrival. His classroom was across the hall from my shop.

As I got to know him, I found out that he was living in South Central, and thus, he was very familiar with its socio-economic environment, including drug use, gang violence, and the ways they have shaped and influenced most of our students at Locke.

Being a part of many local associations and educational organizations, he was, by far, the most experienced teacher within the vocational teaching department. Students feared and respected him a lot. Disruptive activities by his students were very minimal in relation to mine, for I was a new teacher.

So, one day I asked him what methods he used to keep disruptive activities so low in his shop. His answer was very educational and simple: He told me that the first and most important advantage that he had was the fact that he lived in the neighborhood and provided many car repair services to its residents around the campus. So, he knew most of his student's parents. This knowledge gave him a great advantage when threatening to call his disruptive students' parents.

He also told me that when a disruptive student does not listen to your instructions, inform the student that you are about to call his or her parents, and you will see a great improvement. According to Mr. Kemp, this method will work most of the time, but in other cases, it might backfire and result in the student dropping out. That is the worst thing we can do to our students in South Central.

His second piece of advice was the strangest and most amusing. This involved an act of showmanship. At the beginning of every new semester and after taking attendance, he introduced himself to his students while carrying a two-foot-long round steel rod in his right hand. Then, as he introduced his disciplinary policies, he raised the steel rod and hit it against his open left palm. He continued this act while reminding the students of the consequences of fighting, ditching, shouting, running, and cussing in his class. He said that this act of showmanship was most effective for the ninth graders, who had just graduated from elementary school and had never seen such a disciplinary act before.

He said he could hear his students saying, "This teacher is a crazy one. We will not mess with him." He said that he was waiting to hear these comments from his students as it signaled that they feared him and would show complete obedience to his disciplinary procedures.

When I heard this, I began laughing and told him that he really was crazy. He told me to "just try it."

Of course, Mr. Kemp had never physically used the steel rod on any of his students. For him, it was all about scare tactics and showmanship.

After I heard this, I began imitating Mr. Kemp's act by using a 12-inch-long wooden ruler while repeating my disciplinary policies. The comments I heard were, "He is an easy teacher."

But I continued to remind my students, repeatedly, that I would call their parents for any disruptive behavior as well as the front desk, the assistant principal, and the security personnel. By using this method, I thought I would achieve almost the same result as Mr. Kemp.

Another method I used was to shout, louder and harder, over their heads when the students started fighting, cussing, and running in class. The louder you were, the more control you had. I felt that this would instill fear in them and decrease the disruption. I did this a lot until my throat reminded me to cool down.

I followed all of Mr. Kemp's instructions except the use of his steel rod. The machine shop was full of steel rods and other dangerous tools and equipment, so the last thing on my mind was to open their eyes to the use of this dangerous weapon once a fight broke out.

In my opinion, the most effective method was never to snitch on them. I showed them a lot of respect and especially love and continued to remind them of their progress in my class. My students always reminded me of how I showed them sincere care and love, but I do also miss Mr. Kemp.

Oh, Dr. B., I Fucked Up

Antonio was a 12th grade student and the prom's celebration was right around the corner. Prom was then, as it is now, the main celebratory event of most of the high school graduates. Competition among students for choosing their prom's dates was an enduring mystery until a few days before the prom's celebration.

Parents did not fail to pay for whatever it took to make their children look their best. Even the parents who I personally knew had financial difficulties, made sure that they provided for their older kids in this way.

What was amazing to me was not only the amount of money spent by parents in providing the caps and gowns, but the number of pictures taken of the graduates with their parents at the prom graduation party. During the regular school year, pictures of parents were rarely shown to me at all. But something about prom made taking pictures with their parents very important to my students—even more important than taking pictures with their friends.

Being a good-looking young man, Antonio was not an exception to this rule, except that he screwed up, big time, when he tried to show me the pictures he took with his beautiful prom girlfriend, Isabella. He entered the machine shop with his right hand placed on her left shoulder. Then, he pulled his wallet from his back pocket and told me that they had gone to Sears to take their prom pictures. As he proudly pulled a picture out of his wallet to show it to me, Isabella looked at it and slapped him straight across his face, then ran away. When Antonio looked at the picture he had shown me, he realized that there was a different girl in the photo. Suddenly, he said to me, "Oh, Dr. B, I fucked up."

When I realized what had happened, I became angry and told him, "What in the hell did you do? If you love her, run after her right now and beg for mercy. Otherwise, I will kick your ass."

He ran down the hallway like a jack rabbit calling her, apologizing, and begging her to wait for him so he could explain. Soon, his voice faded away, and he never came back to let me know what happened.

A few days after the prom parties were over, Isabella, who was not a student of mine, dropped by the shop and showed me her prom pictures with another student. She told me that Antonio was a jerk and did not deserve her. I told her, "He really loves you, but then, I am not you."

Prom's hidden effect was in leaving so many broken hearts and disappointment for the graduates. Yet, most of the graduating class experienced a great time and cherished memories of their prom. Without my permission, students hung their prom pictures around my table and the surrounding walls. It was more of competition, among them, as well as telling me that they had made it to prom.

Various prom photos given to the author by his students over the years.

Prom time was very confusing but also a very exciting event for all graduating students. It always signaled the beginning of a new and unknown journey into womanhood and manhood. I just wonder how many of them successfully completed their educational journey.

I strongly believe that Antonio was no exception to the confusing excitement surrounding prom time and completing his high school education. He was caught in the whirlpool of conflicting waves that surrounded him from all sides and was unable to steer himself upward and leave behind that whirlpool. It was an innocent mistake in the middle of navigating his entrance into adulthood and with it, his future outlook on life.

Building An Airplane Frame

A student by the name Jerome (I forgot his last name) asked me if it was okay for him to build a replica of his grandfather's airplane frame that he flew during WWII. Jerome wanted to give the frame as a gift to his grandfather for the love and care he had provided him growing up. I told him that it was okay with me, but I did not have any blueprints of airplanes that were used during WWII.

The next day, he brought with him a book that had many miniature pictures and drawings of different types of airplane frames used during WWII. One of those drawings depicted the same airplane that his grandfather flew in Europe. The blueprint drawings were clear and gave exact ratio measurements and all the configurations that were needed to begin forming a miniature body of the airplane.

I told Jerome that I had the right stainless steel flat sheet to begin forming the body of the airplane and for him to start as soon as possible. I also told him that he had full freedom to concentrate on this project and that he did not have to worry about the other projects required by other students. I strongly felt that building such a frame would involve the use of literally all the tools and equipment needed to pass this course.

I did not want to be in his way, but rather, I wanted to encourage him to explore his inner strength, curiosity, and ambition. This was his gift of love and respect to his grandfather, just like my promise to my parents to complete my Ph.D. I only asked him to follow the safety rules and to ask for my help when it was needed.

He immediately removed the stainless-steel sheet from its location and laid it flat on the workbench. Then, he began polishing the surface to make it easy for him to apply a blue color dye that enabled him to start drawing the outside dimensions of the two wings using a scriber, steel rulers, vernier caliper, and other measuring tools. He looked at the book's drawing repeatedly until he was confident to call me for my inspection, prior to cutting it.

I inspected his wing drawings for accuracy and found no errors. Then, I placed the stainless-steel sheet on the flatbed of the band sawing machine and asked him to support the extended section of the sheet so that I could cut as close to his measuring lines as possible. He was not trained yet to use the band sawing machine and I did not want him to get hurt on this very dangerous machine.

Once the two wings were cut out, he carefully placed them between the jaws of the vise and began filing the edges until he reached the exact measuring lines that he drew. After completing this task, he polished the surfaces again. Those wings looked so good and shiny. He wrapped them in a soft sheet of cloth and applied a little oil on the surfaces to prevent them from future rust. With pride, he carefully placed them in his locker and locked it. I was so proud of him and happy with his work.

Now, he was eager to start cutting the lower side of the airplane that needed many more measurements and cutting instructions. After completing the first side, I promised to go over his measurements early the next day, to make sure all was okay before cutting.

The next day, to my surprise, a very good-looking gentleman entered my machine shop dressed professionally in a complete suit and tie and very elegant shoes, a thinly shaved mustache and a well-groomed hair style. He respectfully introduced himself to me as the father of Jerome who was building the airplane frame as a gift for his grandfather. He arrived when Jerome was attending a different class on campus.

I told him that I was very honored to have his son in my class and invited him to see how far his son has come on his own. I told him that his son was destined to become a mechanical engineer or an architect, to say the least. He then told me that there was no need to see anything, that he already knew that his son was a very gifted young man, able to become whatever he wanted. I told him that I fully agreed.

He then took me completely by surprise when he told me that he was taking his son out of my machine shop and also from Locke High School. I was speechless and begged him to keep his son in the shop until he completed his project. When he refused, I told him that I taught on Saturdays, as well, and that Jerome was welcome to attend that class, but again, his father adamantly refused my offer.

He then told me that the real reason behind his decision was to protect his son from being harmed or killed because of the increasing gang violence around school. He was also afraid of other students being jealous of his gifted mind as they were calling him "white boy" and "whitey."

But what hurt me the most was the last thing he said. I still remember it vividly as if it happened an hour ago. He said, "This gang-infested neighborhood does not deserve such an Afro-American bright student. He belongs in a white, safe neighborhood school that can recognize his talent and treat him that way, so I am moving with my family out of South Central. I have purchased a house in a nice suburban white area."

Wow, what a statement! Now, the whites who had enslaved his people for more than 300 years became a refuge for his Afro-American son and family. I am not in any position to question his decision. This statement carries the deep pain and suffering of people whose life experiences were wrapped in "white-only" achievements and arrogance. Maybe his son will be able to break through such a trap and escape its painful chains.

I had heard many comments like this from broken Palestinians' hearts and minds, as well. The pain and humiliation of the victims is universal. Many of my Palestinian people started using the language of their oppressors, a language that demeaned the Palestinian struggle, just to justify their inabilities and weaknesses in facing a much stronger oppressor. Nothing good comes out of victimhood.

Jerome's father then thanked me again and left. This really broke my heart. I do not know if he was wrong or right to take his son out of Locke and move his family out of South Central. After all, I was a father, too, and could understand his need for a safe place for his son to learn. That is our number one job as a parent: to keep our family safe, isn't it?

Yet, by taking such a brilliant mind out of such an impoverished and neglected neighborhood, he also depleted it even further of its smart and hard-working students who needed so much. Imagine what would happen if other parents felt the same and began removing their hard-working and smart kids out of South Central? Who would fill that gap that South Central is so much in need of? One thing is for sure; gangs will move in to fill such a gap.

If I had not studied at a vocational high school, I could have been without a job during the worst time of my life and this teaching position would never have materialized. I did not have the chance to explain to Jerome's father how and why I became his son's teacher. Maybe I could have changed his mind?

Most, if not all the parents I met, wanted their kids to become lawyers, doctors, business entrepreneurs, professors, and engineers. Therefore, vocational education was not the desired future career for their kids.

I do not know how Jerome's career went. All I know is that our country is facing a great shortage in finding qualified employees in machining and welding as well as many other vocational skills.

Maybe his son could have become a mechanical engineer teaching in South Central, where he is needed the most.

Just like Javier at East Los Angeles Skill Center, who was killed by an opposing gang, Jerome was removed because of the threats and fear of gangs. This is the nightmare that surrounds the Watts area and Locke High School and continues to be the same nightmare now. We need a safe place for our students to grow, get educated and succeed.

I kept Jerome's locker locked with my own keys and never permitted another student to use it. When the machine shop was closed and I left Locke High School, I opened his locker and found the wings he had completed, still wrapped in the oily rag.

I just shook my head and locked the locker again and left his work there as a reminder of a brilliant mind and happy memories. I do not know whether his wings still lie in that locker because I had to return the keys to the administration upon leaving.

A Baby Named Gustavo

Like my student, Jerome, whose love for his grandfather led to his unfulfilled dream of creating a miniature replica of the airplane that his grandfather had flown in WWII, Enrique was a hard worker. In his case, it was all about working on the newly- invented machining technology, Computer Numerically Controlled machine (CNC for short).

In the late 1980s and early 1990s, this technology was brand new. I was lucky to convince Dr. Sandoval to purchase a CNC machine for my machine shop. What I received was a bench-bolted, small CNC with its instruction manuals. I had not worked on such machines before as computers were very new to this industry. Thus, I began reading the instructional manuals on my own and managed to prepare a few projects for my students to complete.

In many ways, I had to devote too many valuable hours of my time to learn this technology which decreased my attention on the other machining and welding projects and my other routine duties. Since I needed extra help with this, I asked my students to volunteer to read the instruction manuals for this new machine, in place of completing certain projects. Enrique was the one who volunteered.

I gave Enrique the same full freedom that I had given Jerome. He was then able to read the instruction manuals at his home as part of his homework assignments. Within a few days, Enrique mastered the blueprint reading and how to input the needed measurement for the CNC machine's computer. He learned how to place the proper cutting tools and the feed and speed needed to complete the project. Once all the inputs were completed, I reviewed with him the measuring inputs and gave him the green light to push the Start key.

I have always believed that the country that masters this wondrous technology will have the greatest advantage in moving production manufacturing to a much higher level than we have ever seen yet. Imagine, tightening a piece of metal in the chuck on the engine lathe and with the correct information, feeding the computer those cutting tools that will bore, cut, drill, thread, and polish without any human effort at all. I knew, then, that Enrique would have no problem finding a career in such technology.

He became my right-hand student and I asked him to help train the other students on this new technology. He was very slow but extremely accurate. Machining requires taking your time when measuring and machining at very close tolerances. Unlike Jerome, Enrique missed many classes and was often tardy. I knew that he had a girlfriend but despite these issues, his work was excellent, and he successfully graduated from Locke High School.

One day, perhaps two years later, I saw a brand-new small Toyota SUV parked next to my car, a few feet from the back door of my machine shop. It was Enrique with his beautiful wife, his high school sweetheart, and a newly born child. He rushed toward me and gave me a bear hug and introduced me to his wife.

She got out of the car holding a sweet baby boy and, immediately, I asked if I could hold him. She agreed and handed me their baby. As

I hugged him, Enrique told me that I was responsible for him landing the job that he now held. He said, if it was not for me allowing him to practice on the only CNC machine, and especially using the sophisticated measuring tools, he would not be working there.

When I asked him about his job, he told me that he was now an inspector, checking the accuracy of the measurements of machined parts by other CNC machinists. Machine Parts Inspectors were very well paid at that time. His income allowed him to get married and to purchase the new car that he was driving.

Suddenly, his wife came close to me and asked me to give her back her baby, who was named "Gustavo." Then they both looked at me and asked if I had heard what they had named their baby. I said, "Yes, Gustavo." Enrique then replied that they had named their child after me. In Spanish, Gustavo is the proper name for "Gus."

Now, I asked to hold Gustavo again. While he was in my arms, I began crying and could not let go. Wow, what a lucky teacher I was! Then, they both hugged me and drove away, and I never heard from them again.

Soon after, my machine shop was closed, and I moved to another teaching position and location. What a coincidence that I got to meet Gustavo and hear that story! What kismet! Neither Enrique nor his wife knew that I had been called "Gustavo" by my Hispanic students while at Cal State University.

I considered this an honor to have a student name his first baby boy after me—his teacher! I was in a state of emotional awakening. Even in the darkest corners of Los Angeles, lights always shined. You just had to find them.

Enrique's story is what all teachers dream of accomplishing: a student who graduates and becomes a husband, a father and gets to have a new career and a new life because of classroom experience. Maybe he was listening when I told him that jobs in this field would be plentiful. He proved me right. Maybe, in a mysterious way, Ridah-Al-Wali Dain came to visit me again in serving Enrique as a mentor.

The American Flag—Lost Family Members

The news that the shop was closing and that I would be leaving affected many of my students in different ways. Like many other teachers who lost their positions before I did, my memories of my teaching career did not stop once I left my keys at the front office. While teaching, our students not only take notes about subject matter, but they also observe how we teach. This is especially true if we emanate passion and love from our physical and facial expressions as this affects their opinion of us as teachers.

While some students express their affection to their favorite teachers with gifts, letters, thank you cards, prom pictures, or just simply a hug with tears, I did not receive any letters or gifts. Instead, there were plenty of hugs, tears, prom pictures, and samples of their finished projects.

As I previously mentioned, the taggers displayed my name on top of the 110 Freeway overpass, while those who were in gangs gave me unbelievable surprises of their own. At the end of my Sixth Period, which signaled the last teaching period at Locke High School, they handed me the American flag that had been hanging high in my machine Shop and asked me to unfold it on top of my desk so that I could see the entire face of the flag and what they had written on it.

To my surprise, there were many unfamiliar names written with thick black ink all over the flag. Meanwhile, they stood looking down at the flag, motionless and with solemn respect. One of them told me that he spoke on behalf of all those students who had attended my classes. They wanted to show their sincere love and appreciation for me by writing on the flag, the gang (a.k.a. names) monikers of their fallen gang members who were killed by rival gangs.

Before they folded the flag and handed it back to me, they warned me not to display this flag in any of my future classes if I wanted the chance to teach again. Then they folded up the flag very carefully and handed it to me with tears flowing down their cheeks.

At that moment, they told me that this gesture was the highest honor that gangs bestow on those who they love and respect. They instructed me to unfold it and read the names at home even though I would never know who those beloved (to them) gang members were.

I stood speechless by this gift, then I placed the flag in my briefcase, very carefully, and stood in the middle among them as I embraced them as wide as I could with my two hands.

Although I continued teaching for another 25 years, I never displayed it at any of my high school, college or university classes. But, at home, I showed it to my wife and kids and then folded it up the way they did and placed it in one of my dresser drawers next to my bed.

Years later, when my youngest daughter became a high school teacher, she asked me to show her the flag again, then asked if she could have it as a symbolic gift of my memorable years teaching at Locke High School. She became a teacher because of the impact that my students had on her when she accompanied me to my classes at King/Drew Magnet High School at the age of ten. So, I gave her that flag when she became a teacher. She promised me to frame it in the proper way so that it would last as long as possible without tarnishing the ink colors of the different gang members' names.

That flag was handed to me at age 45 and now I am 74, so almost 30 years have passed, and we are still counting. I do not know who originally hung the flag in my class. It was there when I began teaching in 1985 at the age of thirty-five. For me, this flag carries the pain of a nation that has failed in stemming gang activities and their destructive aftermath on the American people, as well as the pain of my people because this flag had failed in stemming the continued oppression of the Palestinian people at the hands of the Israeli government. I hoped that my daughter's generation with millions of other teachers could replace the names of falling gang members with shining successful names of brilliant students written on our United States flag.

The people whose names were written on it are gone now. The students who wrote those names are now in their early 50s—if they are still alive. Who knows where they are now, how many live, how many finished their education and how many have established solid families? Regardless, their memories, as well as their fallen friends, are still in the hands of an educator and imprinted on our country's flag that will never be tarnished.

Socio-Economic Neglect—Violence, Gangs, and Riots

It is too hard not to mention the recent 1992 Watts Riots. Locke High School and many other neighborhood schools were caught unprepared in the middle of it. The causes of this riot were like many others before it. They were rooted, a long time ago, by the long history of discrimination, racism, and neglect of inner cities' socio-economic conditions that pervaded throughout our country and throughout the Los Angeles Basin.

A major shift was about to take place in the socio-economic relations between minorities and the white dominant citizenry. Massive waves of black and white populations migrated from the Southern parts of the United States to Southern California looking for good and stable work opportunities and a change in their lifestyle.

During the early 1940s, the need for labor intensified because of the massive military buildup in anticipation of the U.S. entering WWII. The main supply of labor was fulfilled by whites, African American and Latinos. At the time, blacks and Latinos were restricted in where they could live. Blacks lived mainly in the city of Watts, adjacent to Central Avenue, while most Latinos lived in East Los Angeles.

The white population lived mainly in the surrounding cities, including West Los Angeles. With the influx of minority labor, the white population feared that those minorities would sooner or later replace them in their own neighborhoods. So, they began forming their own white gangs such as the "Spooks Hunters," as a derogatory term used against the black population. Just like the Spooks Hunters, the Ku Klux Klan (KKK) emerged and began its own harassment against blacks and Latinos.

The U.S. Marines, who were on their way back from their duties, and others who were stationed nearby, began attacking Latinos who dressed in Zoot Suits to instill fear, intimidation, and white racism. This led to the Zoot Suit Riots and both blacks and Latinos began forming their own gangs to protect their people and livelihood.

Following the early 1965 Watts Riots and the emerging Civil Rights Movement, most of the white population left the area and moved to suburbia. Blacks and Latinos gangs became involved in organizing their neighborhoods and most gang activities suddenly stopped. Instead, they turned their attention toward fighting police brutality and discrimination. Parties such as the Black Panthers, Malcolm X Federation, and the Brown Berets emerged.

The police, and to some extent the federal government, feared that those organizations would initiate a massive social movement asking for more income distribution and better socio-economic conditions in their poor areas of Los Angeles and elsewhere. So, the authorities—the Federal Bureau of Investigation—began breaking up these organizations, spying on them, jailing their leaders, and assassinating the most vocal and popular leaders. The above activities were directed by a governmental policy called the Counterintelligence Program, popularly known as COINTELPRO.

The vacuum created during and after the displacement of the above organizations was filled by many different gangs, competing for the control of drug trade, especially the epidemic use of crack cocaine. The two most powerful black gangs were called the Bloods and the Crips. Among the most powerful Latino gangs were the 18th Street, the Soranos (Southerners) and the Norteña's (Northerners).

The proliferation of many other gangs resulted in the increase of gang-related murders, which reached its height at the beginning of the 1990s. This dire situation led to a halt of many progressive programs of the early organizations.

Then, there was the severe beating of Rodney King on March 3, 1991, by the police which resulted in his skull being fractured and teeth and bones broken. It also caused him permanent brain damage.

Watching the beating of King on TV from their own homes ignited the passion of the residents of South Central to stand up and do something against this epidemic of police brutality.

A few days after Rodney King's beating, on March 16, 1991, a young African American girl named Latasha Harling was murdered by Korean store owner Soon Ja Du for stealing a bottle of orange juice. Du was given a sentence of probation with just a $500 fine and did not go to jail for murdering Latasha. This verdict resulted in a deep division by the black community against Asians, especially Koreans.

And when the "not guilty" verdict came back in the police trial of Rodney King on April 29, 1992, by a mostly white jury, the black community erupted. They had had enough, and they took to the streets to riot and loot any business they came across. Their pent-up anger was directed at liquor stores and white and Korean businesses and many buildings and businesses were torched for several days.

Many innocent people were attacked on both sides of the fence. A white citizen named Reginald Denny was attacked by a black man and almost killed. The media went on the offensive showing the brutality of the rioters but did not show the brutality of a similar attack against a Guatemalan immigrant named Fidel Lopez.

The police then mostly left South Central to its doomed fate. This continued for almost three full days until the National Guard finally took over and calmed down the situation with military might. Many more riots took place in San Francisco, Las Vegas, Seattle, Oakland, and Chicago in solidarity with that of South Central L.A. The result of these riots was the loss of 53 lives and close to a billion dollars in damage. The riots were an expression of the blacks' despair of being put down and discriminated against. The socio-economic conditions were the main underlying cause of this and the previous riots, as well.

The day the riots began, on April 29, 1992, I was teaching in South Central. But during my Fourth Period class, I felt a severe pain in my stomach and began vomiting. I called the front office to get a sub to cover my Fifth and Sixth Period classes. I also called the principal's office for my adult afternoon classes and asked for a sub to cover my class that started at 3:00 p.m. Both offices agreed to send teachers to cover for me, so I left during the lunch break.

After arriving home, tired and with a high fever, I took a long nap. When I woke up, I sat down to have a cup of soup for dinner. When I began watching the news, I was shocked to see columns of smoke rising from the direction of South Central very close to Locke High School and its surrounding area. I then rushed outside, and I could also see the smoke columns from my own back yard with my own eyes as my house was located high above the 210 freeway.

As I watched the news, I began comprehending the severity of the situation. Locke High School was in the middle of it. I could not imagine what might have happened to me if I had left in the middle of the riots at 6:00 p.m., driving on Imperial Highway to get to Central Avenue and then taking the 110 Freeway north. I would have been caught in the middle of the riots and who knows what might have happened to me?

I can say though that my stomach pain saved me that day. The School District closed its classes for five days in a row. Upon returning to my regular duties, I could physically see the aftermath of fires: destroyed buildings, accumulation of all sorts of trash, and chain-link fences surrounding most businesses and homes. Some other link fences were busted with large cuts in them and "For Sale" signs were everywhere. Even empty lots were boarded up.

South Central was a ghost town, almost empty of pedestrians and cars. It was so quiet that even the few birds in the tree next to my machine shop building were quiet as their nest had disappeared. But on campus, the noise was deafening, and students' activities resumed. All the students wanted to talk about was what they have done and seen rather than studying.

I for one, gave them all the time they wanted to express their thoughts and feelings about the reasons and causes of the riots, what they have done and seen during the riots, and how they were affected by it. All my students, without any exception, blamed the White man for the cause of the riots. The one thing they always mentioned was the long history of discrimination and racism against Hispanics and blacks by white America as the main driving force behind the riots.

The reasons given to support their arguments were astonishing to me in their accuracy and comprehension. They began asking me why we did not have white students on campus and why they did not have safe streets and public parks to play in. They asked why most businesses were owned by white people, why police officers were unable to control the gangs and why the police handcuffed them, left drugs in their cars, and then used the drugs they planted as an excuse for their arrests. They wanted to know where their public libraries, decent hospitals, and pharmacies were, where were their supermarkets to buy food from and why they didn't have any safe movie theaters.

But what was most astonishing was their observation and alertness to the fact that the teaching curricula at Locke High School emphasized white history over black, and the accomplishments of mostly White scientists and leaders. What about Hispanics and black's contributions to history, science, and their leaders' accomplishments? This was very interesting to me as I was then teaching Political Science and Social Studies at the University, but not at the high school level.

I could fully relate to their pain and frustration since I had seen it and lived it as an Israeli "so called citizen." I, too, had seen how the Palestinian history and identity had been regulated by a racist Israeli public education curriculum that still emphasizes the superiority of the "chosen people" over all others, including the Palestinians.

One student asked me, "What is the value of studying White European history that happened 500 years ago when we are not fully studying the causes of the riots next door?"

I see this as a contradiction. Other students disagreed and said that we should study other people's history while also having our libraries stock books and documents that emphasized the contributions of the African and Hispanic civilizations.

I strongly think that the above questions and conversations must be addressed by our citizens as soon as possible if we are to avoid future riots and violence.

Describing what they had seen was another story. Most of the students told me that they stayed home and watched television as their parents asked them to. The closest they came to the riots was watching the rioters directly out of the windows of their homes. Many described beatings, shootings, and lootings. They made fun and laughed at rioters who were unable to carry what they stole, especially heavy objects such as television sets, air conditioners, fans, and even small refrigerators.

What they fully described was the acts of those students who did not listen to their parents and left their homes to join the gang members or take part in the looting and burning activities. Those students told me that they were involved in many fights against opposing gang members while inside looted stores as each was trying to get to the cash registers and the "good stuff" first. Many showed me their battle scars, and one told me that he liked licking his own blood coming out of his wounds. He even suggested that one day I should do the same.

A 9th grade student proudly told me that when he saw an elderly lady carrying a grocery bag in one hand and her purse in the other, he pushed her to the ground and stole her purse as he ran away laughing at her. A few blocks away, he opened her purse and found only $20 in it.

I became very upset and told him that what he did disgusted me. "How would he explain what he had done to his parents?"

Rather than answering me, he lashed out at me and said he had no parents to worry about, but he had a little brother to feed living at his grandparents' house. He then told me that I didn't know what I was talking about. He said that $20 would feed him and his brother for a whole week. Why should I worry about that old lady when no one gave a fuck about him? And then he ditched my class and ran away. I just stood there speechless. At least he contemplated helping his brother before he attacked this elderly woman.

As far as what they learned from the riots, most agreed that rioting is not the answer to improving their socio-economic condition and that the riots were a buildup of everyone's frustrations over the years. They talked about how the gangs were threatening their learning performances at school and how the images of blood, injuries and killings have scared them and changed their outlook on how human behaviors erupt so suddenly into violence.

In the final analysis, all of them wished that the government could do much more to improve their living conditions, reduce national tensions, and for the police to be more humane, just, and less racist.

My tenure at Locke High School ended at the end of 1995 due to a lack of funding, a lack of students enrolling, and my long leave of absence due to the healing that my right knee required with surgeries, and my other violent injuries.

After that, I began subbing at the beginning of the 1995-1996 school year. By the end of 1995, I had completed all the classes required for both my Social Studies and Administrative credentials, and I received official credentials for both.

I began subbing during the first semester at Narbonne High School and Jordan High School. At Narbonne, I began teaching physically challenged students during the morning's first three periods, and Social Studies during the afternoon, periods 4-6 at Jordan High. During the second semester of that school year, I became a full-time Social Studies teacher at Jordan High School which lasted until the year 2000.

What Disabilities? Narbonne High School: 1995

All the physical injuries and surgeries that I sustained while teaching in South Central, especially at Locke High School, do not even come close to the physical disabilities that my students at Narbonne were born with or suffered later. The three main disabilities that I remember were: the disability to write without mechanical help, to freely move without the help of a wheelchair, and the disability to talk without the help of a language specialist, who accompanied most of my students.

I was not qualified to teach these wonderful people at all. Yet, with the help of other specialists, I managed to do my best, and I learned so much from them. Their high achieving spirit was what amazed me the most. Their determination to overcome their disabilities and to learn deserves a Nobel Prize in itself. I always made them feel at ease and welcome, while at the same time, they tried even harder to let me know not to worry about their physical condition so that they could put me at ease and learn as much as possible from my class.

The history of my own childhood came to haunt and shame me. How could I have done so many bad things to my physically challenged neighbor Nimer? I made fun of his disabilities without knowing the harm that I was inflicting on him. Nimer was not in any kind of school. There were no educational or medical institutions available to treat his condition. He just roamed the streets aimlessly, singing and dancing.

At that time, people were not willing to admit that mental illness and depression could be found among the many families living in Nazareth. Admitting to such illness shamed the family and thus, they looked the other way and buried their heads in the sand.

While Nimer was a victim of such ignorant circumstances, the Los Angeles Unified School District provided our students with the best there is to help ensure that all handicapped students were given the same educational opportunities that other non-handicapped students had.

My tenure at Narbonne lasted only one semester. But the images of those students, their respect and manners in thanking all their teachers and the bus driver, were unbelievable. I still can hear their laughter and feel their energy, which reminded me of Nimer, day in and day out. The teachers and aides who teach them every day deserve all of our thanks and gratitude. They must be compensated for the excellent work they do.

During my last day at Narbonne, the students gave me a gift consisting of two, blue colored plastic calculators, no more than 2" x 4" in size, powered by solar panels. The cost of the calculator was written on the back of the cover: $2.99.

TOP: *the author with his teaching aide and students at Narbonne High School.*
BOTTOM: *the calculator the author's students presented to him.*

Believe it or not, I used them then, and later at Jordan and King Drew High Schools and at Cal State University. Today, almost 30 years later, I still use them while remembering those happy days teaching and being a part of these students' lives.

Jordan High School: 1995-2000

Jordan High School was also located in South Central, Los Angeles in the heart of the City of Watts. My classroom was located at the furthest corner of the campus surrounded by two, high chain-link fences. The classroom was in a bungalow with the number "20" fixed on the top of the classroom door. So, now I was no longer in a machine shop environment adjacent to a huge empty parking lot, but instead, surrounded by high fences. It felt semi-isolated as it was far away from the main center of the campus. On the other side of the fence were the remains of an abandoned battery factory that was emitting unhealthy and unseen fumes beneath its rubble. I always reminded my students not to venture close to the fences so that they will avoid the poisonous effects of touching battery acids as I was on many occasions exposed to while working at the gas station which required me to inspect the acid levels of cars' batteries.

The author in his classroom at Jordan High School (1996).

I taught mainly AP Economics and U.S. Government, World and U.S. History and Geography, among a few other topics. I also began teaching an early class between 7:00 a.m. and 7:45 a.m. before the regular school day began. This extra period was paid for by the District's Urban Classroom Teachers Program (UCTP). These classes were designed to give failing students a chance to complete and pass all sorts of Social Studies classes before graduation.

The teaching environment at Jordan High differed from that of Locke High. There were no humming machines, which meant less noise and much less injuries. With a few long hallways leading to other vocational classes, students were less disruptive when fleeing authority or running to their classes. I did not experience any further riots to disrupt my students' learning. Most of my students were more serious about their education, especially my AP and Honors classes.

While there may have been gangs, their presence was more elusive and much better supervised. Most of the fights took place at lunchtime or outside of campus. I did not hear of any major injuries due to gang violence or shootings. Yet, fighting was normal, as well as the presence of police, helicopters, fire trucks and ambulances. Most drug users gathered under the bleachers to sell, buy, or smoke whatever they had, especially marijuana.

Injured Again

One day during my conference period, I was asked to sub for a teacher who taught seniors only. I entered the classroom and faced the disruptive students who were out of control; a few others tried hard to give me some attention. They knew, beforehand, that their regular teacher was absent and that the front office had sent a sub to take care of their class. Subs always paid a very heavy price because they did not know the students and the students always took advantage of this to make his or her time subbing miserable.

I introduced myself, again and again, and repeatedly asked the students to calm down. Very few paid any attention to me. Among the students, who I did not know, was a very vocal girl whose voice was the loudest. I approached her and directly asked her to lower her voice. She motioned with her hand for me to go away. This upset me very much.

I went to my desk and found an official note packet that we teachers use to write on as a valid pass for students to be sent to the dean's office. I wrote a pass which I gave to her and told her to go immediately to the dean's office because of her disruptive behavior, but she refused to take the note.

So, I opened the classroom door and demanded that she leave the classroom. This time, she continued her refusal and began cussing me out with some very dirty and insulting words. Luckily, while I was holding the door, I saw the dean roaming the hallway, and I loudly called to him to come help me. When he entered the classroom, the student who I had written the note for agreed to leave. As she approached the door that I was still holding, she kicked it very hard against my injured knee where the two previous surgeries had taken place.

I felt an electric shock go through my body and I fell on the floor of the hallway near the classroom door. The dean called security immediately on his radio and escorted the student to the principal's office. Before he left, he helped me up and placed me in a chair where I sat until the pain subsided. At this point, the rest of the students fell silent, and many apologies ensued. The students told me that I was the first teacher to challenge her because she was the Student Body president and this made her untouchable. Of course, I did not know that then.

This incident was almost exactly what had happened to me at Locke High when I was punched in the eye by a student passing by. When that occurred, it was Mr. Anderson, the Wood Shop teacher, who came to my rescue, lifted me up and placed me in a chair. In such an environment, you never know when the next violent incident will take place.

I did what every teacher must do to restore order. Without order, no learning can take place. Additionally, their regular teacher did not leave me with a lesson plan to follow. So, there was nothing I could give them to keep them busy, which was required by our school policy. To the students, this demonstrated that their teacher did not care much about what I, their sub, did while they were out.

Once the class was over, I limped slowly back to my classroom to continue my teaching schedule. Neither the principal nor the teacher who I had subbed for called me to ask how I was doing or to let me know the outcome of the situation with the disruptive student.

The Smell of Marijuana

Since my teaching bungalow was located at the furthest corner of the campus, surrounded by high, chain-link fences with big cuts and gaps in them, it made for a good hiding place for students who wanted to smoke marijuana. This location made it easy for them to get in or out of campus. So, a few minutes after the start of Sixth Period, which was the last period of the day, ditching students regularly drifted toward my bungalow. I kept my classroom door closed to prevent any intruders or gang members from disrupting my students. It also prevented the smelly fumes from entering my classroom from the rubble of the old battery factory. But, a few of the back windows were kept open for ventilation and fresh air which were enough to transmit the unique smell of someone smoking marijuana.

When I smelled it, I always began laughing silently to myself as I tried to figure out where the students were smoking or hiding. Meanwhile, my Sixth Period students, who were ninth graders, would shake their heads and begin breathing deeply while smiling and some would say, "Thank God it is Sixth Period; go get them, Dr. B."

I would then open the door, very slowly, to see who they were so I could report them to the dean's office or call their parents. But every time I opened the door and looked out, those students would scatter quickly in all directions, straight toward the chain link fences and through those gaping holes. The repeated disruptions of such encounters made me ask the dean's office to give me a radio so I could quickly report these offenses once I smelled that energetic odor.

The dean loaned me a radio, and now, I looked like an administrator rather than a regular teacher. I placed the radio on top of my desk ready to be used. When I began smelling the students smoking, I would grab the radio and open the door for better communication with the dean's office. But by doing so, I exposed myself to those students and immediately would hear them alerting each other to flee.

But having a radio also began disrupting my lectures as the other school staff were also using it to communicate with each other and this annoyed the students a lot. I started thinking about returning the radio to the dean but before I could do that, my radio disappeared. Deep in my heart, I knew that one of my own students—a marijuana smoker who attended a different class—had stolen it. But I never had enough proof to turn him in; it was only a hunch.

I reasoned that the student who took the radio wanted me to stop using it. It reminded me of when I used to tie the chain link gaps with my students at Locke High, and those same students, who pretended to be helping me, would cut them back afterward. These were different students at a new location, yet they had the same needs and produced the same results. You never win in that situation.

Now I needed the radio back because I was responsible for it to the dean. What was I supposed to tell him? So, I began telling my students in every period that I was sorry for the continued radio disruptions, and that I was going to return it to the Dean in a few days. It did not take long before the radio suddenly reappeared on my desk, intact. I immediately gave it back to the dean and told him that my battle with the marijuana smokers was lost. I suggested that instead, supervision should be increased outside my bungalow after lunch. He promised to do so and when he did, the smoking decreased for the time being.

Later, when that unique smell penetrated my sixth period classroom again, I smiled and felt a deeper connection and love for those students, as well as those who I taught at Locke High. I'm not sure what it is. To my knowledge, most of the marijuana smokers rarely harmed anyone or were involved in any gang activities or violence. As a teacher, you can only do what is possible by keeping them aware of the harmful effects of smoking marijuana and other substances, avoiding gangs and dropping out of school.

The Blow-Back—The Unintended Honest Judgment

This incident took place while I was teaching my early UCTP class. After I took attendance and began my lesson agenda, I realized that one of my students had her head lowered on top of her desk and was sleeping. I called her to raise her head up but she did not respond. So, I came close to her and told her, "If you are sick, you could go home."

When she raised her head, I saw that her eyes and face were very red which indicated to me that she might have a high fever. Yet, she refused to leave the class and questioned how I knew that she had a fever. I told her to let me put my right hand against her forehead and then I would give her the answer. When she told me that it would be okay, I did exactly that. This told me, beyond a shadow of a doubt, that she had a high fever. This method is not a scientific method. I learned it from my mother who raised seven of us and that was the way she could tell if we had a fever or not. You could really feel the heat once you placed the back of your palm against the person's forehead.

I then told her that I would give her a pass to go to the dean's office so that they could give her legal permission to go home. But she again refused and insisted I give her the pass and let her go directly home. This was something that I did not have the authority to do and I told her this. I insisted that she go, instead, to the dean's office and gave her the official note to leave class, which she took and left.

A few days later, I heard the principal's voice on the intercom during my third AP Economics class saying, "Dr. Bisharat, report immediately to my office and bring your grade book and keys; a sub is on his way."

My students reacted immediately asking why I was being called to the office; some began crying openly. Before I could even gather what she wanted me to bring, there was a knock on the door. When I opened it, a security person told me that the principal had sent him to escort me to her office and that a sub was on his way to take over my class.

I was in complete shock. I followed him to the principal's office and was immediately asked to hand over my keys and my grade book. Then, I was to report to a Cluster Office in the City of Gardena. When I asked what was going on, she told me that she could not say anything more. She was just following the district's policies. She said that a lady at the Cluster Office would let me know more. She then gave me the address and the name of the lady to report to.

I went home broken-hearted. I was very stressed out and began explaining what had happened to my family. They stood firmly with me and told me not to worry if a disgruntled student or parent had accused me of something bad; the principal was just following the district's rules.

I began reviewing in my mind, as I laid in bed, possible scenarios of what could have caused this. The only incident that I could think of was the encounter with that student who was sick.

When I arrived at the Cluster Office, I was met by a very sweet and welcoming lady who invited me to sit down. She told me there was a report that I had taken advantage of a student by trying to kiss her on her face during my early UCTP class. This supposedly occurred when no one else was in class. Once I heard that, I relaxed and began explaining to her exactly what had taken place as there were at least six other students present at the time.

At the end of the earlier semester, this same student had failed my class. One day, she came into class very sad and crying. She asked me if there was anything she could do for me to change her grade. I told her that I am willing to let her complete all the missing assignments during the spring break once school reopens, with the condition that if she did all her work correctly, I would change her "F" grade to a "D" grade, only. She agreed to do that, and all went okay.

Yet, she tried to play the same game during the second semester when she ended up with another "F" as she did not submit any of the work that was required. When she asked me if she could get the same deal as I had given her during the first semester, I strongly refused. I felt that this student was trying to get revenge for my refusal to meet her demands. This incident, that never happened, was her way of justifying her anger toward me with an unfounded accusation.

I heard, later, from other teachers, that she finally admitted that she had made up this accusation. However, by accusing me of taking advantage of her, my teaching career at Jordan High School abruptly ended. I had to stay at the Cluster Office for three months, although I was fully paid for my time while the District's Attorney's Office conducted their investigation.

In the meantime, I was sent out as a substitute teacher, which to me, was quite a contradiction. If I was under investigation, why would the district still trust me to continue teaching? This signaled to me that they did not believe the student.

Meanwhile, the officer who took my report kept telling me that all my students missed me, especially the AP students, who were preparing for their college entrance exams. I felt terrible about this and very sad. When you take the students' regular teacher away for so long and send subs to replace them, the students pay the ultimate price for this lack of continuity and learning concentration. Their quality of learning declines, especially when the investigation occurred just a few weeks before the students' graduation.

When I was finally fully exonerated by the Attorney General's Office and asked to go back to Jordan High, I refused and demanded the Union and the District transfer me to another location. I deeply felt that my reputation at the school had been greatly damaged, and that the principal's handling of the entire situation was unprofessional. She should have arranged a meeting with me first, before launching an investigation on this student's say, so, as well as a meeting with the student's parents so we could have discussed this issue together.

I am sure that what happened to me has happened to other teachers. The only positive thing that I could advise to my students would be to stand up to teachers if they are, indeed, misbehaving. This is their right, but they must have accurate documentation and as much proof as possible. They must also remember that teachers have families to feed, and most are good people who have worked very hard to get their education and credentials. False accusations, like the one against me, can ruin someone's professional career or worse.

I strongly believe that all students have the right and the responsibility to be vigilant toward teachers who commit bad behavior, inside or outside the classroom. Whether this behavior involves lack of genuine teaching, unfair grading, racism, sexism, or other offenses, students must report such behavior to their administrative staff and discuss it with their parents. Standing firm against my teacher's unfair treatment of me when I was only four-years-old is ever present in my mind.

Throughout my teaching career, as well as in my social interactions, I have always encouraged those who were listening to defend and stand tall for what they believe in. Speaking the truth—especially to those who hold power—and defending one's dignity and integrity are values that I learned a long time ago in Nazareth. I believe that we teachers should inculcate it in our students as early as possible.

Alcohol Driven Attack: Gardena High School

While I was under investigation at the Cluster Office, which I named "the dungeon," I was asked on several occasions to substitute for other teachers, which I welcomed without any hesitation. In my mind, these requests to substitute at other schools were the best proof that the administration knew I was innocent. Otherwise, why would they ask me to substitute?

One Friday, I was asked to sub at Gardena High School. The day went well until Sixth Period when three young men approached the door of my classroom and demanded to enter. You could smell alcohol oozing out of their pores. They were very frank and told me that they wanted to beat up a student who was in my class. This was someone who belonged to another gang.

As they stood a few feet away from me, I ran to use the communication phone, but it failed to connect me to the dean's office, and I later learned that this system had not worked for a long time. So, I stood in the doorway and stretched my hands against the edges of the door to prevent them entering the class. Then, I called a student to run to the dean's office and ask for help.

The student took advantage of the situation, and instead of going to the dean's office, he ran home, as he was from the same gang that the potential victim was from. Now, I was left alone to deal with these three young men who meant business. They pushed me violently backward inside of the class and charged toward the student. As I fell, I tried to prevent another hit to my lower back by placing my two palms against my back, but I fell on the sharp edge of the teacher's desk.

I immediately began shouting at the rest of the students to leave the classroom and go ask for help from the closest teachers, or to run to the dean's office. The commotion alerted the school security person who was trying to prevent other students from fighting as they exited the school at the end of sixth period.

The security guard came running toward my class just as some other students alerted the gang members to run, which they did. The guard alerted the principal's office and ran after the intruders, trying to apprehend them. Then, the principal asked me to drop by his office to report the incident, but I declined, telling him that I would do so the next day as I needed to go home.

This new injury increased the previous damage to my lower back, and additionally, I hurt my right hand trying to prevent my fall. The injury to my palm required trigger finger surgery and additional x-rays and MRIs.

Later, I learned from the principal that those same three students had been sought after by the school administration for a long time after committing many other gang-related crimes. Accordingly, I just was an unlucky sub to take the brunt of it. The violence continued even when I was subbing and while I was under investigation.

I am sure that the intruders knew that the regular teacher was absent and that a sub was present that day so they chose to take advantage of the situation. But because of my role that day, they failed.

I think that the luckiest one was the student who I defended. If the intercom system had been working, all this could have been prevented, as I could have simply closed the door and waited for security to arrive. I did what I had to do under the circumstances and that was to protect my students. The fact that I got hurt while doing my job was a part of my teaching obligation, which included protecting my students at all costs. K-12 students are designated as children under the law while teachers are adults, and adults must protect children, period.

After subbing at Gardena High, the Cluster Office sent me on a long-term sub assignment to Eagle Rock High School's Social Studies department. Eagle Rock was far away from South Central, but not that far from gangs, drug use or violence—although the incidents were fewer. I did not see as much of a routine presence of police cars, fire trucks, ambulances, and helicopters hovering above the school grounds as I saw at Locke High and Jordan High Schools.

At Eagle Rock High, I was very content teaching there as it was the closest school to my home and much safer. I made it very clear to my administrators in charge that I would like to continue working there until I retire. The administrator refused and told me that the teacher who I was subbing for would be coming back - and that was that. By now, I was used to being hired and fired.

A few days later, the same administrator called me to say that he had arranged a job interview for me at King/Drew Magnet High School. There, I met the principal and his assistant. By the time I completed the interview, they offered me a full-time social studies teaching position beginning with the 2000 - 2001 school year, which I immediately accepted.

King/Drew Magnet High School of Medicine and Science: 2000-2010

King/Drew (K/D) was a newly built, very modern high school in South Central, L.A. The original school opened in 1982 in a bungalow building across from Martin Luther King Jr./Drew Medical Center, adjacent to Charles Drew University of Medicine and Science. In 1999, the dream of its first principal, Dr. Ernie Roy (who interviewed and hired me), which was to have a stand-alone independent high school named after both Dr. King and Dr. Drew, became a reality.

The high school shared its facilities with a fully independent police station. Martin Luther King Hospital was close by and a constant reminder of the night that I spent there with my former machine shop student, ten years earlier, while at Locke High School.

The campus had no sports fields for soccer, football, or baseball. Students were able to participate in basketball and tennis, as I recall. All the students were bussed in so there was no student parking at all. It was surrounded by major street intersections and active and thriving neighborhoods. A gas station and a Mexican restaurant were located across the street from the school.

The classrooms at King/Drew were extra modern and extremely clean. So were the bathrooms and the hallways. It also had an elevator to get you up to the fourth floor as well as a safe staircase. The front office was extremely organized, and the main entry was, indeed, beautiful. The first floor housed all the administration staff, including the principal, counseling staff and the dean's offices.

My classroom, # 410, was located on the fourth floor with a large window overlooking the main street intersections. There were plenty of storage cabinets for essential classroom needs, such as books and other supplies. Two whiteboards, a computer, a phone and a printer were on and around my desk, as well as an overhead projector. Students' chairs were clean and new. This classroom was the dream of every teacher. It was much better equipped than any of the classrooms that I had used before, including at U.C. Riverside and Cal State Universities.

During our first Social Studies department meeting, I was asked if I could replace the Department's former chair. I accepted and then became the Social Studies Department Chair. My main task, among others, was to attend meetings, keep the Department updated about rules and regulations, and deliver needed books and supplies to all the Social Studies teachers, according to their subject matters, which

I did on my own, before and after school hours, and during my lunch break.

I ran the Department for three years until another teacher took over. The District and the Union's guidelines required that all Department Chairs must serve for no more than three years. I ran it very fairly and democratically. Each teacher chose his or her own teaching subjects, according to seniority of years that they taught at the district. As teachers, we helped each other to have an overall teaching schedule that was fair to everyone.

K/D was a magnet school, which meant that all its students had to pass an entry exam before they were admitted. They also had to meet certain academic qualifications and were the top students at their elementary schools, worked hard and manifested other skills needed for passing K/D's gregarious college preparation classes. The students were asked to dress in the school's dress code, and teachers and the entire administrative staff were asked to dress professionally, as well. This collective effort of following the dress code raised mutual respect and morale among all the students, teachers, and administrators.

My life seemed routine here. I had a full teaching job at King Drew, year 'round, and a part-time teaching career at Cal State. I also was teaching the summer session at Carson High School. This routine teaching schedule allowed me to concentrate on my social life more and I became increasingly involved with all my kids' activities.

To further enhance the quality of education at K/D, I volunteered to participate in numerous educational organizations devoted to the betterment of South-Central student's educational achievements.

Disruptive Students Violence and Bomb Threats

Despite K/D's modern building and its reputation as a magnet school, it was not free of violence, at all. Most of the violence took the form of fist fights during nutrition and lunch breaks. The quad area, where students ate, was not large enough to accommodate free movement because it was too crowded with its hungry students. Security was very tight, as the principal, her administrative staff and other security personnel supervised students' activities. But it did not take much for a small and manageable disagreement among students to grow out of proportion and become a fist fight.

Still, with all of its amenities, gang violence and drug use lurked in the shadows of K/D's beautiful buildings. Most of the fights originated as an unending gang turf war outside the campus to be continued by students inside. On many occasions, these fights began in the quad area, then continued into the hallways as students were on their way to their classrooms. I witnessed many of those fights, and on many occasions, I would break them up while being pushed and pulled accordingly.

I took many direct and indirect hits, but none were very severe. As a result of this violence, I asked the principal to lend me a radio for hallway supervision which helped me communicate faster with the dean's office. With all the injuries and surgeries that I had already sustained, I soon stopped breaking up fights to prevent further damage to my body and especially to my lower back. My reliance on radio communications helped but never stopped those fights.

Once it became clear that I had a radio and was using it, students' fights decreased near my classroom and the hallway. But I started sensing that something would happen to my radio, sooner or later. Then, I began receiving early phone calls, upon answering, the caller hung up the phone. Students began knocking at my door and before I could open it, they would run faster than the speed of light. These activities repeatedly disrupted my teaching practices while I stopped to open the door, hoping to catch the students but to no avail.

As I had intuited, one day, my radio disappeared. I reported it to the Dean but did not get any response. No one returned it and I never found out who took it. I am sure it was a disgruntled student who wanted the hallway fights to continue without my interrupting them. Maybe the same students' patterns at Locke and Jordan followed me here, too. Students kept the gates open, marijuana smoking continued, there were hallways fights and disappearing radios.

The problems teachers encountered with our students at K/D were a little different than those at Locke and Jordan Highs. There were no ugly chain link fences anywhere and rather than smelling marijuana, I began smelling burning paper. Students would burn whatever was inside the bathroom bins to disrupt our teaching activities. Because it happened so often, the principal issued an order to lock all the bathroom doors and only issue keys to the teachers and administrative staff. So, students continually were asking for the keys from their teachers, who kept a record of their names, to guarantee the return of their keys. But even this new policy did not have much effect on the problem because many of the teachers did not keep track of their keys and the students who kept them soon made duplicates, rendering this policy ineffective.

Another dangerous disruption practice was the bomb threat. This threat happened in 2002, 2003 and 2007 when someone called the main office and claimed that a bomb was about to go off on campus. This threat demanded immediate action by all of the school's administrators and teachers to either lock their classroom doors, gather in the quad area, or release students quietly. The threats scared all of us, especially when parents rushed to pick up their children. No bomb ever exploded, there were never any injuries, and the safety efforts were thorough of all adults on campus, including the principal.

My Mother's Eyes Meets a Grandmother's Anguish

At King/Drew, teachers were required to meet with their students' parents twice a year. To do this, teachers stayed after school between 6:00 p.m. and 8:00 p.m. so that parents could meet with us after their workday was over.

When teaching stops, quietness descends on the campus

between 3:00 p.m. and 6:00 p.m. My classroom was too quiet and empty and so was my stomach so, I used to cross the street to an adjacent Mexican restaurant to purchase a very fresh and delicious Ceviche meal. I would get it to go and eat it in my classroom without any interruption by students, telephones or the main office.

After such a quiet meal, I used to take a short nap and then prepare my notebooks, students' grades, and the main assignments, including homework, midterms and finals. I also used to hand out classroom rules and conduct requirements, as well as the main teaching agenda to my students' parents so that they could discuss this with their children.

Soon after 6:00 p.m., parents began entering my classroom to inspect the many graphs, maps, wise quotations, and pictures that I had hung on the walls. A display of the books and videos we used were also displayed on my desk.

Once a handful of parents were present in my classroom, I would introduce myself and go over the grades of their children, discuss their progress, and give them some advice on how they could help them improve their grades and attendance.

At the end of the Back to School Night one year, an elderly lady stayed in my class until all other parents had left. She came very close to my desk, sat down next to me, and took my hands between hers. Then she looked straight into my eyes and told me how lucky her grandson was to have me as his teacher.

Looking back into her eyes, I began crying because I could see in her beautiful, deep almond-shaped black eyes which bore a strong similarity to that of my own mother's eyes. In the case of my mother's eyes, I saw her anguish at seeing me depart her home while wringing her hands. At the same time, I saw this grandmother wringing her hands as she anguished over her grandson's poor grades. I also saw her concern over keeping her grandson safe from gangs and drug use.

When she saw my reaction, she asked me why I was crying. When I told her about how I felt about my mother's pain at seeing me leave, she said, "Son, your mother will always be with you." Then, she began praying while wishing that her grandson would not follow the path of his father who had left him for a life of drug use and abuse.

After this, we held hands for a minute or so and then she told me to hand her her crutches so she could get up and go home, which I did after giving her a very emotional hug. As I watched her departing, her physical body looked exactly like my mother's. Who knew that one day I would meet a very similar African American mother in an inner-city school located in South-Central Los Angeles?

Regardless of being a grandmother, motherhood does not know any boundaries among all the women residing on Earth. It is the beating pulse of humanity everywhere you go. Her love, care, concerns, and anguish were all the hallmarks of motherhood. I still think of her eyes and those of my mother, most of the time.

A Grandfather's Wish

During the 2006 school year, a sad and anguished mother met with me to discuss her son's learning progress. She knew that her son's grades in my history class were poor and could prevent him from walking on graduation day. She asked me if she could drop him off to school early before the regular school day would start so he could complete his missing assignments in the hope of earning a passing grade. I agreed to this arrangement and explained that I already volunteered to teach all my students in need of improving their grades between 7:00 and 7:45 in the morning. She was so thankful she sent me a card.

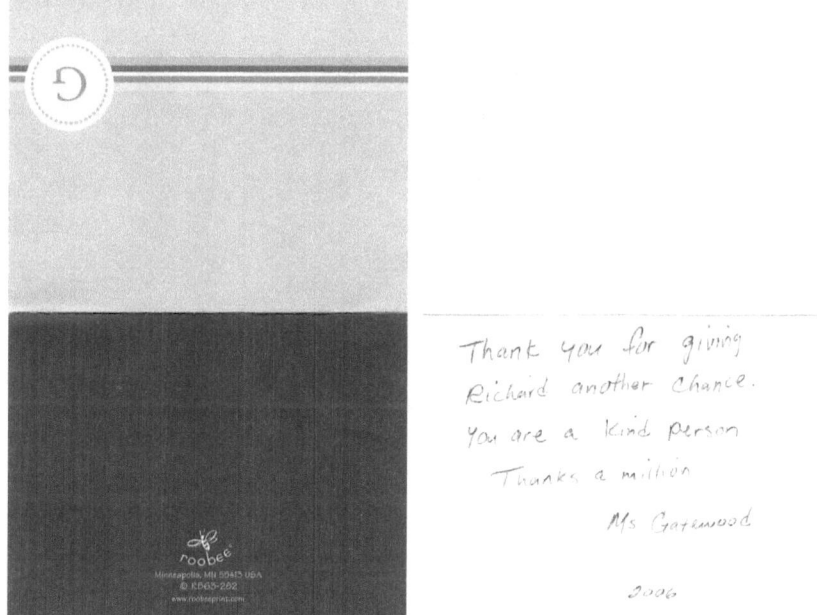

The card the author received from his student's mother after he allowed her son to attend morning class sessions.

Her son attended these morning sessions and received a passing grade. He attended graduation. After the ceremony, I received from his mother another card thanking me for helping her son and noting that his grandfather was able to see him walk the stage before his blindness set in.

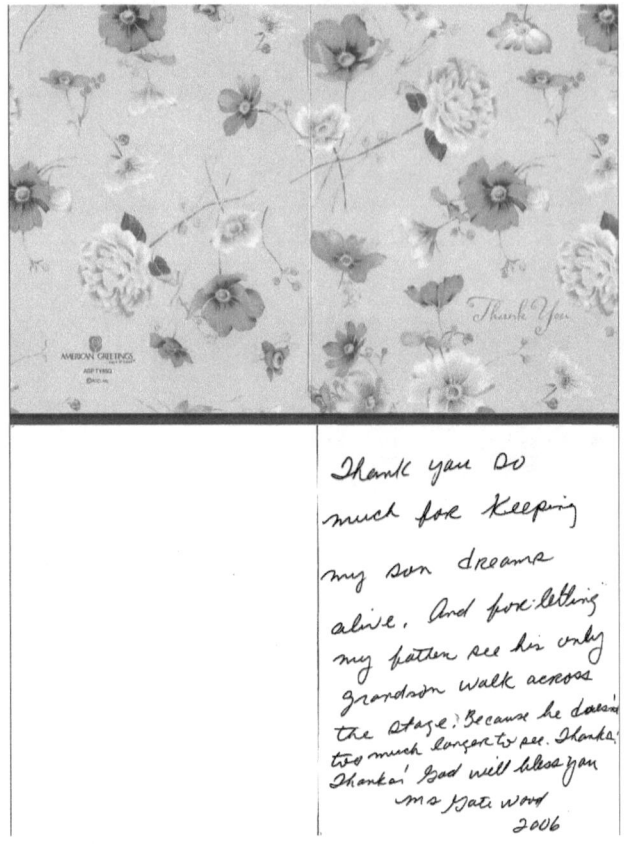

The card the author received from his student's mother after he successfully passed my class and attend graduation.

Reading the card was, on the one hand, very painful, because all I wanted was for my own parents to watch my walk the stage while receiving my Ph.D. On the other hand, I was so happy his grandfather and mother were able to be part of this momentous day.

I will never know whether my parents regretted not being in attending at my graduations—but I do know what it is like now to have seen my children and grandchildren achieve these accomplishments, and I know that my parents were proud of me.

Between the preceding story of the grandmother's anguish and this grandfather's wish, as well as my own parents' love for me and mine for my children and grandchildren, I know that our humanity does not know any limits: all of these people, separated by time and place and culture, and yet we all experience the same love and pride. What a kismet, and a miracle.

Back Injury and Rotator Cuff Surgery

One day, while subbing for another teacher, I was injured while trying to sit in the teacher's chair. His chair was different from mine in that it had five, rolling legs for better stability. As I tried to sit down, the heel of my shoe kicked one of the legs, moving the chair away from me. Without realizing what happened, I lowered my body into the space that had been the chair. All of the sudden, I fell on my lower back and buttocks resulting in a badly bruised and fractured coccyx that was quite painful and took a long time to heal.

I had to take a week off but then I returned to try to teach, however, the pain persisted for several more months. The permanent teacher, who I had been subbing for, told me that a few of the students had attempted to roll the chair away from its position as a joke. So, he had changed the location of his desk to sandwich the chair between the wall and his desk at the far corner of the classroom. It was at his moment that I began questioning whether I kicked the chair or was it an unseen student who did it for a subbing teacher?

My back injury was followed by another one, a month later. One early morning, we had a staff meeting. I entered the elevator with the other teachers, including the principal. There were no signs alerting us that the floors had just been cleaned and waxed.

As I was the first to leave the elevator at the fourth floor, I suddenly slipped and fell backward on the very wet, slippery, waxy, and shining linoleum floor. Trying to protect myself from further injury, I placed my right hand behind my back while holding onto my briefcase with my left hand. As I fell, my briefcase flew away and my right hand became sandwiched between the hard floor and my lower back.

Suddenly, I felt severe shoulder pain while the other teachers were helping me up. The result of this fall was several doctor's visits, physical therapy, and pain. I could no longer sleep on my right side, and I needed to insert my right hand into a soft cloth that hung from my neck to protect it as I was sleeping. Soon, the doctor recommended rotator cuff surgery, which he performed a few weeks later. To this day, my right hand still feels the pain and its functionality and strength never has been the same.

The Heartbreak of Final Grades

Despite many more physical injuries, I continued teaching until the beginning of the 2010 school year when my teaching career came to a sudden end. This unfortunate end came because of the policy that I have always followed in sharing my students' final grades. I did this to avoid any discrepancy between the recorded grades in the computer and the handwritten ones recorded in my grade book.

In fact, my students looked forward to having their teachers share their potential final grades with them before the main office mailed them to their families. By knowing the results ahead of time, students could try to improve their grades before it was too late and the grades were sent to their parents. My students hoped that they could convince their teachers to allow them to complete their unfinished assignments to change the outcome of their grades.

No one forced me to go through this task that required exerting a lot of emotional and stressful pressure. I did it because I loved my students and wanted them to know that I was a very fair and caring teacher and gave them the opportunity to improve their overall grades. This allowed them a much better chance of avoiding their families' retributions as well as advancing their credentials for being admitted to the colleges and universities of their choice. I was always looking ahead on behalf of my students.

Year after year, I never had any disputes with my students whose grades were B's and A's. They always thanked me and promised to do even better. Yet, those with C's, D's or F's gave me a lot of problems which caused my blood pressure to go up. They would always insist that I failed to record some of their grades but could never show any proof of this; sometimes they said that I did not give them the chance to complete their missing assignments.

The most vocal disruptors were my AP students who expected a good passing grade regardless of their poor attendance and missing assignments, including midterms and finals, and their failing grades. Even when I warned them of their poor grades and wrote their names on the board with their missing assignments to offer them enough time to complete their work, many of them failed to do so, and yet, expected a passing grade.

When I showed the students who had bad grades how many of their fellow students had passed with A's and B's, they always attributed such grades to their perfect attendance, due to their parents dropping them off on time at school. According to them, this parental care was not provided by their parents, and it affected their poor performance, even though the school provided bus services to and from campus.

When these students were unable to persuade me to provide them with what they wanted, their responses included violent disruptions with filthy cursing, racial epithets (calling me "white boy"), derogatory comments while calling me by my last name, and throwing objects at me (especially pens, pencils, erasers, crumbled papers, and rulers).

Most of those acts ended when I began calling the dean's office, warning them that I would contact their parents, or when I sent them with an official pass to the dean's office for punishment. Sometimes, students refused to take my signed notes to the Dean; instead, they would rush out of my classroom cursing and threatening me while slamming the classroom door violently behind them.

To solve this problem once for all, I informed my disgruntled students to come and see me, either before class or during nutrition and lunch to discuss their grades again. Of course, few showed up. Why should they give up extra sleep, nutrition, or lunch?

I Will Burn You Alive in Your Car—The Straw That Broke the Camel's Back

It was during one of those periods when a student who was waiting in line with many others to look over her grades caused my career as a teacher to come to an end. This female student had failed my class. When she found out that she would be getting a failing grade, she left her place in line and rushed toward me trying to punch me in the face. I could see her fist coming toward my face when her friend suddenly pulled her back. My heart began pounding. I stood up and gave her a note to go immediately to the dean's office. With the note in her hand, she turned toward me and said, "Dr. B., I know where you park your car, and I will burn you alive in it." Then she ditched my class.

From the way she said it and the way she acted, I knew that she meant business. Her knowing where I parked my car was a real threat. It was, at this moment, when the previous thirty years of violence came back to haunt me. Suddenly, I had a panic attack; I could not breathe.

I called the front office and demanded they provide a sub for me right away. When that sub arrived, I gathered all my belongings and went straight home, never to return again. In that moment, I had an awakening which recalled all the violence that I had sustained and buried for so long in the back of my mind. The trauma of these collective experiences came back in full in that moment, overwhelming me.

Despite all my injuries and surgeries, I had always given my students first priority before my own safety. All the doctors who treated me, especially the psychologist, recommended that I give up teaching in these violent environments. And I did try to persuade the district to give me administrative duties or assign me to a safer teaching location, but it never happened. Even the superintendent, who I met, told me that I only suffered from a "psychological illness," not a physical one, and recommended that I return to King/Drew.

There was no compassion for me from any of the school

administrators, even after my lengthy career teaching in the public schools. No one cared about what I had gone through, no one said "thank you for your service."

After all my efforts to change my situation failed and no accommodation was provided to me, I decided to retire and applied for my pension at the beginning of 2010. The dirty politics practiced in education made me sick, including the lack of union leadership in standing tall with their unionized workers in the face of the district's hegemony over teachers' rights and dignity. I could easily see that the union's leadership involvement was just a show, no more and no less.

True Love

Despite my circumstances when I left teaching, King/Drew was full of many happy memories. The most memorable one was the deafening noise I would hear in the hallways from students, which reminded me of the Christmas church bells. I vividly remember the voices of happy, screaming students calling "Dr. B, Dr. B." at the top of their lungs, while running toward me to give me a big hug and to show me their new Christmas gifts. Those were my happiest days of teaching at K/D.

My students dressed so beautifully. The girls with their new purses, shoes, jeans, sweaters, pants, bracelets, rings, and hairdos. The boys were extremely proud of their sportswear, especially their expensive Air Jordan basketball shoes. They also liked to show off their T-shirts with their favorite team's names, players and numbers clearly displayed on the back; gold rings and necklaces; and jeans and watches.

I saw their generosity in the way they shared their food, drinks, and gum with each other on many occasions. This sharing was not conditional at all. Students shared because they wanted to do something that made them happy and proud. This is something that we can all learn from them.

But what broke my heart was when the school adopted a "no

hugging" policy due to many complaints from teachers, students, and parents that this hugging led to unwanted kissing, which is understandable. Yet, when students saw me after a long Christmas or Spring break and wanted to show me their affection and love by hugging me, I would have to place my hands in my pockets or behind my back to prevent me from hugging them back.

This would cause my students to say, "Dr. B, don't you love me anymore?" or "Is there something wrong with me?"

Such comments were like knives in my heart, but all I could do was explain to them about this new policy. I wonder how many of them took it the wrong way and did not believe me.

There was one memory which stands out from all the rest, and it really broke all bounds of love. On a few occasions, I was sad or angry at some of my students who took their education for granted. They also displayed a total lack of appreciation to their parents' love and hard work; no gratitude to their teachers and administrators; no thanks for their free education, including books and other educational supplies; and a lack of respect for their fellow students who wanted to learn and listen to their teachers.

When I encountered this, I would beg them to take advantage of all that they had been given, and then compare their privileged situation with my own, when I was growing up in Palestine, as well as here, in the United States when I was a student just like them. With the sudden rush of those memories, sometimes I would stutter a little, then my eyes would tear up as I was speaking to them. I just wanted them to know that they did not have to go through what I had gone through; that they should be grateful for what they had.

Suddenly, a few students, both boys and girls, would stand up and walk toward me to comfort me. They would place their hands on my shoulders and say, "Oh, Dr. B., stop crying and getting angry at us. We do not want you to have a nervous breakdown or a heart attack. We love you and you have a family to take care of. We are still young." Here I was, worrying about their future while they were worrying about my health and my family.

This was a stunning example of the heartbeat of South Central, Los Angeles' students. Despite all of the socioeconomic conditions that these students faced, they were the bedrock, the shining lights, and the future of South Central, Los Angeles and East Los Angeles. I saw them as diamonds in the rough.

I told all my students at Cal State, Los Angeles and my family and friends about this experience. I was proud of the love and care those students showed me because of inspiring them to be their best and I am indebted to them.

I do not know where they are now. All I can say is that I truly loved and respected them during the good, the bad and the ugly times that I was with them, and I will take all of my memories with them to my grave.

The Birth of a New Teacher

When I began teaching at King/Drew Magnet High School during the 2000 school year, my youngest daughter, Paola, was ten years old. When she began attending elementary school, I would take Paola with me to King/Drew whenever she had days off from school. Those days that she spent with me were precious.

The author with Paola (1991).

I would wake her up early to avoid the heavy Los Angeles morning traffic. On our way, I would always listen to National Public Radio (NPR) news. We would have discussions about what we had just heard, followed by many intriguing questions that only a ten-year-old Southern California girl could think of.

I remember seeing the changes in her face the minute we arrived on campus. There was excitement and eagerness to soak it all in. I could tell, early on, that she was looking forward to navigating the school campus.

When we would take these trips together, we had a certain routine. We would check-in at the front office and then take the elevator and head to my classroom on the fourth floor. I would make us breakfast: typically, either a Labneh (which looks and tastes like cream cheese) sandwich or ham, mortadella and cheese with cucumbers and tomatoes on the side. We would eat our meal together while I read the newspaper. Meanwhile, Paola would be straightening up my messy desk, wandering around the classroom, and admiring student work and posters on the wall.

Before the first bell rang, we would take our respective positions with me at the front door greeting students as they entered the room and Paola, sitting at my desk. The minute students saw Paola, they would excitedly walk over to her to ask her questions. Often, they would tease her by saying, "How do you understand your dad? He has such a heavy accent. Half the time, we nod and pretend to understand what he is saying, but we love him so much."

It was amazing to see my young daughter interacting with my students. Paola had a natural way of connecting with anyone she met, which reminded me a lot of myself at that age. My students were so sweet to her and genuinely loved her. They gave her the nickname "Baby B.," which to this day she still likes a lot, as a complement to calling me "Dr. B."

While I was teaching, Paola would work on her homework, listen to my lectures, and watch how my students responded to me and their peers. What we did not know then was that she was getting a firsthand lesson on what it takes to be a teacher and the magic that can happen in the classroom. At times, she would even participate in the class discussions and interact with my students. It was a beautiful synergy of students being involved with my "teacher to be."

At lunch time, we would always eat in the cafeteria. It was fun showing her around campus and introducing her to my other colleagues. I usually did not eat in the cafeteria, so it was a nice experience to see what the campus was like during that time.

As she became older and continued attending work with me, the attention she received from boys became more apparent. This was made clear when a certain student took a great liking to her. I can't remember his name, but I do remember him asking me if he could take her as his date to the prom. Of course, she was too young for that, and I told him so, declining his offer.

When her visits became rare, my students—especially the girls, would ask about her and remind me of her care and love for them and the promise she made to one day become a teacher. Their favorite way of teasing me was to say, "Dr. B., you are really her father; now we believe you," which would make me laugh.

Those days spent with her would be the foundation for her future career as an educator. She made this decision, early on, to pursue a career in teaching and spent many days, while in high school, tutoring students at local elementary schools.

After her high school graduation, Paola attended Cal State University, Channel Islands for its excellent teaching credentialing program. Her time spent at CSUCI was incredible. She flourished in her academics and took on a job as a Writing Tutor on campus. She worked extremely hard, taking extra classes each semester and during the summer so that she could graduate early and jump straight into the credentialed Teaching Program.

After completing both her Bachelor of Arts Degree in English Education and earning her Teaching Credential, she moved back in with us and began looking for a teaching position. Soon, she was granted a full, tenured teaching position at Arcadia High School, a prestigious school in our community, known for its high-caliber curriculum and hard-working students.

She began her teaching career at Arcadia High School and worked there for two years before deciding to pursue a master's degree in education back at CSUCI. I was extremely impressed with her commitment to both work and school. Paola would work all day then drive from Arcadia to Camarillo, which is a solid 66 mile one-way. She did this 120-mile round trip, two to three times a week.

During working and going to school, she became engaged to an incredible man, Karim, who I love dearly. So, in her final year in the program she was working full-time, in school part-time, and planning a wedding. And on top of that, she became the valedictorian of her graduating class and was chosen to speak on behalf of the Education Program at her graduation. To say I was proud is an understatement.

Paola continues to teach English at AHS. She has taught all grade levels on top of various extracurricular classes and activities. She has told me on various occasions that she attributes much of her passion for teaching to my former students. They taught her valuable lessons and motivated her to bring awareness to the injustices seen and experienced in various inner-city communities. The compassion and spirit of the African-American and Latino students that she witnessed first-hand at King/Drew had a very humbling impact on her. She always seeks to have pertinent discussions on race relations in her classroom and often shares the stories of my experience teaching and the amazing stories of my students.

As a proud father and a humble inner-city teacher, I strongly believe that Paola would never have chosen the teaching field if it was not for her meeting my inner-city students at King/Drew. The fact that they called her "Baby B," still brings vivid and happy memories to her heart.

Now, as a married young lady, she prefers to be called "Mrs. B." when on campus. What destiny, what an amazing Kismet. Ridah-Al-wali-Dain is again on full display. What began as advice from my mother to attend vocational school has led to an uncharted journey and while I know how it began, I never know how it will end.

Workshops and Seminars

During the last twenty years of my full-time social studies teaching career, I have attended on my own, by invitation, or by request from my principals, many workshops and conferences in and outside California. The following are the most memorable and productive workshops and seminars.

Denver School District

During the 1997 school year at Jordan High School, my principal, Mrs. McMahon, had asked me to represent Jordan High School at Denver Unified School District in recognition of my voluntary work with an educational organization known as "Cross Country Educational Reform Organization." This organization was geared toward serving and enhancing the educational curricula of South-Central public schools.

I was among many other high school teachers who attended. The building where all the workshops and seminars took place was very modern with new tables and chairs. I remember that all those tables were covered by fruit candies donated by a candy factory in Denver. Those candies happened to be my favorite and I consumed a lot and took some to my hotel room.

When we visited West High School, most of its attending teachers and administrators complained about the same problems that most inner-city school districts around the nation are facing: mainly students' violence, drug use, drop outs, gang violence, truancy and lack of respect to the teachers and school property, among other negative behaviors.

Most of those seminars and workshops dealt with these problems as teachers, administrators and students shared their views on the root causes and possible ways to eradicate them. They also complained about the lack of needed school funding, a lack of proper communications between the arrogant District administrators and the school's administrative staff, which according to them, always resulted in a waste of energy and improper funding by the district.

Downtown Seattle was very beautiful, and I enjoyed eating meals there with other teachers at a variety of popular restaurants.

The most memorable one was a restaurant called The Fort. It was built a long time ago with red bricks on indigenous Native American land, as I was told.

Inside the restaurant was a wood-burning barbecue fireplace, which served as the center of activity and was very beautiful. When my turn came to order, the cook asked me if I preferred bison, deer, moose, or rabbit barbecued steak. This was the first time that someone mentioned bison, moose, deer, or rabbit meat to me.

I thought about it for a minute and then said, "Chicken please. Any barbecued chicken will do."

The customers behind me began laughing while saying: "You come to the Fort and order chicken? What is wrong with you?"

I did not listen to them. What I wanted was barbecued chicken. To this day, I still regret that I did not order a bison hamburger.

At midnight, when the bus came to pick us up, a group of about five men started begging the driver to take them with us to the bus station in downtown Seattle. They were drunk and had missed their connection with their tour bus. So, we all said, "Okay" and these five men from Holland entertained us by singing songs while most of us slept. They were finally dropped off, never to be seen again.

I brought with me the documents, research papers, brochures, and other teaching materials and shared it with K/D teachers and its administrative staff. In short, most of the problems discussed could easily be found throughout our country's large school systems.

Georgetown University

After my teaching tenure at Jordan High School, I became a newly arrived Social Studies teacher at King/Drew Magnet High School. My new principal, Mrs. Woods asked me to attend Gillette Economics for Leaders, a six-day program at Georgetown University, which began on June 28, 2003, and ended on July 5, 2003.

The seminars and workshops at Georgetown University were attended by many high school teachers from around the United

States representing their districts. The number of seminars and workshops were immense, informative, and highly valuable in teaching the field of economics to our high school students.

Although I had already taught many economic classes at Jordan and King Drew high schools, in addition to integrating economics in my political science classes at Cal State University, I learned a lot. And I met many high-ranking economic leaders and those representing local and international businesses, as well.

As a group of teachers, we visited downtown Washington, D.C. and gazed at its national monuments. We also visited the Kennedy Center and celebrated the 4th of July at the national memorial park.

Georgetown University's red brick buildings were very beautiful, but the student's dorms were awful. For the entire six nights that I was there, I slept on a wooden bed covered by a very thin mattress. Turning in bed was painful, especially for my lower back and right knee. The blanket was thin, and I could have used an extra blanket as I could feel the cold temperatures of Washington, D.C.

On my return, my wife did not even recognize me when I entered the house. She told me that I had doubled in size and demanded that I lose weight as soon as possible. Georgetown University served us breakfast, followed an hour and a half later with baskets full of fruits, sandwiches, soda and sweets. After lunch the same routine happened again. For dinner I ate at a variety of restaurants and did not pay much attention to the number of calories that I consumed.

Once you add up the above, now you know why I gained at least ten pounds. It took me at least a year to lose those pounds but I needed to lose much more.

The State Department

On June 28, 2005, my amazing and caring principal Mrs. Wood asked me again to represent King/Drew at the World Affairs Council Workshop on Education. This one-week workshop was one of the most memorable workshops that I attended.

As with the other two workshops, this one was also attended by many other teachers from many other school districts around the nation. In addition to many lectures by well-known economists, corporate executives, and economic professors, the main focal point was to introduce us to the evolution of the European Economic Union, popularly known as the EU.

We visited the main E.U. building where many of our lectures and seminars took place. Most, if not all the above lectures and seminars, were structured around the usefulness of such a union in its pursuit of a better European economic integration following the collapse of the Soviet Union at the beginning of 2000.

As a Political Science student, I could sense at the time that this Union was another strategic decision that the United States supported to encircle the collapsing Soviet empire. The move was to make its weak economy dependent on the might of the United States and its Western allies. This Union was protected by the North Atlantic Treaty Organization, popularly known as NATO, which is the military side of such a Union and was to be dismantled as we promised the, then, Soviet leaders.

Many of the speakers alluded to my hunch but not directly. Nevertheless, I gained a lot of insight and it was worth it.

We also visited different foreign embassies and met many of their officials. The two, most memorable embassy visits, for me, were the Irish and the Turkish Embassies. At the Irish Embassy, we met the assistant to the ambassador. She was dressed elegantly in a green skirt and scarf. Her eyes were green, too, as I recall. The meeting room was in an old building covered with a lot of brown-paneled wood. She offered us iced tea, lemon juice and some pastry. She was very polite, smart, and diplomatic. After a brief question and answer session, we thanked her and left.

The Turkish embassy, on the other hand, was a newly built building with a statue of the Modern Turkish Leader, Ataturk, standing by the main entrance. We were greeted by another ranking embassy diplomat, but the ambassador was not there to see us. The diplomat greeted us very warmly and insisted that we join the rest of the embassy staff for lunch. And what a lunch it was: coffee, sweets, fruit, juice, chicken and beef shish-kabob, rice, and other foods which were laid out on a long table located at the far side of the hallway. Afterward, they gave us a short history of modern Turkey and its desire to join the European Union. Then, we thanked them for their hospitality and generosity before leaving.

Meeting Secretary of State, Madam Condoleezza Rice

One of the most memorable incidents I experienced on this trip occurred during our visit to the State Department, where we were invited by our guide to have lunch on the fourth floor of the building. While I was eating lunch there, I saw Secretary of State Madam Condoleezza Rice walking in the hallway in front of our dining room. Right away, I hurried to the table where our State Department guide was sitting and asked her to invite Madam Secretary to meet us. She was completely taken aback because no one in the room, including her, paid any attention to the dignitaries.

So, she told me that she would try her best. A few minutes later, she called me over and told me that Madam Rice would be accepting our invitation to meet with all of us teachers. Shortly after, the Madam Secretary entered the room accompanied by her bodyguards and stood at the front door, thanking us for what we were doing as teachers. She then told us that her parents were also high school teachers.

As she turned to leave the room, I stood up and asked her if she could take a picture with us. She agreed to do so and approached our table. I then placed my hand on her shoulder and told her that I was responsible for all this trouble as I had spotted her walking in the hallway. She thanked me and told me that it was great for her to be among us before leaving to attend to her official duties.

The author (right) wit Former U.S. Secretary of State Condoleeza Rice (center).

Despite her accommodation to us, I was not aware at that time about her previous stance in supporting the invasion of Iraq (there were obviously others in the Bush Administration who pushed for it, but at least at that time, she seemed distanced from the decision-making process). It was only later, when investigations and reporting bore witness to her support of the invasion, that I realized her culpability in the Bush Administration's decision to invade Iraq. Being a part of the lies and deceptions that the Bush administration invented to destroy Iraq decreased my respect for her, and her shameful stance towards the Palestinian tragedy saddened me even more. But at that time, she was the Secretary of State, and so I thanked her for being with us teachers and for allowing us to take pictures with her.

Family Reunion

My adventures at the State Department building did not stop with Madam Secretary. When our guide realized that the name written on my badge was "Bisharat," she immediately realized that she had seen this name before. She called me to her front desk and asked, "Do you know a man by the name of Henry Bisharat?"

I said, "Yes, he is the son of my first cousin."

Then I asked her if I could see him. She said, "Yes" and sent an aide to his office asking him to report to her. She happened to be his Administrator in Charge. What a small world!

A few minutes later, Henry entered the room confused and with a fearful look on his face as if he had done something wrong. When he approached her desk, she asked him to look around the dining tables. When he recognized me, he came running over and hugged me tightly. What a moment! Two cousins meeting at the United States' State Department building. He then thanked her, and I could see his relief on his face.

The author with his cousin Henry at the U.S. State Department.

That same day, he invited me to have dinner with him, which I accepted. We discussed how we ended up at the State Department building that day, our social lives, and our future careers, as well as how both of us had ended up studying Political Science, despite our age difference (I was much older than him). The irony was not lost on either of us: we had both dedicated our careers to public service in a country where its government actively worked to undermine the establishment of the state from which we came. Indeed, I taught students the virtues of this government, while Henry worked to advance its interests abroad. What a tragic kismet.

After dinner and after our discussions, he gave me a brief tour of the surrounding area and then dropped me off at the University's campus. We hugged each other again and both left for our destinations. A few years later, we met again and ate Italian food at my house which my Italian wife prepared for him. I am very proud of him.

Volunteering—Neighborhood's Educational Organizations

During my teaching years at Jordan and King/Drew High Schools, I was asked by the principals to get involved with diverse educational organizations whose main purpose was to enhance and strengthen the educational experience for all the students residing in South Central and East Los Angeles' neighborhoods. (I do not remember attending such meetings while teaching at Locke High School.) As a result, I began volunteering during the last few years of teaching at Jordan High School and then accelerated my involvement while at King/Drew Magnet High School.

Some of those meetings took place at the homes of those who began these organizations, some were held in the late afternoon in adult classrooms on LAUSD campuses, and some, at City civic buildings.

The participants were organizers, parents, teachers, students, and occasionally civic leaders. The energy of the debates was always present and our concerns about our South-Central students were central to all our efforts.

I was not privy to the outcome of such endeavors, but I was, and still am, very proud and very thankful to all those concerned parents, teachers, and students. The passion and compassion with which they presented their points of view was very remarkable indeed.

I learned a lot from them, and I hope that they also learned something from me, especially my experiences teaching university and college students. Most of them were looking forward to seeing their neighbors' kids attend colleges and universities. After all this, hope was at the center of their organizations' mission.

Here are some of the names of those organizations that I was involved with: 1- LA Pass, 2 - Workforce LA, 3 - The Achievement Council, 4 - Watts/Century Latino Organization (WCLO) and Parents and Students Organized (PASO), 5 - Cross Country, 6- Facing History and Ourselves. All of them thanked me and presented me with Certificates of Appreciation.

The founding father of Watts/Century Latino Organization, Mr. Arturo Ybarra passed away very recently. His legacy with the organization was recognized in his obituary in Los Angeles Times' August 18, 2023, column. When I saw his face, I immediately recognized him and my memories of him popped up. What a man.

Los Angeles Trade Technical College (LATTC)—1983-1990

The teaching machine shop technology at LATTC was totally different from that of Locke. All my students were adults and took their training very seriously in the hopes of finding well-paid jobs as soon as possible.

The machine shop, itself, was at least five times bigger than that of Locke High School. The amount and variety of machines were unbelievable to me. I had never seen so many machines, including the ones at Masoneilan Industries or back home at both ORT or Don Bosco's.

Undated photo of the author with his students at Los Angeles Trade Technical College.

Here I was to oversee all those machines while instructing my adult students on how safely to operate them. The excellent high school vocational training at ORT and Don Bosco paid me back its dividends. Yet, without listening to my mother's advice, none of this could have materialized. Ridah-al-Wale-Dain was at its full display.

Among the many memorable and teachable experiences, two are still cherished in my memories:

WESTECH

To keep my students updated with the latest machining technology, I used to accompany them with other students attending LATTC's Industrial Department to the Los Angeles Exhibition Center. There, we watched, in real time, the wonders of machining technologies presented by "Western Technologies," better known as WESTECH.

Unlike all the machines that I have manually operated during all those years, this new technology was using Computer Numerically Controlled Machines, for short CNC. This technology was computer-controlled rather than a manually driven machining operation. Seeing all this opened the eyes and ears of my students to the possibilities of excellent job offers.

I have always believed after teaching, seeing, and using such technology that whoever controlled this technology would, without any doubt, control the future of human progress. Additionally, this gathering helped most of the Industrial Department's students get to know each other as well as, we, teachers. We all looked forward to next year because without such an exhibition, students and teachers alike could have rarely met. I repeated this visit four years in a row and every year, the CNC technology became more advanced and more productive.

A Strip-Tease Bar:

By the end of 1989, I had decided to quit this beautiful part-time job due to exhaustive work and family obligations. As a thank you gesture, my students invited me to a late dinner with them. The man in charge at that time was the eldest student in my class and was at least twenty years older than me. He insisted that I leave my car parked at the college so we could all stay together in a van that they had rented.

After I agreed, he drove the van while I sat with the rest of the students, not paying attention to where he was driving me, however, the rest knew exactly where he was heading. When he stopped and we all got out, the place he had taken me to looked scary, unmarked, and dark. As we entered this so-called restaurant, I could see dancing women on top of a stage with a long and shiny steel pipe attached at the bottom of the stage that ended at the ceiling. The women were nearly naked while performing all kinds of exotic and sexy drills. Many in the audience placed money under their so-called underwear while laughing, drinking, and singing.

I just could not believe what I was seeing. Meanwhile, my students were laughing their hearts out. I had never ever entered such places nor was I entertained by this type of thing. What surprised me the most was that they had arranged for a belly dancer to perform for me who asked for me by name while gesturing for me to tip her in her underwear. I was ashamed to be there watching this with my students. Yet, I managed to stay for as long as I was able to until the leader of the bunch realized that I had to go home.

He then drove us back to the parking lot. He told me that, as the representative of my students, they often did this as a final thank you and as a gesture of love and respect to me as their machine shop teacher. Ridah-Al- Wale-Dain had struck again, albeit in a different way, for I know that my mother would never approve of such a gesture.

California State University, Los Angeles: 1985-2010

I have called CSULA my second home for personal and sentimental reasons. It was where I completed my B.A. degree; got to know foreign students from many countries who also were able to enter the United States on Foreign Student Visa like mine; met my wife; completed my dissertation research and writing at its John F. Kennedy Library North, began teaching at its Department of Political Science in the same classrooms that I had sat as a student, and especially, in the same classroom where my wife and I met when we were students; and had the privilege of being a colleague of many of its outstanding and caring faculty members and staff.

Twenty-five years of teaching and working in the same place is, by its implication, a home away from home. You just become part of its environment and a driver of its destiny.

My students came from all corners of this globe. They all were there by choice and by paying their tuition. Doing so, most students were more serious about their learning and more respectable toward their professors. The difference in ages was astonishing; it ranged from nineteen years to seventy years of age. Women, on many occasions, outnumbered the men taking my classes, which was a sign of increasing women empowerment and taking an equal place in society with their fellow men.

The author in the office of his colleague, Dr. Urquidi, at Cal State Los Angeles (January 1997).

Most of my classes were located on the third and fourth floors in the largest hall on campus. It was named after our civil rights leader, Martin Luther King. Thus, it popularly became known as "King Hall."

During all those years, many teachable events took place. Four of them remain with me to this day, thus I would like to share them with you.

September 11, 2001

The 2001 Spring quarter began at Cal State on September 17th, six days after the tragedy of 9/11. A week or so after 9/11, a store owner of a Middle Eastern grocery store was shot and killed barely a mile or so from my home at the intersection of Las Tunas Boulevard and Rosemead Boulevard in Temple City. I had frequently shopped at that store and knew the owner, himself.

He was an Egyptian citizen belonging to the Coptic Egyptian

Church. This killing was, as I recall, motivated by a vengeful person in retaliation for the horrors of 9/11. The proximity of this killing to my house and the fact that I, too, was an Arab/American, brought fear and anguish to my heart. I was on the alert all the time, especially with my family.

Six days later, my Spring quarter began at Cal State. It was a late 6:10 p.m. - 8:00 p.m. class. I went to the chair of the Department and asked him to accompany me to my class just in case harm was waiting for me. When he asked me why, I told him about what had happened to my neighbor and all of the other retaliatory killings across the United States of mainly of people of Arab background with the Muslim faith. He brushed aside my request and reminded me that I had already been teaching for the previous six years and he had full confidence in my ability to weather such circumstances.

Having no other choice, I carried my briefcase containing my books and fifty copies of my syllabuses to my class. As I entered the classroom on the third floor, I could immediately detect a wary silence and changes in my students' facial expressions. I placed my briefcase on top of the table, took my books and syllabuses out, and placed them next to my briefcase. I then turned my face toward the board and wrote my name in Arabic, and next to it, my name in English like I had been doing since my first day of teaching at the high school, college, and university levels.

I then faced my students and introduced myself without denying my Arab/Palestinian heritage and advised them that there were seven more classes covering the same subject. So, if they felt uncomfortable with me, then they could easily take the same class with other professors. I told them that their interest comes first and that leaving my class would not result in any bad feeling at all. I then said that I was about to give each student a syllabus and asked them to look at it and read it carefully before making up their minds.

There were forty-five seats, all full, in addition to five more students standing next to the wall hoping that someone would drop this class so that they could attend. And even though none dropped it, I added the five extra students because I didn't want to disappoint them, and they greatly appreciated it.

I then began my lecture by covering, briefly, what took place during 9/11 while promising to cover this incident in more detail as the quarter progressed. After all, I was teaching American Government and Politics and that was my #1 job and I made that point very clear to them.

A few weeks into the quarter, the students began reminding me of my promise to explain the causes and consequences of 9/11 more fully. I then devoted one of my sessions to show them the documentary *The Secret Government*, which was produced by Bill Moyers. In this documentary, Mr. Moyers covered the CIA's secret wars with many countries including President Reagan's war against the Sandinista Guatemala government, which later became known as the "Iran Contra Affair."

In the following class session, we discussed the documentary's main lessons. Many of my students stated that they understood now why those people attacked New York rather than other countries, including Saudi Arabia, England, or France.

As is the custom at Cal State and being a part-time professor, I needed to be evaluated by my students every quarter. So, over 25 years—multiplied by four quarters each year—students evaluated me as their professor. The results of those student evaluations were used to determine whether my teaching contract would be renewed for the following year or three years.

The result of all the student evaluations was that they considered me to be outstanding and that is why the Department kept me for so long. Regarding the above class, I could only read and find out about my students' evaluations three weeks after the beginning of the following quarter. Now, I was anxious to read those evaluations.

What a surprise I had in store for me: their evaluations exceeded my expectations. In addition to giving me a stellar evaluation on my teaching abilities of the subject matter, the common theme written on the back of their evaluation was that despite 9/11 and the fear engendered toward Arabs like me, I did not deny my heritage or who I was for the sake of being safer among them or for being more Americanized. They emphasized that people like me are the ones who are less likely to betray this country. Whereas those who deny who they are for the sake of their own interests are more at risk. Thus, they said that people like me deserved their respect and admiration.

Additionally, Moyer's documentary made them understand the many war crimes that the American government had committed in their name. They also emphasized that they would follow the news and keep themselves informed about the government's investigations into the causes and consequences of 9/11.

I do not know how many of them have followed the news or not. All I know is that they were listening, studying, and evaluating our foreign policy in a totally different light. I only hope that their hatred of Arabs and Islam has decreased, since that tragedy. Otherwise, I am proud of them.

Mr. Gonzales

As a result of the many injuries and surgeries that I sustained while teaching in South Central, the doctors who treated me for those physical injuries and surgeries helped me obtain a handicapped decal to avoid parking too far from my classes or climbing stairs, among other physical hardships.

At Cal States, there was a handicapped parking space next to King Hall and my office building. One late afternoon, as I was parking my car, I saw Mr. Gonzales exiting his brand-new Mercedes Benz, parked in the handicapped parking space.

I began wondering why he was taking my Political Science class that late and at that age. He was at least in his late sixties. After the class session ended, I asked him if I could see him for a moment and he agreed. Having the class to ourselves I told him that I had observed him parking his brand-new Mercedes Benz in the handicapped parking space. I said, "That indicated to me that you were not taking this class to find a job, am I right?"

He then looked at me with tears running down his cheeks and admitted that I was right. He said he was taking the class to be an example to his two grandchildren whose father—his son—had abandoned them due to his heavy drug use and gang activities. He then posed a question to me by asking how I could lecture my grandchildren to go to school if there was no one for them to emulate as an example? Therefore, he said, "I am here to let them physically see me going to school at this old age so that they can follow my example and not that of their father, who dropped out and never went back to school."

After hearing this, I gave him a big hug and cried with him. Then I told him that his brave example was what education was all about. In my eyes, he passed the class and there was no need for him to keep attending the class at that late hour; that he could go home and be with his grandchildren.

He thanked me but refused my offer. He told me that as a veteran of our armed forces, taking shortcuts was not what he learned at the academy or during his service to our country. He said, "My responsibility as a grandfather requires committing myself to the right thing. Regarding what my son has done, I would not be able to bear the pain if I saw his children going the same path."

I told him that I fully understood, and we both left the classroom. What a caring and loving grandfather he was. We need millions like him. Now that I am a grandfather myself, I always keep Mr. Gonzales' story in mind and hope to be as caring as he was.

A Mother and Child

In one of my 8:10 p.m. - 10.00 pm classes, there was a female student who was unable to afford a babysitter for her six-year-old son. Thus, she asked my permission to let her son sit next to her in class, which was against the university's policy. Instead, I placed a chair next to the classroom door and kept the door wide open so that we both could keep an eye on that beautiful child.

The student was taking this class to fulfill her last requirement to obtain her teaching credentials and start a teaching career with the LAUSD. The teaching position was promised to her by the LAUSD after successfully completing all the needed classes and obtaining her credential.

This brave and loving woman reminded me a lot of Mr. Gonzales' predicament. As a father myself, I knew that she was not happy seeing a six-year-old child waiting in a lonely hallway until ten o'clock at night. She was compelled to do what she had to do to keep the lights on and feed her family. This hard choice was not her choosing, just like me accepting all the jobs that came my way to keep the lights on and feed my family. She did so because of her love and commitment to her family. I was proud of her but kept it to myself.

When the time came to calculate the final grades, I found out that she was twenty points short from passing the class with a "C". I began searching my heart and my conscience while asking myself, "Who am I to give her a C-, which means repeating the class again. That would compel her to bring her child with her and again deprive this child of sleep?"

I just could not dismiss her tenacity to attend this class with her child and felt I needed to grant her the "C" grade, indicating passing the class. I did this without her knowing.

To this day, I believe that I did a moral and courageous act. Being in school at that late hour with her child alone deserves an A+ grade. Who knows what my decision at that critical moment resulted in? I strongly believe that teachers must and should teach from a beating heart and compassionate conscience.

We are educating the future generations at all levels, they are the roses that we should nurture with loving water and care, without which, our school kids will grow up being orphaned by love and compassion and they will go on to lead a dysfunctional society. If you want to change the world for the better, go home and love your family first.

The Aftermath of the United States' 2003 Invasion of Iraq

Following the illegal and fabricated invasion of Iraq, in March of 2003, many Iraqis were desperate to immigrate to the United States whose own act produced such desperation in the first place. One of those Iraqis was a beautiful woman who said she had been serving as a high school principal in Iraq's capital city of Baghdad.

At the time, she was taking my class to complete her teaching and administrative credentials so she could find a career with a school district in Southern California. Her problem was her son, who lived with her as a refugee. He was under constant surveillance from both the FBI and the CIA. That's what she told me at the time. She requested that I allow her to not attend the class, but instead, to complete all the required class work at home so that she could be close to her son.

I refused because I felt this would be direct discrimination against the rest of my students and against the University policies, as well. She then asked me to allow her to take the final and the midterm in class, but to submit all the required homework while not physically attending the rest of the classroom sessions. As far as the required research paper, she promised to write a comprehensive research paper about what she had witnessed during the U.S. invasion of her country.

I agreed, for this is a very teachable firsthand account witnessed by a living Iraqi person, describing the war crimes that the invading American troops had committed. These were not only committed against the Iraqi Army but also Iraq's infrastructure, civilians, and in particular, the Iraqi children. In exchange for her submitting all homework, midterm and final work, I felt that the class assignments for passing were fulfilled.

I then waited for that research paper as well as the rest of her class assignments, but none ever materialized. This student dropped the class and never came back. Why? I do not know. Maybe she and her son were another human casualty of this criminal war against Iraq. I never saw her or heard from her again. The grade I gave her was an Incomplete.

Western University of Health Sciences: 2012-2019

Although my teaching career at both the LAUSD and Cal State University came to an unfortunate end before my intended retirement at my 65th birthday, a friend of mine informed me of a job opening at Western University of Health Sciences to teach in its Interprofessional Education (IPE) program.

When I first met the IPE program administrator and gave him my resume, he was very impressed with my entire teaching career. He asked me a lot about my teaching experiences at the university and paid special attention to my endurance teaching in the inner-city schools for so long.

In my mind, what impressed him the most was my continued emphasis on my students not dropping out of school, and the way I persevered in completing my Ph.D. after the theft of my first three dissertation chapters at Cal State University. He immediately hired me for the job.

When I asked about what I would be teaching, he introduced me to the IPE program, which involves meeting students from all nine colleges in small groups with a faculty facilitator. We would be discussing non-clinical aspects of symptom presentation in complex cases, including interprofessional knowledge and awareness, financial or ethical challenges, and communication barriers.

He strongly emphasized to me that many doctors, throughout the nation, do not communicate with each other to solve a medical problem associated with a patient. This is especially true when it requires not only his or her specific training, but the understanding of other health professionals, specialized in their own fields, to help treat such patients. He said that this teamwork was an essential ingredient in saving lives and treating patients.

When I began my Faculty Facilitating job in 2012, my students represented the nine colleges on campus, including: physical therapy, dental, nursing, optometric, osteopathic, pharmacy, podiatric, and veterinary. They hailed from all over the world and the females outnumbered the male students. They were all highly educated and many with Master's degrees and few had already been practicing doctors in their respective countries.

The medical cases that I facilitated with them were given to me by the IPE program administrator. Most of these cases required teamwork among my nine students representing their individual specializations in those nine colleges. I made sure that they followed all the instructions outlined in each specific case as well as respecting the space and the opinion given by each student.

I met with my students once a week for two hours, mainly on Wednesdays, four times a semester. Each calendar year was broken in two semesters. Thus, my yearly facilitating hours totaled sixteen. Their stellar performance amazed me all the time. Sometimes I wished that my own doctor could be as thorough and knowledgeable as they were. Their outstanding performance was mirrored by the passing grades that I gave them.

Throughout those seven years, what amazed my students about my career were the stories that I shared with them regarding my high school students and their struggles to complete their education. I had always stressed not to drop out and to be very thankful to their families and all others who were helping them to pay their very high tuition, which averaged between $250,000 and $400,000 by the end of their four years of medical training. Thus, they were always concerned about finding jobs after graduation to pay for their tuition. I assured them that this country has a dire need for thousands more doctors and nurses.

I used to cut out articles for them to read that covered recent literature on a variety of medical issues and research. Those articles included the latest research on a variety of medical issues, the pay scale of recently graduating students in their medical fields of specialization, the influence of politics in determining their pay scale and the interest rates that they would pay on their student loans, the spread of the opioids epidemic and the Covid-19 epidemic, and many other subjects. I placed all those articles in a folder and invited them to look at them or take them.

In class, we watched many short documentaries that were recommended by the administrator in charge relating to their subject matter using a program called TED. These documentaries always generated many in-depth analyses and discussions among us.

However, the spelling and the pronunciation of the medical terminologies made my head spin. I used to tell them that they deserved a medical degree for just writing and pronouncing all those terminologies. It is no wonder why most, if not all the doctors who examined me (I will say at least thirty) shared poor spelling skills. I think that they forgot how to spell correctly when prescribing my medications—hoping that the pharmacist would decipher them correctly.

I could sense in their demeanor how lucky they were at not having to go through what I had to complete my mission. My happiest days at Western University were the days when a former student would tap me on the shoulder while I was walking on campus to remind me of how he/she refused to give up or drop out after listening to my struggle and perseverance. Now they were dressed in their white medical uniforms as if they were fully accredited medical doctors in their respective field of study. What an honor to be among them all.

My career at Western University came to an abrupt ending when Covid-19 struck the nation and most universities momentarily closed while some others used online instruction instead. After classes resumed, I never heard from the University and never received any termination notification. I called the IPE office many times, but no one answered. I do not know if the IPE program is still going or not. By then, I was almost seventy years old, and I reasoned that I had done enough teaching, but never enough educating.

During those seven years, I officially became an employee of the University, so my payroll deductions included Social Security, state taxes, federal income taxes and Medicare taxes. I did not take this job for the money, but rather, to help students complete their educational missions. I learned a lot from them, and I hope that they also learned a lot from me.

What do all the above stories have in common, regardless of if they took place teaching at UCR, East Los Angeles Skill Center, Locke, Jordan and King Drew High Schools in South Central, LATTC, Cal State University or Western University of Health Sciences? That teaching is one of the most, if not the most, rewarding careers there is. Our job as teachers is to reduce or eliminate ignorance in our midst and around the world. What an honor to be a teacher among the millions of others, here and around the world, and doing so with an open and loving beating heart.

Conclusion
My Life's Highest Highs and Lowest Lows

During my teaching years, I found that for my students to understand subject matter, the best teaching method was to provide them with simple, clear, and related examples of what I was lecturing about. This helped them comprehend and relate to subject matter, so, I will attempt to do that here.

The Israeli/Palestinian Peoples' Tragic Kismet (TIPPTK) is no exception. This ongoing TIPPTK has haunted me all my life, especially since my arrival to the United States as a foreign student in 1971. The decisive roles that the United States has played and is still playing in its pursuit of global hegemony, has deepened, and prolonged this tragedy's inherent pain and suffering at the expense of the Palestinian people.

I never imagined that as a high school student who defended the United States' foreign policies against my classmate's support of the Soviet Union's, that I would one day fundamentally alter that stand. Seventy-three years is a long, long time for me to keep waiting for a ray of hope coming from the State Department or its Congress that could shed light on the Palestinian's hopes for a just and everlasting solution to this tragedy.

Looking at this tragedy from thousands of miles away, in Greater Los Angeles where I have lived most of those years, I have come to the realization that I was looking at the canopy of the forest of the United States' foreign policy, rather than seeing the individual trees that made up that canopy. Among them were the Palestinian and the Israeli trees, as I viewed U.S. policy when I was back home. My view then came largely from my surroundings in the city of Nazareth. I was not as worldly then as I am now. I had not yet studied politics or any of the many fields of studies associated with it such as international relations and global politics. Back then, I did not know anyone who ever mentioned the study of politics to begin with.

Although I was living in one of the most politically contested regions in the world, my meager knowledge was mainly built around what I had heard from my family, friends, and teachers about how Israel was born in 1948. This directly resulted in the death of a very vibrant Palestinian society and culture at what the economists coin the "take off stage," encapsulated in what became known as our Nakba.

Additionally, the aftermath of the 1967 Arab/Israeli War and the Cold War between the United States and the Soviet Union were also on the lips of most, if not all those, who I knew at that time. Their meager knowledge came from what they had heard on the radio and read in the newspapers. There were no scientific analyses or documentaries to watch for a deeper understanding. Few, at the time, owned televisions but most owned radios—like my family.

This meager local knowledge of global and international politics comprised the shade of the trees in the larger political canopy, which I was unable to see or understand living in Nazareth. But this canopy came into view and became clearer in my mind when I began studying politics here in the United States. Studying politics then led to studying history, a subject that I have always loved.

History taught me that since recorded history began, all empires and kingdoms have shared a common denominator: the quest for power and hegemony over other people's lives, cultures, natural resources, and their rights for a better and more prosperous future. Greed was always at the center of it all.

My history studies about the United States' empire differed from other empires' historical studies. It talked about how the U.S. empire was guided by a living Constitution that, in theory, limited its hegemonic desires and domination of others when conducting its foreign policies. This Constitution enshrined the protection of human happiness and wealth. It also stood for defending freedom, liberty, justice, equality and the dignity of all men and women.

As I understood it, the Constitution was and is a living document. And just like all living things on earth, it is in a constant state of change toward achieving those goals without being greedy. But what I did not understand is why the Constitution stopped changing and growing and completely froze in its tracks when it came to the question of TIPPTK? When, on a daily and hourly basis, the freedom, liberty, justice and dignity of men and women are violated by the Israeli dominant culture and its brutal armed forces against the Palestinian people.

This question drove me crazy and left me sad and bewildered, to say the least. But I found that these answers were not that hard to find. The United States is just like any other empire that came before it, and I will assume, that will come after it. When it came to its hegemony and greed, the U.S. put the Constitution on the back burner in its pursuit of global political, economic, and military hegemony. Our TIPPTK did not disrupt, nor did it contribute to such global hegemony, so why should the U.S. care about solving such a tragedy?

The Palestinian people have nothing to offer to this empire's quest for domination. The enshrined Constitution's words cannot be applied to the Palestinians, but for the Israelis, this is another matter. Israel can offer more useful tools to strengthen the United States' empire. Israel's usefulness to the United States became very clear after Israel's victory in the 1967 Arab/Israeli war. This victory supported, financed, and militarily equipped by the United States, and its Western allies, made its outcome possible. Thereafter, the United States never looked back. Israel became the obeying and darling vassal and subservient state in the service of the U.S. empire.

By keeping the Middle East in a state of no war and yet no peace, eliminating the success of any nascent and decent Arab nationalistic movement, and safeguarding the flow of oil and gas from the obeying Saudi Arabia and the Gulf states became Israel's main obeying task, which she fulfilled with a great success. That is why it receives the unquestioned support of the United States despite its criminal and genocidal acts daily against the Palestinian people, in addition to becoming a full-fledged apartheid state for all to see. Israel is but another super healthy tree among many others that make the United States' foreign policy canopy large, green, and healthy.

This tree is also nurtured by the tens of millions of dollars that the powerful and numerous wealthy pro-Israel organizations give and donate to whoever is attempting to run for a U.S public office, especially in Congress, the White House, or the governorships. The U.S. Supreme Court made such political donations legal by arguing that a political donation is a form of free speech and protected under the first amendment of the Constitution.

Thus, most if not all, those who run for public office find themselves in a dire need for funding their campaign and accept donations from all those organizations and individuals who support and love Israel, including at least seventy million Born-Again and evangelical Christians. The main request of those who donate is to blindly support and even fund the State of Israel regardless of its brutality, inhumanity, disregard to both the international norms and conducts and to the principals of our own Constitution toward its victims: the Palestinian People.

In another world, regarding TIPPTK, the subservient and obeying partner is no longer the Israeli Knesset or Parliament, but the American Congress and the White House. Israel's indirect and clever use of those donations obligates the receiver to become subservient of Israel and not the other way around. Just follow orders and look the other way or you will no longer be receiving such donations and the hopes of being re-elected again, in addition of being accused of being antisemitic, thus becoming an undesirable candidate.

But the Palestinians have nothing to offer to this expansionist empire like that of Israel's. The Palestinian tree is short, leafless, and dying. The shadow of its neighbor, Israel, keeps it lifeless and unseen from the top branches of the United States' overarching foreign policy canopy. Thus, why should congress and the white house give a damn about the Palestinians, period, full stop.

Yet, the ongoing war in Ukraine made me think twice about the above conclusion. Many if not most of the experts who have analyzed and fully examined the causes and the consequences of the Ukraine proxy war between mainly the United States and Russia have concluded that the United States empire is fighting Russia "to the last Ukrainian." Could this simple conclusion apply to the United States relations with Israel?

The empire of the United States, like all other empires, does not care in its pursuit of its global hegemony and interests about morality, Integrity, or the value of human lives to achieve such hegemony. The subservient Israeli state's proxy role in serving the United States' pursuit of its hegemony over the entire Middle East's energy resources, strategic waterways, and huge consumer markets is a fight that the United States is pursuing "to the last Israeli and Palestinian" alike.

Once both the Israelis and the Palestinians realize that they are but two disposable pawns in the empire's chess game and that both trees are among the other one hundred and ninety-three trees that make up the United States' foreign policy canopy, TIPPTK pain will decrease tremendously and the two peoples will quickly reconcile their differences and concentrate instead on their similarities, leading to a just and lasting sisterhood, brotherhood and peace.

But back in Palestine and until the age of twenty-one, I did not see any canopy at all. I was living as a branch on top of a healthy

Palestinian tree nurtured by the unconditional love of my family and all my surroundings. My mother had always said that the United States is the "world mother." Like mother, like son, I also defended the U.S. against the Soviet Union during my high school years at both ORT and Don Bosco.

With just a second-grade education, I do not know what stand my mother would take if she could fully comprehend the United States' role in keeping our Nakba going and in knowing that the destruction of her village and the pain of its Mukhtar, who was her father, have a lot to do with the U.S. foreign policies in pursuit of its global hegemony. Knowing her beating Palestinian heart, I will predict that she would still believe in what she had always believed in: that the United States is the "world mother."

But then, why don't the members of our Congress, which includes so many mothers, fathers, and grandparents, listen to the cries of my mother, father and grandparents who were but a small sample of the rest of the fifteen million Palestinians scattered around the world? The answer is simple and clear: there are no donations, there is no Arab or international progressive support, they are not following what the Talmud and the Torah teach and have no sympathy or compassion for the Palestinians. Again, greed and selfishness are at the bottom of it all.

So, where is my Palestinian green and lush branch residing within the hearts, minds, and conscience of the American People, who are represented by a constitution that I so much admired, taught and believed in? Am I a part of that canopy that represents the U.S. foreign imperial domination or am I just a drying branch on that Palestinian tree? I do not know, but instead, think about it all day.

Writing this memoir has been one of the most difficult yet rewarding experiences of my life. It has provided me with an opportunity to relive the highest of highs and the lowest of lows, and to look back on my life with pride in what I have accomplished.

Yet, there is a deep sadness, as well. I have struggled for almost a year in trying to draft a concluding chapter that fills the biggest hole in my heart: the space where TIPPTK resides. It should come as no surprise to the reader that international conflicts shape the experiences immigrants to this country bring with them, and I hope it is not a shock to hear that living in safety and security in America does not make those past experiences disappear. If anything, it augments them.

Growing up as a Palestinian/Arab in Israel was a painful experience. Setting aside the Nakba, the "catastrophe," as Palestinians call the loss of their homeland and their displacement in 1948 to the creation of the State of Israel, I grew up as part of a religious and ethnic minority. But by mere accident of geography, Nazareth fell within Israel proper, so I lived in conditions relatively better than my fellow Palestinians in the refugee camps, West Bank and Gaza. That reality has never been lost on me.

While teaching in inner-city schools in Los Angeles, I was constantly reminded of this reality as even here in a land enriched with a constitution that purports equality, democracy, and respect for the rule of law, I was confronted with the fact that ethnic minorities experienced the same pain as I did. In some ways, at least the Israelis were honest: they made (and continue to make) clear that it was/is only a Jewish State, with all the benefits accrued to those who embodied the same ethnic and religious identity. But the United States does not do this. It claims to be colorblind, to separate church and state, and to treat everyone with dignity in society and under the law, but that is not practiced in most places I encountered.

My students did not enjoy the same freedom or equality as the dominant culture and ethnic group. They lived lives in which the erasing of their indigenous ancestors' heritage and culture and the slave ancestry of their forefathers and mothers continued to create an unjust society. They earned less, died earlier, and were more likely to suffer the ill effects of crime, poor health, and racism. They grew up in a city bearing Spanish as well as indigenous Indian names that were originally part of Indian / Mexican land, and yet their heritage was constantly used against them to insinuate they were poor, uneducated, and illegal.

Many lived lives in which foreign policy decisions made in this country directly resulted in the overthrow of their countries' governments and/or societies. We fought wars on their shores until we decided we were too tired to continue, and when they came to our shores seeking refuge, they were often treated like ingrates. Then, when these children succeeded in pushing past all these barriers to become star athletes, model students, or successful business entrepreneurs, they entered a society that implicitly believed they had only gotten to where they did because of Affirmative Action or the unspecified "help" of their own communities.

In short, my sadness is one of frustration and anger: that this country not only did no better than Israel in its treatment of the Palestinians, but it also actively made my students' lives and mine much harder than it should have been. Here, I was teaching the American Constitution as a tool of empowerment for my students to emulate while the overwhelming majority of our 535 Congressional Members always support Israel without paying any attention to its policies toward my people: policies that are contradictory to the teaching of our Constitution's main premises.

The White House, the State Department, the Pentagon, and most of our fifty states' governments just follow suit and look the other way when it comes to Israel's treatment of the Palestinians and very few of them are willing to admit that Israel is an apartheid state.

The question then is why this same congress which is fully empowered by our constitution to add a new state to our union not add Israel to our union as our new fifty first state and finish with this charade before Israel drag us into an unknown future including the possibility of a nuclear war engulfing the entire region and may be beyond? All that congress and the white house need to do is to bluntly ask both the Israelis and Palestinian peoples to ratify a referendum asking for an admission to our union. Once our congress approves their referendum's article as being compatible with our constitution's democratic principles, then congress sends its approval to add Israel as the fifty-first state to the president's desk who upon signing it "Israel/Palestine" becomes a fully functioning fifty first state.

The entire conflict will stop immediately. Both the Israeli and the Palestinian governmental agencies will come under our control and the war in Gaza with its human suffering will come to an end. You break the law, you go to jail. Now both peoples become American citizens who must follow the American laws and regulations. By doing so, our congress will add at least sixteen new members and two senators. This proposal will bring about an earthquake and ignite an increase in the American people's political civic duties thus increasing their total participation in our democratic voting power at the local and national levels.

Since the ratification of our constitution, the American citizenry has grown at least four-fold thus the number of our congress must reflect that growth. Therefore, the American people could ask for increasing the number of house of representatives members to be increased from 435 to at least 500, the senate with a new mathematical formula could be increased from 100 to 150 senators, and the supreme court from 9 to 15 judges. Why not? This proposal sounds like a pipe dream but under the present circumstances when all other plans for ending this conflict have failed, this proposal sounds the most promising.

But like the popular American proverb says, "the chicken always comes home to roost." In late 2022, Israel's elections led to massive civil unrest (which remains ongoing) when those who benefitted from the Palestinian Nakba were faced with the new socio-economic and political realities created by the election of far right and extremely conservative Zionist religious parties under the leadership of Prime Minister Benjamin Netanyahu.

Netanyahu's government has been labeled by many Middle Eastern scholars, human rights organizations, and others as being fascist and pro-apartheid. This government is bent on taking away many socio-economic and political privileges that most of Israel's population have enjoyed (all while ignoring the bad deeds that they have committed against the Palestinians).

Now the chicken came home to roost. When Israelis opened their eyes to their new realities and began to feel what it might be like to live under a government that would use religious authority and military might to curtail freedoms, liberties, and civil rights, they began demonstrating by wrapping themselves with Israeli flags and taking to the streets. Of course, many ignored the fact that they served in the same Israeli Army and supported the same government that had supported the destruction of freedoms, liberties, and civil rights for the Palestinians. In other words, they woke up to feeling what Palestinians feel every day and rejected it—just as the Palestinians have since the start of this conflict. Wrapping themselves with the Israeli flag has added more insult to the Palestinians. For them the flag has always symbolized the destruction of Palestine itself.

Unfortunately, as I have been writing this memoir, a war between Hamas and Israel broke out on October 7, 2023, following an attack by Hamas on several southern Israeli towns that border the Gaza Strip. The scale of the Hamas attack is unprecedented: the Strip was sealed off 16 years ago behind the world's most sophisticated human barrier, a collection of watchtowers, fences, concrete moats, and human/electronic surveillance systems, paid for by U.S. and Israeli taxpayers.

Over two million people—half of whom are under the age of 18 (meaning they have literally known no life other than living under this blockade) were crammed into an area that has been widely recognized as a modern concentration camp.

Hamas managed to not only breach this barrier in numerous locations, but to destroy communication towers. Then, they used paragliders to circumvent areas that weren't destroyed and landed their fighters from the sea. Hamas did not use this opportunity to march on Tel Aviv, or the West Bank, or to openly engage the Israeli

Army in direct combat. Instead, they attacked Israeli towns and public gatherings, resulting in the Israeli government claiming over 1,200 civilian deaths, thousands of injuries, and 200+ kidnappings.

As I type this, Israel has responded with a human catastrophe on a scale not witnessed since the 1948 Nakba: an air, sea, and ground invasion into Gaza that has resulted in the displacement of over one million Palestinian refugees (who were already refugees from 1948, so I don't even know what to call them at this point) and tens of thousands of Palestinian deaths and injuries. Entire towns have been destroyed, including civilian infrastructure, such as roads and medical facilities. They have cut off all food, water, electricity, and diesel imports collectively punishing 2.2 million people for the actions of 1,300 Hamas fighters in what is becoming a slow-moving cleansing of the Palestinian people from the Gaza Strip.

How this tragedy will end is unknown at this time, but how it began is clearer. Hamas grew out of an arm of the Muslim Brotherhood, which itself began in Egypt under its colonial rule. The Brotherhood had a charity arm and a political arm, but it couched its positions mainly under Islamic teachings. It spread throughout the Middle East and was widely viewed by every autocratic regime in the area as a threat to their legitimacy.

Because of the realities of the Israeli occupation, the Palestinian branch underwent its own unique evolution. Over time, the Brotherhood's teachings in Palestine became a sort of Islamist "liberation theology"; it became highly militarized through the writings of a cleric named Sayyid Qutb, and it developed a charter that sought to establish an Islamist caliphate throughout the biblical Holy Lands, thus espousing the Palestinian cause in religious (not national) terms and deeming the removal of Jews from the Holy Lands as a necessary step to accomplish the creation of this caliphate.

This removal was said to be necessary, not just because they sought a Muslim state, but also as a matter of justice: the Muslims, themselves, were removed by "the Jews" through violence and terrorism (i.e., the 1948 Nakba), and thus, they justified their use of force. In other words, in Hamas' eyes, the Israelis were the terrorists—not Hamas.

Despite their charter, throughout the late '80s and early '90s, Israeli leaders (in particular, leaders like Ariel Sharon) viewed the Islamist groups as potential deterrents against the secular Palestinian Liberation Organization (PLO) under the leadership of Yassir Arafat and his political party, Fatah. Israeli leaders reasoned that while Hamas was openly anti-Jewish in its views, it was not openly nationalist in the way the secular PLO was, and they bargained that Hamas would content itself to remain in the mosques and out of the streets in exchange for funding and social power.

Furthermore, the Israeli leaders reasoned that the overt anti-Jewish language in the charter was just anti-Israeli sentiment—something they understood given their conflict with the rest of the Palestinian nation and Israel's own messianic rightwing groups who espoused anti-Arab and anti-Muslim ideologies (one of whom would eventually go on to assassinate Yitzak Rabin, and many of whom now run the current Israeli government and settler movement).

It soon became possible to drive a wedge in the Palestinian national movement by fomenting division between the two factions, essentially toppling Fatah's unitary control of the Palestinian national cause and creating space for Hamas to arise as a political party. But this strategy soon failed: After the PLO and Israel signed the Oslo Accords, Hamas did not simply disappear content to stew in mosques.

Instead, it declared Fatah and the Palestinian Authority traitors to the cause. It began ramping up attacks on Israel, utilizing suicide bombings and militant raids to force the PLO (and the slowly growing Palestinian Authority) into the bind of abiding by their security assurances to Israel while simultaneously representing the national aspirations of the Palestinian people who continued to live under military occupation regardless of the Oslo Accords. From 1993-2000, when the second Intifada erupted, the number of Israeli settlements had doubled, and the number of settlers had doubled—

thus belying the Israeli argument that they intended on abiding by a two-state solution in the first place.

The result was that Arafat, and the PLO were blamed throughout the 90s and through to the Second Intifada for both not striking peace with the Israelis and for failing to stop Hamas. The Palestinian Authority spent large amounts of its time policing Hamas militants within the West Bank, and thus, soon began to appear to many Palestinians as nothing more than a second Israeli police force, while Hamas continued to enjoy popular support as the only Palestinian faction willing to stand up to Israel and provide social services, especially education and medical care to the beleaguered Gaza's citizens.

Then, in 2005, Israeli Prime Minister Ariel Sharon made the decision to pull Israel's settlements out of the Gaza Strip. This decision was made entirely for political reasons: it was simply not tenable to maintain settlements for a few thousand Israeli settlers who were living amongst almost two million Palestinians. Also, much of Israel's left and secular population and its military refused to continue funding and serving rightwing religious pipe dreams.

Israel's departure was widely viewed by many Palestinians as a Hamas success: by making the occupation untenable, Israel ultimately quit the Gaza Strip, while the Palestinian Authority languished in the West Bank with nothing to show for the so-called peace process.

But then, Israel immediately cordoned off the entire Gaza Strip, stringing numerous military installations along its border to separate it from numerous kibbutz communities and towns in the south. As was the case in the West Bank, construction began on a separation barrier, but a basic conundrum remained: who governed the Gaza Strip?

The Bush Administration's neoconservatives (who at this time were unwilling to admit the folly of their "democratization" efforts in the Middle East) pushed for the Palestinians to hold "national" elections; Fatah won a majority in the West Bank and Hamas (which is based in Gaza and took credit for Israel's withdrawal from the Strip and ran largely on issues like combating corruption and increasing social services) won a majority in the Gaza Strip.

Israel and the United States immediately decided that the Palestinians in Gaza got democracy wrong and sought to unwind the Gaza elections, but by then the die was cast Hamas and Fatah fought one another for control of the Gaza Strip, with Hamas emerging the victor and purging Fatah party members from the Strip (and this remains the biggest intra-Palestinian conflict to ever take place).

The Western countries, and especially the United States, branded Hamas as a terrorist organization, thus accepting Israel's view of Hamas. Hamas's view of Israel was known for a very long time as being a state-sponsored terrorist organization, as well.

After additional Israeli/Hamas battles broke out in the Gaza Strip in 2006 (and in Lebanon, where another militant group, Hezbollah, is based), Israel ordered a massive blockade of the Gaza Strip, effectively declaring unilateral control over the entire area and its people who were now concentrated to this sliver of land.

Since then, Israel has maintained exclusive control over (1) all imports and exports; (2) access to and from the Gaza Strip via sea, air, and (except for one crossing with Egypt) land; and (3) all sources of clean drinking water, electricity, natural gas, petroleum, diesel, and food.

Meanwhile, Hamas has run the Gaza Strip using funds received from Qatar, Iran, and other Arab governments (with Israel's acknowledgment and approval—an odd arrangement given that Israel considers Hamas a terrorist organization and visa-versa) but with little done to improve the lives of the Palestinians they ostensibly represent. (It is debated how much Hamas could do given the blockade).

This last fact cannot be stressed enough: Israel (and specifically, longtime Israeli Prime Minister Benjamin Netanyahu) has known and tacitly approved of Hamas' growth, gambling that it would remain "contained" behind its blockade.

Meanwhile, as is always the case, the Palestinian people of Gaza suffer as they are, quite literally, caged in; they cannot leave, few are able to get out to work, they live in impoverished, overcrowded conditions, and they are the victims of a blockade that would be considered an act of war under any definition of such in international law. They have lived like this for 16 years, and then some, if you count their actual dispossession as far back as 1948. What little government they do have is run by Hamas, which governs like an authoritarian, religious organization.

Concurrent to all of this, the Israeli left effectively ceased to exist as a political force, and the rightwing religious extremists in Israel have grown in power, unchecked. Openly anti-Palestinian/Arab/Muslim attitudes that were discretely discussed by the settlers and certain "fringe" elements in Israel, have become tolerated, accepted, and institutionalized in a way that, coupled with Israel's military, has made the Palestinians and their cause a non-issue. The degree of daily violence visited on the Palestinians has continued, unabated, unchecked, and with no end in sight. The Israeli policy of "mowing the lawn" that it proudly executed several times has killed and maimed thousands of Gaza's residents including children and women. Now the inhabitants of Gaza are nothing, but grass and weeds need to be cut so that no grass can grow taller than what Israel deemed safe. No human or natural force can stop grass from growing. Even on a busy freeway, grass grows as a reminder of its everlasting presence.

Despite every country and expert stating that, short of a single binational state, a two-state solution is the only way to end the conflict, we are no closer to that now than we were in 1993 when the Oslo Accords were signed.

This summary of a very long history is necessary to understand the present war because in the eyes of both Hamas and Israel's governments (which again, has been largely led by Prime Minister Benjamin Netanyahu during this time), each side had ostensibly struck "a deal with the devil," in that each worked with an opposing party it considered to be run by terrorists: Israel allowed Hamas to grow on its doorstep, reasoning that it would divide the Palestinians between governance under that organization in the Gaza Strip and governance under a feckless, useless government in the West Bank, thus providing it with an excuse to claim there was no credible party with which it could negotiate for peace and under which a Palestinian state could grow.

Thus, why should the Palestinians follow the Oslo Accords promises that were agreed to in establishing an Independent Palestinian state when the far-right Israeli settlers are continuing to steal more Palestinian lands and terrorizing its citizens?

Meanwhile, Hamas worked within the confines, set by the Israeli government, to become a dominant political party and de facto ruler over 2.4 million of people while channeling money and arms into both securing its authority and building up its armaments. In the name of battling the "Israeli/Zionist State terrorist organization," Hamas has been arguing that its citizens are living in a concentration camp like condition, on top of being branded as a terrorist organization, and they have used these reasons to justify their autocratic rule and the worsening socio-economic conditions of Gaza's 2.2 Palestinian people.

But at the root of this so-called cooperation (between the Palestinians in the Gaza Strip and Hamas) has always been the idea that the other side (Israel) were the terrorists: Hamas views all the Israelis as terrorists, and Israel's political and military establishments treat all the Palestinians as terrorists, not just Hamas. By dehumanizing the other side, in this way, each has essentially given itself carte blanche to take "any means necessary" to defeat the other.

That is how you come to have "resistance fighters" murdering children at a concert and a government acting in "self-defense" by carpet bombing civilians while cutting them off from food and water.

I cannot predict where this war will go, but this current wave of violence and destruction was sadly predictable—maybe not the scale of Hamas' violence or Israel's assault, but to those informed of these facts, it should not surprise anyone given that both sides struck these unofficial bargains with the other knowing that one cannot "win" while the other exists. And, as always, it is the innocent civilians on both sides who suffer.

As Israel mounts its response against the innocent people of Gaza as revenge for Hamas' attacks, and as Israelis mourn the victims of Hamas, and vice versa, it would be best to remember this lesson and work to stop the cycle of violence rather than creating conditions that are doomed to repeat it. The international community and especially the United States must stop Israel before it is too late: the level of starvation, malnutrition, disease, homelessness, and death amongst Gaza's population has already made it one of the most destructive conflicts of the 21st century. Indeed, the destruction is so great that South Africa (long a champion of the Palestinian cause) brought charges of genocide against Israel in the International Court of Justice, and for the first time, the court held that Israel must prevent acts that are banned under the 1948 UN genocide convention, including indiscriminate killing of Palestinians and deliberately inflicting on them "conditions of life calculated to bring about its [the Palestinian community] physical destruction in whole or in part." It also reserved judicial review over Israel's actions—including ordering it to preserve evidence, report on that preservation, and report on how it will be punishing those within Israel who have called for incitements to genocide. Finally, it ordered Israel to ensure basic services and aid get into Gaza. Hopefully this ruling will be the beginning of the end to the violence.

I do not condone the killing of men, women, and children, no matter if they are Israeli, Palestinians, Jews, Muslims, Christians, or any other religion. So, I cannot condone what Hamas has done nor what Israel is doing and will do in response. These are the actions taken by groups that have come to view the other as terrorists who are to blame for the other's suffering; that suffering turned into hate long ago, and that hate and suffering have been fed by decades of uprisings, suicide bombings, occupation, and violence. This is not to blame the victims of Hamas' attacks on October 7, 2023, for their own deaths or to say they "deserved" it—that is a barbaric way of thinking, and I reject it.

Nor is it to blame the people of Gaza for Hamas' actions in that they "should have known" Israel would respond "by any means necessary" and thus deserve the genocidal hell they are experiencing. That is equally barbaric, and I reject it.

Rather, the lesson here is that hate and the violence it inspires are learned and cultivated. They are not innate to the human condition, and they do not grow in absent conditions that allow them to bloom. My parent teachable examples are what the whole world needs to learn and remember now for the bloodshed to stop. Otherwise, history will repeat itself: as one example, just as I grew up hearing horribly racist comments from Israelis about Arabs when I was young, so too has that same language revived itself amongst rightwing Israeli—many of whom now occupy positions of authority within the Israeli government.

The so-called "deals with the devil" between the two sides must end—and real peace, built on equality between both peoples, is the only way to stop them. Martin Luther King Jr. once famously said that an injustice anywhere is a threat to justice everywhere, and nowhere has that been clearer than in what Israel is currently experiencing. What goes around comes around: one cannot purport to live in a democracy in the service of your own interests while denying it to others who are living next door (and amongst) you. Eventually, the cancer of illiberalism spreads: it does not remain contained to just "those people."

David Ben-Gurion, Israel's first prime minister and its most celebrated, might have been able to avoid the present socio-economic and political crises had he met with the remnants of the Palestinian political leadership following its defeat in 1948 and sued for a just peace with them. [8]

A very different country would have arisen had he done so—one less committed to seeing their neighbors as enemies, and one able to better situate its need for security in the context of its democracy. He did not, and the Palestinians, Israel, and the world is worse off as a result: the chickens have come home to roost and the survival of Israel and Palestine now lies in the hearts of Israeli citizens and their resolve in pushing against the rise of fascism and apartheid, not just in Israel, but throughout the Holy Lands.

This whirlpool of contradictions, frustration, sadness, and anger makes me seriously question the stand that I took at ORT Amal and Don Bosco High Schools when I enthusiastically supported the United States' values against those of the Soviet Union, even as I was being challenged by the rest of my classmates on my views.

At the age of eleven, I was happily carrying the grocery bags of our Jewish elderly neighbors to the bus station. Then, in my adolescent's years, I threw away the warm tea that my mother had prepared for the Israeli soldiers rather than be subservient to them. Now, as an adult who has experienced life on life's terms, I refuse to change my attitudes toward our "unfinished" Constitution which is still the best document ever written for empowering people around the world to achieve their best potential. But it is in constant change.

The United States of America was the country that I freely chose to become a citizen of but not that of Israel. My Israeli citizenship was granted/ imposed on me without my consent. This citizenship is my direct proof of my heritage as a Palestinian. Without it, I can only claim so, but with it I have a documented proof of being a Palestinian because I was born in Palestine when Israel was born as well.

Therefore, my attitudes toward my American students and that of the United States' society will never change. I deeply believe that, sooner than later, our support of Israel will diminish and that of the Palestinian cause will increase. Either way, a changing attitude and a welcoming of the Palestinian causes could help lessen the memories of the tragedy that befell our people.

I am grateful that this country gave me the opportunity to better myself with a good education, which was inculcated in me before arriving on its shores. Hard work and perseverance were running in my bloodstream as a testament to those of my ancestors. I have paid a very heavy price for my education: physically, financially, and emotionally, and never received any help toward that goal. (It was all from my blood and sweat.)

The United States afforded me the chance to become a high school teacher and a professor, to buy a home, and to live in one of the safest and most desirable places in the world. I have raised a family here and my children are now raising their own families, all of whom are happy, healthy, and successful in ways I could never have imagined. I'm surrounded, every day, by people from all over the world who have shown that there is unbridled strength in our differences and if given a fair chance, we can all have life, liberty, and the pursuit of happiness.

To experience all of this, while seeing that Palestinians continue to die every day at the hands of the Israeli police and military, is difficult. To see that my people are no closer today to having their own state than they were a decade or six ago is heart-wrenching. And, to see that the United States actively encourages these politics leaves a hole in my heart. This hole, to some extent, has since been filled with the dreams and successes of my students, the joys of my family, the growth of my grandchildren, my life's long labor of love mirrored by leaving my dissertation and my memoir behind for future American students and my kids, and grandkids to read and learn from.

And finally, I also want to acknowledge all of my family that have also migrated to the United States and Canada, both before and after my arrival. Like me, they have all sought to make better lives for themselves and their loved ones. They have settled across the continent, from east to west and north to south, including in Canada, California, Washington, Virginia, Tennessee, Idaho, Ohio, Illinois, Florida, New York, Georgia, Nebraska, Texas, and Nevada. This growing family is comprised of law-abiding citizens, each with their own successful stories of becoming doctors, professors, lawyers, pharmacists, priests, teachers, archbishops, diplomats, nurses, pilots, school administrators, engineers, members of the US armed forces, and business entrepreneurs.

No matter our experiences, the one common denominator that bound and continues to bind those of us who migrated to the "new world" is the intergenerational trauma of the Nakba. Each of us has her/his own story of pain and anguish to tell, and it remains an ongoing link to our Palestinian roots no matter how different our endeavors here have been.

In this way, we are bound with Jewish people all over the world in a similar tragedy of history: just as they are haunted by the intergenerational trauma of the Holocaust, so are we haunted by our Nakba. Just as they say "Never Again" in response to their historic horrors, so do we. Just as they weep for what has been lost, even as they seek to build something new and better, so do we. Just as they love their children, so do we.

It is my sincere hope that Jews here and in Israel understand that peace will come for both sides with an understanding that this shared human experience can bind us together as one Semitic family. We will not always agree—no family ever does. But to recognize our shared histories and humanity requires a recognition of our equal dignity and right to self-determination. There simply cannot be peace through violence—it can only come with equality for all.

In the meantime, knowing that my family here is carrying the torch of the Nakba's memories helps to keep the hole in my heart from growing. I believe a complete healing will come when my people have gained an independent and sovereign country like all others.

My grandkids have always called me Sido—grandfather in a Palestinian dialect. This Sido's life was well-spent in service to my United States' Constitution, family, my community and in memory of the promise I made to my parents so many years ago.

Appendix

Footnotes:

1. Nakba: Is a word that was coined by the indigenous Palestinian population to describe the horrors of their displacement from their ancestral land by the advancing Zionist/Israeli Armed Forces mainly in the years 1947-1950. Nakba's best English translation could be: "catastrophe, disaster or cataclysm." Regardless of which English word you use, it all boiled down to the war crimes that the Zionist State of Israel's Armed Forces unleashed against the Palestinian people culminating in the ethnic cleansing and forced displacement of over eighty percent of Palestine's total population at the time. Some estimates put the number at 800,000 others at 950,000. Most mentioned repeatedly the number 800,000 people being forcefully displaced. Add to the above, the complete destruction of at least 450-500 villages, as well as partial destruction of too many other towns and cities.

At the time Palestine's economy was at the stage of what economists term "the take off stage." Its vibrant and healthy cultural and civic

societies were at their pentacles as an example of what the future of the middle east will look like. But, Israel has destroyed all things period. In addition to the traumatic catastrophe, the Nakba manifested itself in many other psychological, emotional, physical, and cultural cataclysms for the Palestinian people that manifested itself in an intergenerational trauma to this day including myself.
It is in my opinion our muted Holocaust that neither the Zionist State of Israel nor its Western supporters are willing to admit. I am not in need of their admission, I know that I am with the rest of my people including the Jewish people who are the victims of two Holocausts that took place during the 1940s.

2. Israel: Is a name that was first mentioned in an Egyptian Merpentan Stele erected to Pharaoh Merneptah in 1200 BCE. Until the creation of the fairy tail story of the bible 2000 years ago, the word Israel remained obscured and unrecognized. The creators of the bible have mentioned Israe's name l many times as the promised land for the Jews without even knowing the geography of that land.
The Zionist leadership cleverly wedded its Jewishness to its racist ideology that made the birth of Israel, in 1948, possible, at the expense of Palestine's indigenous people. Therefore, I deeply believe that there are many differences between the words: Jewish, Israel and Zionism. For me Jewish is simply a religious belief that does not advocate the creation of an independent ethno-nationalistic Jewish state. As an atheist, I have no problem with all religions if they leave me in peace and do not impose their teachings on me. Israel, on the other hand, is a fictional invention in direct violation of Judaism's principles and teachings of never establishing an exclusive State for the Jews. In my mind, once a person says that he/she is an Israeli, then his adherence is more to Zionism, which created Israel, than to his Jewish religion. You just cannot have it both ways.
Looking at it from a different humble and objective perspective, a person can be a Zionist but not a Jew, a Jewish person can be a Zionist once he/she refutes the teaching of Judaism and accepts and

defends the creation of an ethno-religious Jewish State. Whereas an Israeli is a person whose main job is to defend Israel regardless of its Zionist ideology. He/ she sees Israel as the protector of his/her safe well-being among the nations of this globe.

I am an American/ Israeli/ Palestinian humble citizen, and above all, a human being. I have no problem with the above definitions if all my Nakba's wounds are fully recognized and fully addressed by the State of Israel with full equality to people like me who hold an Israeli citizenship and to all other Palestinians who do not hold that citizenship, especially the refugees. Then, what is written on my passport is of no consequence to me.

3. Tabbouleh: Tabbouleh is a very simple and refreshing salad popularly found in the Levantine region of Lebanon, Palestine, Syria, and Jordan. Its main ingredients consist of parsley, tomatoes, cucumber, green mint, onion, lemons, olive oil, salt and pepper. While chopping the parsley by hand, you soak uncooked bulgar that you will add to the tabbouleh once it becomes soft. Then you add a lot of lemon juice, extra virgin olive oil, salt, and pepper and mix thoroughly. You could also add chopped tomatoes, onions, and cucumber, as well. The above ingredients are all dependent on your taste, yet parsley is the star of this salad. I always add at least 70% of parsley to the above. Normally, you use a spoon to scoop the tabbouleh up. In my case I also use the leaves of romaine lettuce. I place the tabbouleh inside a curved romaine lettuce leaf and make a tabbouleh sandwich (try it, you will like it).

4. Jewish: In my opinion, a Jewish person is a person who believes in Judaism, which is a religion based upon the teachings of the holy books of the Torah and the Talmud. I was taught that a Jew adheres to the holy teachings of both holy books. Additionally, I learned that Judaism does not advocate the creation of an ethno-nationalist independent and sovereign state for the service of the Jewish people only. Peace, justice, mercy, equality, and love of humanity are at the core teaching of Judaism, Christianity, and Islam.

5. Taghribat- Bani-Hilal: Is an Arabic epic oral history of a long and dramatic journey of adventure, occupation, and settlement of a Bedouin tribe of Banu Hilal, from the present- day Najd region of Saudi Arabia. This tribe faced famine quite frequently, so they were always on the move to find other regions to live in, thus the adventures. Their journey took them to present-day Egypt, Tunisia, and Algeria. In doing so, they encountered severe resistance from the local population under the leadership of their hero El Zenati Kalepha who bitterly battled Banu Hilal's hero Abu-Zed Al Hilali with another military leader named Ibn Ghanem. This oral history is mainly recited in the form of musical poems that reflect Arab folk history, customs, symbolism, and beliefs.

6. Zionism: At its core ideology, Zionism is a racist ideology developed during the middle of the eighteenth century by wealthy and highly rich and educated white Jewish men (sorry, no women) in pursuit of finding a national, independent, and sovereign country exclusively for those men and women who adhere to the Jewish religion, culture, and norms ONLY. Despite the fact that Judaism did not advocate such a creation, the evolution of such an ideology went through many twists and turns culminating in the successful establishment of the present-day State of Israel In 1948 with the lifesaving help of England which occupied Palestine following WW1. In doing so, England demanded that in exchange of such help, the future Zionist State of Israel will be a vassal state in the service of the interests of the British empire.

Following the British empire's demise following WWII, the emerging United States Empire replaced that of the British, and Israel became a vassal state serving the new empires' interest throughout the Middle east. To this day, Israel is successfully fulfilling its vassal duties thus the immense United States unquestionable economic, political and cultural blind support.

This settler colonial project produced two innocent victims: On one hand, the Palestinian people have paid and are still paying an untold suffering of displacement, the destruction of their culture, and heritage that became known worldwide as the Palestinian "Nakba." Meanwhile, the European countries that supported such a project claimed that by granting Israel its creation, that they have shown their love of the Jewish people, thus who cares if the Palestinians paid the price.

This deceitful argument has resulted, on the other hand, in the abuse of the innocent Jewish peoples' traumatic Holocaust suffering by offering them no way out but to immigrate to Palestine. This was despite their overwhelming choice of immigrating to the United States and other countries, which was blocked by the Zionist leadership in cahoots with the British empire.

Now, both people are locked in an ongoing human suffering neither of whom have asked for in the first place. What a tragedy.

7. Eastern Bloc: The term "Eastern Bloc" refers to a group of eastern European countries that were aligned militarily, politically, economically, and culturally with the Soviet Union from approximately 1945 to 1990 and formed what is popularly called "The Warsaw Pact."

8. Ben Gurion: While taking my upper division class on the causes and consequences of the Cold War at U.C. Riverside, I read in a book (whose title and author names I have since forgotten) in which the author was describing a meeting that took place at Yalta that included Churchill, Stalin, and Roosevelt, to discuss the state of the world after defeating Hitler's army. The author made an excellent point that, had these three leaders chosen reconciliation rather than confrontation among their conflicting ideologies, the world could have pursued a more peaceful coexistence that would have benefited all humans on this Earth. It could have saved trillions of dollars spent on nuclear deterrence and instead they could have used those trillions in utilizing human ingenuity to create a more efficient and environmentally friendly, intelligent consumer goods that could have benefitted all humans on this earth.

This excellent and teachable point reminded me of an article that I have recently read where the author pointed to the fact that when the Israeli military commander informed Ben Gurion about what to do with the defeated Palestinians national leadership? Ben Gurion motioned with his hand, without uttering a word, in a way indicating to the commander to drive the Palestinians out of Palestine.

At this critical moment in history, Ben Gurion could have asked the commander to invite the remaining Palestinian national leadership and to share with them a reconciliatory plan allowing the defeated Palestinians to stay where they were in the hopes that both people could live in peace and harmony by sharing the land for the benefits of both.

Here, at this critical moment in history, neither Ben Gurion nor the victorious Allied leadership showed real charismatic leadership. By failing to do so, TIPPTK is still with us today, and the looming nuclear confrontation between the East and the West is also still with us today. No one knows what the consequences of the present war in Ukraine, which is in reality a war between the United States and Russia, nor that of the bitter confrontation between the Taiwanese government (again with the support of the United States) and China, which claims that Taiwan belongs to "Mother China," will be. With that in mind, the recent genocide in Gaza and the aftermath of Hamas attack on October 7th, could have completely avoided had Ben Gurion displayed the real charismatic leadership at the time.

9. Watts Towers: An Italian immigrant named Sabato Rodia spent over 35 years constructing the towers that has included many shapes, colors, length, width, and heights. He built them using a variety of discarded items that he found around his watts surrounding neighborhoods including broken glasses, tiles, pipes, wires, empty soda cans, broken pottery, bricks made of variety of cement, and other ceramic items. Sabato worked non-stop for 34 years between 1921-1955. Although at the time Watts was its own independent city, but in 1926 it became part of greater Los Angeles city- The City Of Angeles. His towers became very popular among the almost all African American citizens of Watts who at the time were prevented from living in other areas due to racist housing covenants. Those towers became a symbol of pride of the entire surrounding neighborhoods . It was no surprise to me that the Los Angeles Unifies School District has strongly advocated for all its schools to encourage its teacher to take their students on field trips to visit those towers, which I did with my students on many occasions. Due to their significant, those towers were added to the National Register of Historical Places, to the Los Angeles Cultural Monuments, to the California Historical Landmarks, and to the U.S. National Landmarks.

Acknowledgments

This memoir was a years-long project in the making, and it could not have happened without the support of several people:

- My wife, Lina, who provided invaluable help and patience with locating pictures, assisting with the timeline and identification of friends and relatives both here and in Palestine, and listening to me talk about this memoir constantly;
- My editor, Pat Kramer, for helping to bring the text to life, and my publisher, Stephanie Larkin, and all the good folks at Red Penguin Publishing for bringing a lifelong dream into reality;
- My daughters, Stefania and Paola, for their patience in putting up with my bragging and complaints;
- And last but certainly not least, my son, Nabil, who has been by my side from the start with helping me organize my journals, go through the initial, mid-stage, and final writing processes, edit my text, scan the photos and assist with drafting the captions, organize (and debate!) my theories on war and peace, and generally getting this project to move from my desk and into the hands of you, the reader.

A special thanks to my students for giving me the pleasure and privilege of being a part of their lives.

And to my parents, for whom this story is written and to whom my life's work is dedicated. They believed in me, and I know they are proud of what I have done.

About the Author

Ghassan S. Bisharat, Ph.D.

Dr. Ghassan (Gus) Bisharat was born on June 23, 1950, in the city of Nazareth, Palestine/Israel. His early years were shaped by stories of his family's original home, the village of Ma'Alool, which was destroyed in 1948 by the advancing Israeli armies. Memories of the *Nakba* mixed with daily reality: as a Melkite/Catholic Palestinian, Dr. Bisharat grew up a minority within a minority. However, the injustices, humiliations, oppression, and discrimination he experienced could not quench his love for learning and the belief that education was the key to uplifting the Palestinian struggle for a just and lasting peace and an end to their tragedy—views his family embraced and one that ultimately led him to leave his homeland for the United States.

Arriving in California on March 21, 1971, with a one-hundred-dollar bill, Dr. Bisharat experienced the harsh realities that many immigrants face: low-paying jobs, high living and education costs, and heart-wrenching distance from his family. He spent many years toiling at his cousins' gas stations and rental car offices and later, working as a machinist and welder. His education journey began at San Gabriel Adult School in the City of San Gabriel, California, followed by East Los Angeles College, and then Cal State University, Los Angeles where he earned his B.A. in Political Science and met his future wife, also an immigrant (from Italy).

Dr. Bisharat then enrolled at the University of California,

Riverside where he completed both his Master's degree and his Ph.D. in International Relations and Comparative Politics. Dr. Bisharat eventually began a full-time job teaching machine shops and welding, first at East Los Angeles Skill Center, and later at Locke High School in South Central Los Angeles, as a means of supporting his growing family and paying his bills, especially his tuition fees.

After an extensive and lengthy job search, all doors were closed in his face to pursue a governmental and/or university teaching career. Failing to do so, he then accepted his kismet and began teaching in the Greater Los Angeles Inner City Basin where he spent the next two and a half decades teaching social studies at numerous high schools throughout the Los Angeles Basin while simultaneously teaching part time as an assistant professor of Political Science at Cal State University, Los Angeles.

His journey inspired him and helped him connect with his students—many of whom were minorities from impoverished backgrounds facing daily discrimination, poverty, racism, neglect, and violence like what he had experienced back home. Dr. Bisharat used his life story to help connect with his students, steering them away from gang violence, drug use, and the neglect of their education while instilling in them the love of education and pride in their heritage.

This memoir is based on decades of personal journals in which Dr. Bisharat recorded his daily activities, and it exists as both a family history and (he hopes) as an inspiration to current and future students to not give up on their dreams. Long retired, he and his wife now spend their days enjoying their three children and five wonderful grandchildren. He can also be found in his shed teaching his grandkids how to use tools and other equipment, in his home office studying current events, on cruise ships, or at a local casino trying his luck.

The author with his wife, children, and grandchildren in Tehachapi, California - November 2023

www.ingramcontent.com/pod-product-compliance
Lightning Source LLC
Chambersburg PA
CBHW060546080526

44585CB00013B/462